THE ART OF MINISTERING
TO THE SICK

THE MACMILLAN COMPANY
NEW YORK · BOSTON · CHICAGO · DALLAS
ATLANTA · SAN FRANCISCO

MACMILLAN AND CO., LIMITED
LONDON · BOMBAY · CALCUTTA · MADRAS
MELBOURNE

**THE MACMILLAN COMPANY
OF CANADA, LIMITED**
TORONTO

The Art of Ministering
To the Sick

BY

RICHARD C. CABOT, M.D.

AND

RUSSELL L. DICKS, B.D.

NEW YORK

THE MACMILLAN COMPANY

1947

PREFACE

We have written this book because of our interest in the subject, and because we have not been able to find any adequate book about it. We hope it will be of interest to all who care for the sick: to doctors, nurses, and social workers, and to the sick themselves, as well as the ministers to whom it is addressed primarily.

R. C. C. is chiefly responsible for Chapters III, IV, VII, VIII, IX, X, XII, XIX, XX, and XXIII. R. L. D. wrote most of Chapters XIII, XV, XVI, XVII, XXI, and the whole of Appendix A. In Chapters I, II, V, VI, XI, XIV, XVIII, and XXII, our ideas are intermingled so closely that we cannot tell which of us wrote what. During the three years of our partnership in work for the sick we have felt again and again the strength of the alliance between doctor and minister. We have felt it still more while we have been writing this book and criticizing each other's work. R. C. C.'s experience with sick people has been the longer; but R. L. D. has had far more experience in the attempt to meet the religious needs of the sick in a hospital.

Note for reviewers and critics: We should be especially grateful for criticism of nine ideas which occurred to us during the preparation of this book, namely:

1. The Growing Edge (pages 13 to 16).
2. The Sense of Growth (pages 99 to 101).
3. Directed Listening (pages 197 to 202).
4. The use of Quietness to influence some one else (pages 206 to 211).
5. Evil and Futurity (pages 109 to 112).
6. *Vis Medicatrix Dei* (Chapter IX).
7. Two Must Face a Third (Chapter XII).

v

8. Note-writing as Creative Work (pages 247–252).

9. Rituals of the Sickroom (Chapter XX).

We are grateful to several friends for criticisms of our MS., and to Miss Alice G. O'Gorman for devoted care in its preparation and in proof-reading.

R. C. C.

R. L. D.

Massachusetts General Hospital

CONTENTS

PART V. CRITICAL OPPORTUNITIES

APPENDICES

PART I
PREPARATION

CHAPTER I

WHY THE MINISTER SHOULD VISIT THE SICK

HAS the Protestant minister of today any good reason to visit the sick? The doctor diagnoses and treats them. The apothecary prepares their medicines. The nurse or the family give bedside care. The social worker looks after domestic, legal and industrial difficulties. The librarian supplies books. The occupational therapist gives manual work. The Catholic priest hears confessions, gives absolution and administers extreme unction. But can the Protestant minister be anything but a nuisance? Many physicians doubt it. They fear he will excite or tire the patient. The patient himself may dread to see the clergyman. "Am I as sick as all that?"

By what authority, then, does the minister go to the sickroom? Why should we expect that he can lend courage to the sufferer, confidence to the dying? Has he suffered? Has he seen anyone suffer? Has he seen the fear of dying? Has he felt the fear of death turn into confidence? Has he worked shoulder to shoulder with those who have seen it and are helping to bring it about?

It is the purpose of this book to answer these questions. In this chapter we describe three aims which call the minister to the sickroom: (1) To counteract the evils of specialism. (2) To give a devotion such as only religion can permanently inspire. (3) To care for the growth of souls.

i

Religion has always been an antispecialistic force. It deals with all men's interests in their relation to the eternal. So it was natural that when the Christian church endeavored to carry out the commands of Jesus Christ it should include his ministry of healing. Priest, doctor, and nurse were all one person until comparatively recent times, and the priest was that person. For centuries the Christian church was the chief imitator of the Good Samaritan. About 300 A.D., when Christians made painful pilgrimages to Jerusalem, the first hospital was founded there. A hospital was a place for Christian hospitality and now and then a place to care for sick people. It was a hostel where pilgrim met pilgrim. After a long hard journey pilgrims came weary, starving, or sick to Jerusalem. They had to be cared for, and the hostels took them in. Later, as hostels or hospitals were founded along the route traveled by the Crusaders, each had a part set aside for the care of the sick. These sections were called "infirmaries." Some of the old hostels with their infirmaries can still be seen at Rhodes.

Quite independent of pilgrimages, the monasteries cared for the sick and for the poor. There was little or no medical care for them, and nursing as a separate profession has developed only within the last century. For nineteen-twentieths of the Christian era it was done by priests and nuns. Till very recently the Christian church alone has carried modern medicine to the Orient, establishing hospitals, training native doctors and nurses, studying the cause and cure of oriental diseases. Since modern medicine came into its own, since city, state, and private hospitals have been built, the church has given up most of its responsibility for the physical care of the sick, though it still maintains hospitals and continues the rôle of spiritual physician.

Why are doctors so slow to welcome ministers in the sickroom? Because the work of Darwin, Pasteur, and Koch has brought "scientific medicine" to the front by leaps and bounds. Corresponding changes of thought in the church have come too slowly to suit the doctors. Christian Science disgusted them (rightly and wrongly), and as soon as they were used to this they had to face what they thought quackish competition from church clinics, and more lately still from clerical psychiatrists.

Medical sensitiveness to "interference" has been somewhat allayed since 1905, when it turned out that the new medical-social workers were allies, not enemies. This discovery makes the doctor now more ready to accept the minister as part of the medical team. By the patient's wish the doctor still heads this team. But though medical-clerical relations are improving, the clergy still find themselves tolerated, seldom welcomed, by the medical profession as allies in the struggle against suffering. Medical opposition, sensed if not often heard by the minister, has often kept him from visiting the sick. But many physicians are ready now to welcome him as they welcome anyone who can be of genuine assistance to the patient.

Dr. James H. Means, Chief of the Medical Service at the Massachusetts General Hospital and professor of Clinical Medicine at the Harvard Medical School, said recently, "I believe the patient should send for his minister when he gets sick just as he sends for his doctor." Yet most ministers and most doctors are not ready to accept this view. Why? Because neither group understands the spiritual needs of the sick nor how to meet these needs. Too few doctors and too few ministers have been sick themselves!

We are persuaded that the minister has a place in the sickroom, a place not that of the doctor, of the psychiatrist, of the social worker or of anybody else. The minister's duty there is to rouse the great energies, certainties, and faiths of the Christian religion. If he has Christian faith, and otherwise he has no business in the ministry, he has a great asset, perhaps the greatest asset that a person could have in dealing with the sick. His peculiar privilege springs from the fact that he has a living and sometimes a contagious belief in God, in immortality, in the saving qualities of the Gospel of Jesus Christ, and in the soul's endless power of growth.

Most of the sick in hospital wards have no familiarity with the words or with the habits of religion. You cannot evangelize a dog. You cannot convert an idiot. Many patients who need the minister have scarcely more capacity to realize his usefulness than a person under ether or dead drunk. Nothing could be more fatuous than for the clergyman to assume that he can present the Christian religion in terms of belief to the great majority of persons whom he meets in a hospital. He is not dealing with members of his own parish who may be presumed to have some interest in religion. Yet he should not confine himself merely to the few devout persons who happen to be within the hospital walls. They need him, and he will go to them. But he is more needed by many others to whom the words of religion mean nothing.

They need the minister because the sick do not live by bread alone, nor by the most appropriate diet, medication, surgery, nursing, and hygiene that can be brought to their aid. They need the clergyman because the appendix, the gall bladder, the heart, lungs, and other organs are not independent machines but are linked in their adventures with a nervous system and with a conscious mind which usually integrates, though it sometimes disintegrates, their behavior in sickness and in health.

It is stupid to help a patient in one respect and hurt him in another. To give him good medicine but bad food would seem too idiotic to be borne. But at present we do something as bad as this in many cases. We work hard to improve the condition of the sick man's body, but we allow conditions to exist which hurt his mind and through his mind check the healing of his tissues. Mental and spiritual food is a crying need. Yet in long illness the mind usually starves or hungers, because man is not so one-sided a creature as our medical treatment assumes. We ignore the patient's view of hospital sights, sounds, and smells, of the doctor's significant silences and half-heard conversations with assistants and nurses. We let poisonous fears act on his body and on his mind, because no one stops them or neutralizes them. He fears death oftener than his doctor and his nurse realize because they know so well that his disease is not a mortal one.

Doctors aim to banish, to curb or to prevent suffering. But the doctor has not always the skill to diagnose or to treat the mental part of illness. In many cases he can discover nothing to do for the mental suffering, emotional starvation, occupational upset, that exist in heart disease, lung disease, and other common maladies. Sometimes he can lessen these psychic burdens of illness only by healing the physical tissues. Medical treatment is then the whole task, as it is

especially in mental disease and in the fevers which blunt consciousness. But this is rare. Usually we can attack disease both through
the body and through the mind. A man carries into his illness the
interests, affections, emotions, conflicts that have governed him
hitherto. They raise his blood pressure, they upset the movements of
his heart, his stomach, and his bowels. They pervert the chemistry of
his digestion and of his metabolism. The medical profession sees these
connections better today than twenty years ago. Doctors are beginning to recognize the emotional and spiritual element not only in
mental disease but in all disease. Psychiatrists are being called upon
to minister to it in some hospitals, but we have still a long way to
go in this direction. Whose job is it?

We who write this book believe so little in specialism that we
would rather see doctors treat *all* their patients' ills, instead of turning over some of them to the nurse, some to the social worker, and
some to the minister. We believe the sick man would be better
nursed if he were moved in bed by a doctor's anatomically erudite
hands rather than by a nurse's. He would be better fed if the doctor
rather than the nurse or the dietitian planned his meals. If the
doctors understood social work as they do medicine, they could do
social as well as medical work, and do it better than any one else,
because the facts about the patient would then be organized in a
single mind, instead of being passed back and forth between two or
more. If the doctor were an "old-fashioned country practitioner,"
that almost mythological being now extinct in many places, he
would know the patient's family, his work, his character, his income,
and his amusements, so that he could do all the social work that
conditions permit.

If the doctor were an all-round man like Dr. Schweitzer in West
Africa, Dr. Grenfell in Labrador, Dr. Alfred Worcester in Wal-
tham, Massachusetts, or Dr. Torrance on the Sea of Galilee, he could
take the minister's work as part of his weekly routine. But as doctors are now selected and educated, most of them lack the time, the
interest, and the skill to make the social and spiritual diagnosis, or
to give social and spiritual treatment to their patients.

Will anyone dispute this? Will anyone say that the doctor of the future will learn social work and theology as he now learns anatomy and use them as indispensable elements in his grasp of the patient's troubles? Possibly; but we see no prospect of it. Until the medical man is surer that the minister has something important to contribute, in sickness and in health, there is no chance that medical interests will be broadened to include theology.

The nurse was once a "sister," ignorant of the technique of modern nursing, but persistently concerned about religion. She grasped much of what now seems to us the minister's opportunity. She made bad blunders in asepsis or in medical care, but she was everlastingly concerned about the patient's soul and, therefore, she often refreshed both his body and his mind in ways which the modern nurse is too busy and too exclusively medical to consider. That is not wholly her fault. If the nurse is to earn her living she must please the doctor. Therefore she looks to him as her leader in all that she does for her patient. It cannot well be otherwise. But so long as it is so the nurse will do little or none of the minister's work.

The social worker might do the minister's work if she conceived her job in that way. But the social worker is so busy with the patient's economic problems that she does not know much about what is going on in his wandering, listless, frightened mind. She is afraid to touch religion because she fears sectarianism, proselyting, and conflicts with the hierarchy of some particular branch of religion. Moreover, she is not trained for the minister's work.

Doctors, nurses, family, friends, and the patient himself are too close to the situation to evaluate it comprehensively. Who can praise the doctor so judiciously, who can admire the patient so discriminatingly, as the minister? Who can weigh complaints so dispassionately? Who is so apt to see what is missing in the total set-up? With malice toward none, with charity for all, he can interpret the efforts of each actor on the stage. None of them can see himself with sufficient detachment, with sufficient humor, nor judge the rest with sufficient charity. Routinism should have no more dangerous foe and no more compassionate forgiver than the minister.

If the minister is to counteract the evils of extreme specialism he must not become another specialist like the doctor or the social worker. His job is to focus attention on two points: the patient as a whole and the ground of his being in God. The minister is also interested in the patient's physical welfare, in his economic security, in his family life, in his hobbies, his friends, his fears, his hopes, his disappointments, his sins, and every other aspect of his life. But he should do nothing that any available specialist can do better. He should see that the patient gets care but he should not care for him medically, psychiatrically, economically or politically. The outline of the patient's entire life is the minister's concern.

Is that outline clear? No. You cannot see it or touch it. G. K. Chesterton long ago lamented the lack of any standard outline of a human soul. If a man is smashed by a high explosive, the doctor sees in an instant whether he has lost an arm, a leg, an eye, or an ear, because the doctor knows the normal physical outline. With more expert study he can find out whether any important internal organ is injured. But who can survey a human being's mind? Who can state authoritatively whether all its proper powers are present, whether any of them are rudimentary, atrophied, hypertrophied, or perverted? The psychiatrist has no authoritative list that he can check up as the doctor checks up our physical organs. No one has such a list. But it is more nearly the minister's business than any one else's to make one, and then find out by intimate acquaintance whether some of the patient's proper but invisible faculties are starved, poisoned or exhausted.

If the sick man can eat and sleep, if he moves all his muscles and performs all his excretions, if he talks sensibly and does not cry, curse or complain, he will probably be taken for normal by his medical attendants. The huge total of what he keeps to himself, all that he cannot express, or fears may be ridiculed, what he dreads, what he depends on, what he takes for granted, what he loves and now misses, the hopes and affections that he lives by, the frustration and successes that have shaped him—these and many more, further or impede his convalescence. Wound, starvation or atrophy in some of his invisible powers may even destroy his desire for life, which is notoriously a factor in physical recovery.

We do not assume that the minister can get adequate information about the patient's soul in a few minutes, or that he can ever know the whole of it. But we believe that, unless he makes the attempt to collect a workable knowledge of it, no one else will. No one else will give the time, no one else has the detachment and the interest in human personalities that the minister's profession demands. For the minister who is worth his salt has an *energy of interest* in a human being that springs from the belief that he is a child of God, a poor relation of the power that moves and governs the universe.

This interest sometimes comes into a patient's life at a critical time. We have known several persons in whose lives the period of hospitalization has been a turning point. Primitive people from remote rural districts sometimes meet in the hospital for the first time in their lives a relatively civilized standard of good manners, of cleanliness, of respect for women. They see for the first time a delicate and refined nurse do a dirty and repulsive job as if it were a privilege. "I didn't know there were such people in the world," he would say if he were articulate enough.

Thus the emergencies of illness may force a patient to turn over a new leaf and to acquire for the first time a reasonable amount of self-control, of regularity in his physical habits, or of insight into his own emotional crises. At such a turning point he can profit by the counsel of a minister. A young mother known to us had been told that there was no hope for her diabetic child eighteen months old. In desperation she carried him across the United States to the clinic of the greatest specialist on diabetes in the world. There she found that there *was* hope. There her child received not only expert but devoted care. There she saw him set upon the road to health. Somewhere in the early days of this reprieve from threat of death there was an opportunity for a clergyman to share and to augment a great spiritual experience. But no clergyman was there.

Someone is hungry, thirsty, sick or in prison. He needs food, drink, healing, enfranchisement, so far as compassionate humanity can give them. Permanent food as well as instant relief may come out of these misfortunes. It has often come out of them. In that rebuilding of the sufferer's life the minister may take a part. At any rate he must try, because his business is the advancement of people's lives along the path laid down in the build of their natures.

II

In 1890 I (R. C. C.) said to the doctor whom I was assisting in a hospital clinic, "When one starts in the practice of medicine how does he get any patients?" The doctor answered, "By devotion to the few he has already, perhaps free patients in a clinic like this." If a minister asks how he can get a chance to free souls for the Christian message, one true answer is this: By devotion to such opportunities for service as he can find in any hospital or among the sick of any parish. Devotion opens people's minds through their hearts. Any interested person can show devotion to the sick, but the minister ought to be able to give a more complete and convincing service than any one else.

Devotion in visiting the sick person shows itself in preparing oneself better for the visit, in remembering more about him, in imagining his needs more vividly, in collecting more of what he wants brought to him and in giving up more for him. (All but the last of these points are dealt with in the chapter on Note-writing.)

The quality of the minister's devotion is shown in what he sacrifices for the patient. Others will think of sitting up with him at night when all the family are worn out. But the minister will do it. Others will talk of staying at the bedside on a holiday so that the family may go off and get some refreshment, but the minister will be most apt to do it. He is laying siege to an enemy: depression, fear, bitterness. His mining operations may be countermined, ex-

ploded and destroyed. There is no certainty of success and if he
fails his time will seem to others, perhaps to himself, wasted. He
will lose some people's esteem and be in danger of self-pity. But
these risks are part of his sacrifice. If he takes no risk to his own
reputation for good sense and good judgment, even when the patient
needs that he risk something, he will be false to his call. Doctors
and clergymen learn to be terribly careful to avoid criticism of their
good sense and of their good judgment. But now and then the
patient needs a devotion that is ready to risk even prestige, even the
reputation for good sense. Devotion is the minister's badge of office
when he goes to a sufferer. Devotion answers the challenge which
he should always put to himself:

By what right am I here? By what right do I see you in the
intimacies of your pain, your humility? By what right do I see the
unfinished picture and the artist in his longing, the unfinished poem
and the poet in his brooding? By what right do I dare hold up
an ideal for you in your pain, or express your longings in prayer?
Only by right of serving you.

If I may straighten your sheet, adjust your pillow, quiet you by
standing by, then I have a right to see you. If I may strengthen
you by my confidence, if I may encourage you by my patience, then
I may come to you when you are ill. But how do I attain this
knowledge of the sickroom? How do I know that your sheets need
to be straightened, when perhaps even you do not know it? How do
I know, despite the fact that a pitcher of ice-water stands near-by,
that you are allowed to drink only a little of it? How do I know
you are restless because of boredom or moody because of fear? Only
by having suffered or by having served where I could watch others
suffer. Only by learning to be steady of nerve, self-forgetful, resourceful because I need to be so and have practiced it. Your need,
my understanding, and my desire to help are my authority for
coming to you.

The minister goes to the sickroom because he is the duly recognized representative of Him who said, "For I was hungered, and

ye gave me meat: I was thirsty, and ye gave me drink: I was naked and ye clothed me: I was sick and ye visited me: I was in prison and ye came unto me." (Matthew, 25:35-36.) This whole passage can be read as a description of the mental and spiritual anguish of any sick man. To be sick is to be a stranger, naked, stripped of vigor, weakened by lack of determination, feverish by helplessness, bared by broken confidence; a stranger among strange people, even one's clothes changed for a queer abbreviated gown. To be sick is to pass through strange places of the spirit: the night before an operation, with its haunting dreads and imaginings, the taking of an anesthetic, the struggle with post-operative discomforts. To be sick is to face the uncertainty of diagnosis, the loneliness of con-valescence, the difficulties of facing life as a cripple or an invalid. These are new paths of our spirit: "A stranger and ye took me in." To be sick is to be in prison, imprisoned in one bed, one room, ward, building; imprisoned within one's helplessness and one's handicaps, chained to the threat of death.

The minister goes to the sickroom by authority of the needs of the patient, needs which will not be met otherwise. By right of the heritage which is his he must go to the sickroom, and by right of the needs of the spirit, he may be trusted by doctor and patient, after he has trained himself. By virtue of the special methods and of the devotion which are his heritage he may minister to the sick to their advantage, to the advantage of the doctors and nurses who care for the sick, and to the advantage of his own spiritual welfare.

III

In his antispecialism and in his devotion to the sick the minister's goal is always *the growth of souls*.[1] If he is to help on this growth he needs to face three questions: Is all growth spiritual growth? What are the foods of growth? Why is one man's growth-food another's poison? We shall attack the last problem first.

A person can assimilate spiritual food only when it feeds his

---

[1] For the definition of "growth" as the word is used here and elsewhere in this book, see Appendix C.

"growing edge." A soul like a muscle grows from a frontier which registers the point reached thus far on its march into the unknown. Not many years ago it was discovered that we can cultivate a bit of human muscle or kidney outside the body and watch the details of its growth. The tissue puts out new columns of cells like the rows of bricks added as we build a brick wall. Thus in a week's time a fragment the size of one's little fingernail lengthens itself a fraction of an inch. The growing edge, jagged and irregular, is the surface out of which new cells sprout. Something like this happens in the sapwood of a tree just beneath the bark and at the edge of every fresh leaf.

The soul has a growing edge. It can advance only from the point where just now it is. But teachers and ministers sometimes invite it to start from where it is not. When kind friends try to tell us the way to motor to some point across country they usually start not at the growing edge of our ignorance but at a point a good deal farther on. "Take Montgomery Avenue and follow it till the road turns off to Morristown, then go on till the road forks, etc." This assumes (1) that we know how to get to Montgomery Avenue, and (2) that when we get to it we shall know which way to go on it. In fact, however, we have difficulty in finding Montgomery Avenue, and when we find it we go to the right instead of to the left, and so land miles from our destination. The growing edge of our knowledge of the country is much farther back. The direction given us is correct but it does not start from the point where we need to be picked up. We cannot go forward from where we are not, so we go backward or wander in a circle.

This ludicrously simple illustration has far-reaching parallels. Those who try to explain a point about physics, about the insides of an automobile, about music, mathematics or theology, are apt to start some distance ahead of our growing edge. They assume that we know more or care more than we do. They use terms that we do not understand. Often we do not even know that we are off the track until we have gone some distance and have wasted time and energy without fruit.

College education as I (R. C. C.) have seen it in fourteen years' teaching at Harvard, wastes a large amount of money and time because the faculty have no clear idea about the growing edge of the student's mind. A boy of eighteen is ready to push on in certain directions and not in others. Teachers find holes in his knowledge and are ready to believe that they abhor the vacuum and will take in the needed filling. But in fact they cannot. It is like trying to fill up the hole made in a man's leg by a fragment of shrapnel. We cannot fill it from the top down. We have no living flesh to put into it. The hole must fill itself from the bottom up with material transferred from what the patient eats, drinks, and breathes.

So it is with the holes in a student's knowledge. They cannot be filled satisfactorily unless we go to his growing edge, that is, to the point where he demands an answer to a question of his own. He will assimilate knowledge which answers his questions, those he spontaneously asks or can be roused to ask. He will not assimilate the answer to any question that happens to interest his teacher. Nevertheless we continue to fill our college courses with answers to questions which the students never asked and cannot be induced to ask.

The growing edge of anyone's knowledge is at the point where his questions push out like the edge of a tissue culture. Perhaps on most college subjects the student asks no questions at all. Then he will get no living knowledge of those subjects until his curiosity can somehow be aroused. Is it any better with our attempts to develop his character? The growing edge of his character is what he now wants to make of himself. A college student wants to become popular, athletic, and fit to earn a living. Till he gets other ambitions he will not grow by taking the college courses which his tutor approves, even though he gets good marks in them. He may attach bits of information to the surface of his soul just as he can fasten false teeth to his jaws, but no growth takes place in him.

We conceive that every patient who is not feeble-minded or senile has a growing edge when he enters the experience called illness. To find and to cultivate that edge is the minister's task. It is often an impossible one, humanly speaking. None the less it is his task.

.   .   .   .

Each person must do his own growing in sickness as in health. What can we do to help it? *We can supply the atmosphere in which growth is favored.* That is the business of a teacher, and especially of the kind of teacher whom we call a clergyman. A gardener of souls, he tries to supply the environing earth, moisture, air, light, and chemical reaction. That is much. Can a minister do that? He can, if by good listening he can find the growing edge of a patient's life. As in medicine, our only reliable and permanent way to prevent people's sliding down hill is to invigorate their tissues so that they begin to go up hill.

It is not so terribly hard to help a person to grow, provided we like him and he likes us, and provided we can find out where he is. The trouble is that his development often reaches out in such different directions from our own that our experience does not help us much to find him.

What are the foods of growth? We do not ask about the "best growth," the most direct growth, or growth in the right direction, but about any growth, even that spiral, groping progress in which most of us move, through mistakes and misunderstandings, through wrongdoing repented, through sudden revelations of opportunity or of heroism. We shall mention five very familiar foods which, as we visit sick people with one sole object, their spiritual growth, we try to bring, even though we know how far off we are from discovering to them the great riches of the Christian religion.

1. Whenever people sincerely *love* anything or anybody, they grow. They grow more when their love has to reach up to what is above them, in science or art, in human personality or in social endeavor. But whoever loves anything is enlarged by that very act. We are often uncomfortable when clergymen quote the familiar words of Scripture, "God is love," because God is many other things besides. He is beauty and wisdom, opportunity and chastening.

But because love is part of His nature, anyone who is governed for a time by a love that is not selfish or merely sensuous, advances along the path in which it is the minister's object to encourage him. If he can discover, through good listening and good questioning, an interest or an affection that can be deepened, the minister has done something for the cause that he represents.

2. If he can help the patient to *learn,* if he can so light up his interest that a new fact, or a new truth, takes root, the minister has assisted, no matter how little, the divine process of his growth. Even if he has made two interests grow where only one grew before, then he has planted something which may branch out in unexpectedly valuable directions.

3. We live in a country in which *beauty* is perhaps less appreciated than in any other, but if even in America we can help anyone to appreciate more of this great kingdom of beauty, we are favoring another side of growth. In the field of beauty we include humor. Part of the minister's vocation is to secure for himself and for others the right sort of detachment, not aloofness, from life. Humor refreshes us because it gives us detachment.

4. *Service.* What we have said so far about growth may sound self-centered. The sick need to know that they are of use to some one else. They do not grow naturally by self-culture. The crippled seamstress, whose story we have told on page 63, found her happiness in teaching others to sew and later in managing a shop where only cripples worked. Her own suffering gave her knowledge of other cripples' needs and patience with their foibles. With their help and God's she has made herself useful in the industrial world for over twenty years.

Mere utility is not enough to nourish growth. It must be such utility as can be articulated with a branch of the sufferer's own crescent life. Otherwise useful work becomes mere routine.

5. In my own life (R.C.C.) it is *suffering,* frustration, humiliation, grief, remorse, that have best nourished growth. This is not always so. The searching wind that invigorates one man chills another. Our dose of suffering may be too great for body and soul.

But as we look back along the path of our lives, do we not see our sufferings as our best teachers? Especially if those sufferings did not have to be borne alone. "Man's extremity is God's opportunity" to teach what we are too stupid, too self-satisfied, too habit-bound, to grasp at other times. The burnt child avoids fire. Suffering taught him. But the pleasantly warmed child may never learn fire's mordant tooth.

We asked, What are the foods of growth? We answer, Love, learning, beauty, service, and suffering well borne. Some may object: "This is all very well, but what has it to do with religion or with spiritual growth? Has the sufferer any better hold of God, any stronger habit of prayer, by reason of the useful but mundane activities that you have described?" Our answer is that the best proof of religious life is not in the facile use of religious terms or even in clearness of religious belief, but in a certain quality of thought and action of which any earnest person has some and no one has enough.

Growth is the ethical absolute.[2] The only good life is growing, *not toward a goal but in powers* such as sympathy, courage, honesty, perspective, tenacity, knowledge. Spiritual life means the growth of each soul along the plan of its individual nature. That plan steers us toward depth and away from superficiality in knowledge, away from shallow emotion and from vapid struggles with ourselves.

If we have gone but little beneath the externals of our fellow men's lives, if we see them as walking automata, as means to our ends, as amusements or as enemies, we treat them so. When we penetrate deeper by study, by sympathy, and by sharing hardship, we find it possible to return good for evil. We see good in men that they do not yet recognize, and play up to that good. This is a more spiritual relation to men because it is less superficial, nearer to the reality.

Prayer as we see it is a part of a thoroughgoing effort to grow, to learn, to get beneath appearances. "Prayer is the heart's sincere

2 See Appendix C, p. 377.

desire." Men great and good have said that only once or twice in their lives have they "really" prayed. They mean that the heat of their desire for Reality has risen but seldom to the boiling point. But that desire is there all along in those who grow. The naming of God is not important so long as we do the will of our Father in heaven. That will appears in us as the will to learn, to treat men as men and not as means, and to kill self-deceit. Jesus guides us best in such matters and if we keep close to his spirit prayer will go out of us whether we call it prayer or not.

To sum up we conclude, then, that the minister's opportunity in sickness is to devote himself to the growth of souls at a time when pain, sorrow, frustration and surprise, bring experiences that invite a new start in life. What these opportunities are and how he can meet them is our subject in the rest of this book.

Chapter II

SPECIAL ADVICE ON WORK WITH THE SICK

I. SPECIFIC

1. Take an opportunity to ask the doctor's advice about how you can best help the patient and let the doctor realize that you wish to forward his plans.

2. Before you see any patient who is seriously ill collect from the family or from the nurse the essential facts about the patient's last twenty-four hours. Study his temperature chart if one is kept; inquire about his night, his spirits, and about previous visitors if he has had any that day. Be as nearly up to date as you can. Make allowance for any drugs that he may be taking. Clergymen are sometimes puzzled or alarmed by mental and spiritual dullness due not to moral lapses but to drugs.

3. Let the patient know on what day and at what hour he may expect your next visit and be punctual in keeping the appointment. Visits help the patient to furnish his empty days with definite anticipations. Your visit can at least serve as an interruption and a change in a long, empty stretch of time. Knowing that you will come, say at five o'clock, the other hours pass more quickly. But if then the visitor does not come and has sent no word, the sufferer's disappointment is proportionately keen.

4. Don't stay too long. Short frequent visits are best. It is a common complaint that the minister tires out sick people by staying on after he should have known enough to leave. This is especially annoying in acute disease and after operations; but it happens also in chronic troubles such as broken bones and broken hearts. How shall he know when to go? He should watch the patient's face and movements. He can learn to read there his signal. As a check on

his own judgment he should ask the nurse or an intelligent member of the family to come into the room or to make some move as a suggestion that he has stayed long enough. It is a good rule that when in doubt whether to stay or to go, he should go, and should pay only polite attention to polite invitations to stay longer. Ten minutes is often long enough with patients acutely sick, and few visits should exceed twenty minutes.

5. Don't allow any alarm, horror, or sorrow to appear in your face or in your voice. If the patient is a close friend and has been much blanched and thinned by his illness, it may be hard to conceal your feelings at the first visit. But it is imperative. We have known visitors to break down and cry or to be shocked into a distressing silence when they came face to face with a patient who was jaundiced, distorted, or swollen up by disease. Practice in a hospital will give the minister control of himself, and he should acquire it before he begins to visit the sick in his own parish. A patient often wants to show you his wound, to exhibit his diseased appendix in a bottle, or the gallstones that have been extracted from his gall bladder. Nurses and doctors, if they are friendly, are very apt to show the minister highly repulsive specimens in which they are interested. He must school himself to be interested too, and not to show his natural feelings of disgust.

6. Sympathy can be given in a way that does harm. The sufferer should be made to realize that you share his pain; but if you dwell on his feelings you can unman him. He does not want to go to pieces or to break down. That undermines his self-respect. He wants to know that you are close to him but especially that you are close to his endeavors to make something worth while, or at least something bearable, out of this encounter with his enemy. He wants to play the game, as soon as he can learn it, and he wants you to play it with him. If it is bereavement that has hit him he wants you to talk about the person he has loved and lost, and now loves more than ever. To share admiration helps him to rebuild. To share the emptiness of loss pulls him down. If it is pain that has gripped him we can increase that pain by dwelling on it. We

can better help him to make headway against it by making sure that he has every available medical aid, by doing the little in our power to make him more comfortable, and then when everything possible has been done, by helping him to turn some part of his attention off his pain.

7. Remember that the sick have often a sharpened awareness of sights, sounds, and smells. An odor of tobacco may distress a person when sick though she would not mind it if she were well. A loud laugh, a loud voice or a specially harsh one may do harm for the same reason; yet one should not purr or croon. Sudden swift movements in the sickroom are sometimes annoying. Nervous, jerky or restless shifts of position have the same effect.

8. Don't kick the bed in entering or leaving the sickroom. Don't lean on it or sit on it. The slightest jar may hurt the patient. Certain people in a sickroom are like a bull in a china shop. Let not the minister be counted among that group.

9. Stand or seat yourself in such a position that the patient can see you without having to strain himself by looking up at an angle to his natural line of sight. By following the direction of his eyes as you approach his bed you can place your chair conveniently for him. Be careful not to make him face a strong light from a window behind you. Don't sit in a rocking chair and rock. Rocking tires some patients very much.

10. The chief object of a visit is to make the sufferer feel that somebody cares about him, if possible that many people, his neighbors and friends, care about him and are interested in all that concerns him. The minister can carry this further, if anyone can, by making the patient realize that God cares for him, suffers in his suffering, understands it, and plans for him in sickness as in health.

11. One should rarely if ever apologize for one's deficiencies, for the fewness of one's visits, or for anything else. Apologies require answers, and often difficult answers, from the patient.

12. In your first moments with the patient be as alert and as watchful as you can to pick up your clue to what is in his mind and to what has been there in recent hours:—hopes, disappointments,

boredom, bitterness, irritability, or simply lassitude and blankness. Feel your way as cautiously but as rapidly as you can into his present state of mind. Go slow and listen hard at the outset in readiness to accept his lead. You *may* need to give the lead and not to take it, but the opposite is much oftener the case.

13. When you choose topics exclude all that require close or prolonged attention or that range far from the interests that the sick man may be expected to keep alive despite his illness. Choose topics near him in space, time, and affection, and near the familiar subjects of his interest. His family and friends, his own past and future, objects in his own house or in his own room, his favorite hobbies and familiar tastes are the best starting points.

14. Sick people like variety, change, little surprises. The more thought and ingenuity the minister puts into providing them, the more he will excel the average visitor who has no "inspirations" in such matters. Of course he has none, because he gives no thought to the visit until he starts to make it. A small morsel of variety means much to an invalid, and most of it has to come to him from outside his own house, when a visitor brings him some gift or some news. This does not mean, of course, that the sick like to be rudely startled.

15. When the illness is chronic but not incurable the patient often suffers from a false though natural belief that he will never get well. In such a case the minister, well fortified by the doctor's positive assurances, can do good by painting the future. Imagine and describe in whimsical detail what the patient will be doing in a month or in six months, whom he will be serving, how he will then look back on his present condition and laugh at the doubts that now torment him. Thus with skill and preparation one can so dramatize the sufferer's future that for a few minutes he lives in it. Here as in so many other instances the minister can show by his ingenuity in preparation a quality of devotion that proves him a man of God and so proves God to some who doubt Him. He can show the devotion that only a consciousness of God and an impetus from God explain.

16. Occasionally the sick like a visitor who will chat for a few minutes without looking for a response, and then take his departure. He has given a fresh current to a tired mind or at least something new to look at. Yet he has called for no effort at a time when the patient is not up to it. Such a visit is not very different from a brief period of reading aloud. Some prefer the latter because it obviously calls for no response. Others want to be talked to even though they cannot hold up their end of the conversation.

If we read aloud and if the patient drops asleep while we read, it may be important to go on reading as long as our time will allow, because the patient needs the sleep and will usually wake up if we stop. We have to know the patient's habit about this, for some people do not wake when reading ends. Then we can harmlessly slip away for another call.

17. Don't talk of depressing or alarming subjects. A doctor visiting a patient who had been hurt in a motor accident was led to tell her, naturally but stupidly, of another and more serious accident to a child whom he had recently been called to attend. After that he talked pleasantly of other topics. But the impression which stuck in the patient's mind after he left was the horror of the child's injury. Nurses often talk about their lurid hospital experiences in a way to neutralize any good that their services confer. The minister is not so apt to make these blunders, but should be warned by them.

18. Sometimes sick people want nothing but a friendly presence without any effort to carry on a conversation. Most often this "presence" will be that of some woman in the family who knits by the sickbed or sews by the window. But if there is no mother, sister, or daughter to do this, any friend can be of use. We have often sat silent for hours in a sickroom reading or writing and now and then exchanging a smile with the patient or shifting a pillow, and we have known that it was our best service.

19. The minister should not take any part in the treatment or practice any special psychotherapeutic technique. If he does so he will at once embroil himself with the doctors of his neighborhood

and so will soon spoil his chance of usefulness. It is conceivable that he might do a better job than the doctor, but it is hardly conceivable that he will be ready to take the main responsibility for the patient's illness and to bear the blame if he does not improve. Since the doctor must bear the responsibility he should have a free hand without any interference from anyone.

20. The minister should never let himself be drawn into any discussion with the patient or his family about the value of the doctor's treatment. If they have doubt about it, it is for them to ask the doctor to bring a consultant. They have a perfect right to suggest this and to suggest also what consultant they would like to have. The doctor practically never makes any objection. In the extraordinarily rare instance in which the doctor refuses a consultant, the family or the patient can always discharge him and engage any other doctor whom they prefer. But in all this the minister can take no part unless the family is so ignorant that they think they must stick to the doctor whom they have called first. Then the minister should inform them of their rights. But except in cases of flagrant abuse or neglect he should refuse to discuss the question of whether the present treatment is effective or whether better could be had.

21. The minister like the doctor must keep many secrets and hold much in reserve, but he must tell absolutely no lies to or about the sick. This is not alway easy. Some doctors believe in deceiving patients—of course for their own good—and if the minister is to keep on good terms with the doctor it is sometimes hard not to take part in such plans of deception. If asked by a patient or by his family any question about the disease and its prospects of cure, the only safe course for the minister is to "decline jurisdiction." "Have you asked the doctor?" should be a question very often on the minister's lips. It is not his business to have any opinions about diagnoses or treatments.

"Do you think I am going to get well?" "That's what we are all working and hoping for, but I know nothing of such matters. I'm often scared by illnesses that the doctor knows are not serious at all.

I do know, because doctors all say so, that your determination to get well will help to cure you."

22. Don't whisper or speak in low tones to a nurse, to a member of the family or to any one else in the sickroom or near it, if there is the slightest chance that the patient will see you or hear you. Your conversation may have nothing to do with him. It may contain only what you would gladly have him hear. Nevertheless he is apt to think that you are saying something too alarming for his ear. Such a belief is like poison to him. It will do him far more harm than any visit can do him good. Say what you have to say about the patient *in his presence* whenever that is possible. Don't let him fall to wondering what you and they are saying about him downstairs or in the next room. Leave the house, and if possible close the street door loudly enough to let him know that you have left it, soon after you bid him good-bye. When you need to talk at length with someone in the family have him come to see you.

Don't walk on tiptoe unless the patient is dozing or asleep or unless you know on reliable authority that the patient prefers you to do so. Many patients are irritated or alarmed by it.

23. Pass on to the sick man's family what you have learned about visiting the sick and especially the shut-in, or other chronic sufferers, provided you have previously won your welcome as a teacher by showing that you can practice what you teach. To train the family for their tasks as nurses and tonics to the sick and especially to the dying, is one of the most useful services that a minister has a chance to perform.

24. The minister's preparation for visiting includes finding what are the especially trying times for the patient and planning the week so as to come then. If the patient has just let his nurse go he will need help in filling the gap.

II. GENERAL

1. A Christian minister can never be insulted or more than momentarily irritated by the patient, because he *is* a patient. The minister can never be enraged. He can never get his feelings hurt

or become antagonistic. Why not? Because the patient "knows not what he does." His stomach or his nerves betray him. It is his sick organs that say sharp cutting things to us and fail to show gratitude for our endeavors. So it is in the vast majority of instances. So we should assume it to be always. Even in the exceptional case where the sick man really wants to hurt us it is our business to return good for evil and to conquer ill nature by good nature.

2. There must be something likable in him no matter how cross-grained or degraded a surface he shows. The deeper his goodness is buried the more unconsciously he hopes that you will recognize it, and will insist on it against all reason.

These two dogmas are fundamental to Christianity. They are as familiar to the minister as his own name. We list them here merely because they are hard to act on no matter how much we are convinced of their truth.

3. We need also to prepare our mood, and to get rid of the dust and leaves still clinging to it from the last thing we have been doing. We carry over far too much from visit to visit, not of our permanent ideals but our chance associations. When we bring our minds and our bodies to the patient's home we are apt to bring along also portions of our last committee meeting, of our recent brush with the tax assessor, or of the newspaper that we have just been reading. What is on the top of our minds, what colors our mood, is largely a matter of chance unless we form a habit of recalling, just as we start, the present needs of the person we are going to see, the point at which we have now arrived in our relations to him, and the essence of the Gospel of Jesus which we need to keep in command of our lives. Ten seconds' prayer on the doorstep of the patient's house or on the threshold of his sickroom arms us and cleanses us surprisingly if we are in the habit of it. Few prayers are more effective.

4. Play no favorites. In a parish or in a hospital a minister's influence is dwarfed if he seems to concentrate his interest upon a few. He may have no such intention but he must be shrewd to avoid even the appearance of it. Fulsome praise of any particular

person is apt to be repeated and spread about the parish as evidence
of favoritism. In emergencies no one resents his devotion to a single
family. But it must be clear that this ceases with the emergency.
He is bound to work for the good of everyone who wants his help.

5. Don't argue; listen. Argument is a powerful engine to get at
truth latent in the mind's recesses. The shock of another's challenge,
the call to defense, the stimulus of ideas that are strange to us, are
good exercise for healthy combatants. But argument is not good for
the sick and it puts the minister in a false position even when the
patient leads him into it. Irritable weakness which is common in
the sick makes them apt to contradict and leads to disputes unless
the minister is on his guard. Even when persuasion is his duty, he
should try every maneuver of countersuggestion, apposite story and
humor rather than be drawn into argument. Often enough the
patient will set himself right if we listen.

6. Don't carry parish gossip. We who visit the sick are sure to
hear racy gossip which will spice our conversation agreeably. People
try to draw it out of us by shrewd questions. But if we yield, we
weaken our position from the first. Few of us need to guard our
tongues so strictly as the minister. A useful rule is this: Repeat
nothing unfavorable to the person it concerns and say nothing
behind his back that you would be ashamed to have him hear.

7. Don't preach about the sick or repeat stories about them. Like
the doctor, the minister hears confidences and becomes conversant
with many secrets. Some of them would make admirable illustra-
tions in a sermon. Most of them feed people's idle curiosity about
their neighbors. People soon find out who keeps confidences and
who does not. We believe that the minister's experiences with the
sick should enrich his sermons as all his experience does, but this
need involve no violations of confidence, and no anonymous stories.
They are sure to be recognized.

8. Work with the doctor. The minister who visits the sick should
go out of his way to get on friendly terms with the doctors in his
parish, to study their peculiarities and to assist them whenever he
finds a chance. If he can work with the doctor on a committee for

some object that interests him, if he can get acquainted with him in a civic club, town meeting or at a golf club, the minister will find ways to make it clear that co-operation and not rivalry, respect and not antagonism, is his desire.

9. Train parishioners to have you called when they are ill. Perhaps the last incumbent of your pulpit did not care to visit the sick. Rather few ministers do. People need to be informed through various channels that you regard sick visiting as one of your privileges. This should be said from the pulpit and by printed notice repeated at suitable intervals. When a call comes, the minister should send word when he may be expected and should keep the appointment punctually.

10. Let your people know that you consider sick-visiting as important as the preparation of sermons. Each helps the other. People will get more from your sermons if they know you in the sickroom. Your visits will mean more when they exemplify principles and texts familiar in your sermons. It will take less time to write a good sermon if your mind is stored with material and your zest increased from your experiences with the sick. People want to hear something that proves their minister's acquaintance with hardship at first hand.

Chapter III

INSTITUTIONAL PROBLEMS

I. COMPLAINTS

To hear complaints and to be neither gullible nor callous, needs training. Patients complain of their doctors, of their nurses, of the medical students whom they see in the hospital, of their relatives, friends or acquaintances, and of other patients. They complain of their diet, of hospital rules, and of many other matters. The minister who hears complaints should land his mind in one of four positions:

1. That the complaint is justified and that the matter can be set right.
2. That the complaint is justified but that the matter probably cannot be set right.
3. That the complaint is unjustified.
4. That the complaint may or may not be justified, and should be further investigated.

One gets clues to a belief in one of these four diagnoses from one's past experience. One hears the same complaints again and again. But one must beware of "snap diagnoses." Twenty patients may have made a certain complaint and twenty investigations may have shown that nothing could be done about it. Yet the twenty first case may convince us that something *can* be done.

We begin with the commonest of complaints:

1. *Against the institution and its rules.*
   (a) That patients are waked and washed too early.
   (b) That the food is bad or badly served.
   (c) That too many noisy or dying patients are left close to the complainer.
   (d) That the rules as to visitors and visiting hours are inhumanly rigid.

(e) That there are too few experienced and kindly nurses.

(f) That the floors are too slippery.

(g) That there are too many medical students at work on tasks beyond their capacity.

Almost all hospital patients complain that they are waked, washed, and fed too early in the morning and that they are expected to go to sleep earlier in the evening than they can. Against this complaint plausible defense can be made. The patient should know this defense and be aware of the extenuating circumstances. But in the end we cannot defend a practice which sacrifices patients' comfort to doctors' convenience.

Ordinarily when patients complain of it it is the minister's business to explain (a) that doctors' service in hospitals is often given free, that their convenience is therefore to be consulted, and that many of them want their hospital patients to be ready to receive them on a nine or ten o'clock visit. (b) This visit is satisfactory only if the interne has previously received the night nurse's report, visited each patient, examined a good many, and familiarized himself with the laboratory reports, X-rays, etc., so that he can report on them to the visiting physician. (c) This in turn is possible only if the patient has been waked, washed, and fed at an early hour. So there we are.

If the visiting physician came in the afternoon there would be no valid defense for the custom of waking patients early. They need all the sleep that they get, and they should not be disturbed unless they sleep exceptionally late. Of course one cannot be serving breakfast to patients all the morning.

Besides the doctors' convenience we have to remember the night nurse's fatigue. If she does not begin to wake, wash, and feed her patients at an early hour she will not be done with them in time to pass over to the day nurse her reports on each patient's progress during the night, before she goes to her much needed sleep. Nevertheless the whole process could be pushed on an hour or two were it not for the fear that the doctor will arrive and start his visit before the nurses and internes have booked themselves up sufficiently to

make his visit profitable to the patient and not too long for his other
engagements.

All this it is often the minister's business to explain to outraged
or wilted patients, not defending what is indefensible but explaining
the complex interlocking machinery of the hospital and the difficulty
of changing it. There is some alleviation for the patient in knowing
that he is not being waked so early because of an individual's hard-
heartedness or merely because it is the hospital rule. There is reason
behind the rule, though, we think, a poor reason.

On hearing this complaint one should make no attempt to reform
the hospital routine unless one is prepared to go very far. One
would have to undertake a campaign of education with trustees,
superintendents, perhaps even with the general public. The evil is
ancient and very widespread. Many have attacked it without success. Some palliation of it has been obtained here and there. But it
still remains an aggravation to the patient's illness wherever doctors
make their hospital visiting in the morning. Patients get used to it
as to so many other irritating items in their hospital life. They learn
to sleep earlier and so are less sleepy when the night nurse begins
to bother them in the morning.

About food the minister's explanation will be roughly the same.
It is hard to deliver good food, hot, nicely served and properly
adapted to the needs of each patient as they vary from day to day
and even from meal to meal. Moreover it is costly to do this and
hospitals are usually in debt and losing money. If they are tax-sup-
ported the taxpayers, often including the sufferer himself, do not
want their taxes any higher. Food prepared in large quantities, as
it must be in hospitals, does not taste as well as food cooked for a
few. Dainty service takes more time, more taste and more money
than hospitals can afford. They cannot cater to the tastes of individual patients nor predict how much each patient can eat at any
particular meal. Yet to be served too much often destroys what
little appetite the sick man has.

Many a patient has to feed himself when he is hardly strong
enough to do so. But no hospital could afford nurses enough to feed

all the patients who on some particular day might need it. And it has to be admitted that despite all these difficulties the vast majority of patients do somehow get nourished, recover, and go about their business.

Discomfort, often considerable, yes. Disaster, very rarely.

The patient shares the services of a skilled and experienced physician in a hospital ward, and is able to have these services only because the doctor can go quickly from bed to bed instead of slowly from house to house. So the patient must share also the discomforts unavoidable in a ward. Most of the time ward patients are not noisy or close to death. If they were they would be moved to a private room. But emergencies upset predictions. Mrs. B. had been taking her pneumonia quietly thus far, and when she began to be delirious last night the nurse thought the hypodermic would quiet her as it did the night before. When it did not the night nurse knew that Mrs. B. should be moved. But the night ward tender was unusually busy and could not get round to moving her for nearly an hour. So everyone in the ward was aroused and some of them frightened. This happens about once in so often. If it happened every night some different arrangement would be made, but it had not happened before for a good while.

Rigid rules about visiting hours are necessary, first because nurses have to watch visitors and make sure they don't stay too long or smuggle in food or drugs; also because doctors and internes cannot go on with their needful jobs (examining, questioning, doing surgical dressings, giving special treatments) while visitors are present. The process of study and treatment has to stop while visitors are there and this interruption has to be reduced to a minimum. Hence visiting hours.

Too few good nurses? Yes, but good nurses are rare and expensive. No hospital can afford enough of them. Moreover nurses have to be trained. They cannot learn much out of books. They must learn by doing what they can safely do for the sick under competent supervision. Some can never learn and go on from minor to major blunders, but it is impossible to predict this from their looks, their previous education or their behavior in the class-room. They learn by trial and error. Some of these errors are distressing to patients and a few are serious, but no way has yet been found to get training for nurses without some blunders. No one wants to pay for a hospital served wholly by the best type of trained nurse, and if they did no new ones could be trained to replace the others as they retire.

Tell hospital architects and hospital superintendents how to find floor material that wears well, is cheap and easy to keep clean but not slippery. They will make you rich and famous.

Medical students, like nurses, can get the most vital part of their training only by direct experience with a great many sick people. They can learn much by watching physicians at work. But there remains much that they can learn only by doing it, at first inexpertly. Good hospitals provide enough supervision to prevent students from doing harm to patients or making them suffer unnecessarily. But the best of supervision cannot see everything. Mistakes, of omission and of commission, will happen. They happen even to the expert. Even he in very rare instances makes a blunder that costs a patient's life. It happens only once in many thousand cases but it does happen. Knowing this every hospital superintendent acquires a statistical fatalism that seems like callousness. Once in so often, he knows, something will go wrong in any big institution where sickness that needs infallible accuracy is treated by fallible human beings.

Not every patient can have the best service of the best men and women all the time. Only a few can have that and for part of the time. Unless a good many had the service of the fallible, multitudes would go without any service at all, as in most countries they still do. Division of labor means a chain as weak as its weakest link. Sometimes it breaks.

2. *Complaints about the doctors and the internes.*
   (a) Neglect, owing to hurry and inattention.
   (b) Heartlessness, mechanical behavior. Carelessness.
   (c) Roughness of hand or voice.
   (d) Vagueness and elusiveness when the patient wishes to talk over his troubles, their future and their treatment.

(e) Too much research and teaching; too little personal interest.

(f) Procrastination.

(g) Personal unattractiveness, *e.g.,* odor of tobacco, of alcohol, or of ether.

(h) Commercialism.

(i) Defending all that subordinates do and being defended by all subordinates. Conspiracy against the patient.

Complaints about medical care should usually go straight from patient to doctor. Complaints about the institution and its rules cannot often go directly from patient to hospital superintendent because the latter is usually invisible. His assistants are not so invisible but are harder to identify in the maze of the hospital hierarchy. But the patient ordinarily sees his doctor every day, and should be urged to speak his mind directly. The doctor does not always welcome complaints, sometimes because he is human, and sometimes because he is unpaid and so prone to feel that any service that he gives is a favor. Sometimes he is spoiled because he hears so much praise and so little blame from his awed or admiring patients.

Nevertheless the patient should be urged by the minister and by his other friends to speak of what displeases him, provided there is any reasonable hope of correcting it. The doctor probably cannot improve his looks or his voice, but he can give more time and more explanation if he is brought to see the need of it. The minister should be discriminating when he listens to complaints. He can see better than the patient that many of his apprehensions are not well founded. In our experience most complaints about the doctor's neglect or callousness are not well founded. Yet they are quite natural. The doctor *is* a very queer being and needs to be explained to the patient. He cannot explain himself. The minister can do good service by explaining him. The minister too needs explanation and should be grateful to anyone who will tackle the job in a fair-minded way. Meantime, this is what he may well say to the patient about the doctor: [1]

When he seems hardly to notice the patient's sufferings or even

---

[1] See also Chapter IV, What the Doctor Is Like.

his complaints, he has in fact taken them into his mind and passed quickly to the next act. He has blended them with a multitude of other facts given him by nurse or interne before he entered the ward. His mind is now so busy on plans to relieve the suffering that he seems to ignore the suffering altogether.

While he is so intensely at work, he often frowns, not at you but at his job. He may speak coldly or roughly, not at you but at his own thoughts. We admit that he would be a better doctor if he could pursue his rapid-fire calculations internally and still keep his full attention on the men and women before him, but that is asking more than his best. Try it yourself and you will not blame him. He is acting for your best interests.

"But sometimes he walks by my bed without a minute's pause and then spends fifteen minutes with the man in the corner bed."

Yes, because the nurse and the interne have already given him the facts about your previous day and night. The doctor has reflected on these and tried to think what more could be done to hurry things up or to improve the symptoms. He has failed to think of anything, and as he is a careful and experienced man, his silence means that in all human probability there is not anything more to be done.

But here comes in a point in the doctor's psychology that the minister (or some one else) ought to interpret to the dissatisfied patient.[2] It is not pleasant for the doctor to feel nonplussed as he does when he stands beside this patient for whom he can do nothing. He cannot be at his ease unless he is in the process of finding out what to do and then doing it. To be at a loss, as he often is, is not comfortable. Therefore he moves quickly past the beds of those for whom he can do nothing more, and focusses his attention on the patients who call his resources into action and so give him the chance to feel and to be of use. "That he can do nothing for you," the interpreter adds, "doesn't mean that you are incurable or that you are not rapidly getting well. It usually means that in your case nature has cut him out of a job and is doing all the work."

[2] See also Chapter IV.

"Well then, why doesn't he stop and tell me *this?*"

Because, like you, he is human and does not want to feel his helplessness acutely, as he would if he stopped to talk with you empty-handed, his mind empty of any helpful remedy for your ills. He does not want to face your reproachful eyes. All this he sums up in the act of being busy with other patients. He has not conversation enough to go round or time enough to get round the ward if he stops to speak with those whom, today, he cannot help. He is not a brilliant conversationalist. He is a brilliant surgeon. He cannot be everything.

It comes to this. Doctors do far more thinking about their patients and are far more busily engaged, behind the scenes, in the laboratory or elsewhere, on their interests than there is any time to explain. We think it would be better if they explained this oftener. But doubtless they do their best. So let me explain for them.

When the minister says something like this he acts on the good old maxim, "Defend the absent." Good for everyone, that maxim, but used by few. The minister has to make up for others' forgetfulness by working that maxim hard. He defends the absent because they are not there to defend themselves. He tries to imagine what the absent would say if they heard the charge which slips out so boldly in their absence. Perhaps it is a true accusation, but no one should believe it without hearing the defense. If the accused is not on hand some one else ought to defend him. Not if there is no defense. We should not say, "I'm for the absent right or wrong," but tentatively, interrogatively, we should rouse doubts about his crimes: "Who knows that he did this or said that? Is the evidence conclusive? And if it is might he not have a good reason or at least a defensible motive? Could we fairly expect him to do differently considering the situation, his traditions, and the light he had to see by? Hasn't he usually done the best he could, and done pretty well too? Would you want to be condemned for what he did without a chance to explain yourself?"

So much we can often say without defending the indefensible or whitewashing any crime. Strong currents of human nature flow toward criticizing or condemning. Censorship is in the air. If you are ready to maintain that most of your absentee criticism is just, test it by imagining as vividly as you can how you would feel if you suddenly discovered that the man you criticize has heard your words, accidentally, not as an eavesdropper, perhaps through a third party. Probably you would then maintain that the substance of your remarks was just, though you would have phrased them differently in his presence. Perhaps. But isn't it possible that you would have omitted them altogether?

We believe that one should say nothing about the absent that will not bear the test either of his presence or of the presence of a good friend of his. The doctor may speak of the sick man's coming death in a way that he would not want him to hear. But he is ready and anxious, to tell some relative or friend what he believes is coming to the patient. It is the hostile not the painful truth that we are most apt to express when we should not. And why shouldn't we? Because we should not dare to do it in the presence of the accused. We should be ashamed and probably attacked if he suddenly walked in.

Returning, after this intentional digression, to the complaints that ministers often hear against the medical staff: Can we defend the doctor for his elusiveness? He is hard to pin down when we need to know his plans and his expectations about our future. Yes, and often he has good reasons. First, he knows that patients, given the chance, sometimes ask questions that they are not ready to hear truthfully answered. Like the artist who asks what you think of his pictures, they want an agreeable answer. If the truth as you see it is not agreeable, if it is terrible, they sometimes do not want it at all and may be all the sicker because they have heard it. Knowing this and being unwilling to lie, the doctor often evades.

Often rightly. Sometimes without good reasons. Occasionally he plans an operation for a patient but gives the patient no such insight into his condition as would make him desire the operation. The social worker is then asked to make arrangements so that the patient can come into the hospital for the operation. The social worker has no right to tell the patient that he needs the operation because he has, say, cancer. That is the doctor's business. Yet so long as the doctor has told the patient nothing, the social worker can give him no good reason for the financial sacrifice and domestic rearrangements which his hospitalization will involve.

When this situation arises someone has to remind the doctor as gently as possible that he has forgotten something. The social worker, the nurse or the minister may have to do this. They will neither condemn nor approve of the doctor. They will assume that the matter has slipped his mind and will remind him accordingly.

Research and teaching in hospitals are right and valuable but easily abused. Someone must be constantly watchful to prevent their abuse even when the physicians concerned are high-minded and disinterested men as they usually are. Scientific enthusiasm is a noble trait but it sometimes runs away with the scientist and makes him forget the rights of patients. I (R. C. C.) have seen experiments —harmless but annoying experiments—done on hospital patients without asking their consent. Consent will be gladly given in the great majority of cases. But it takes a little time and trouble to ask it and so it is often forgotten. I have seen a patient with an "interesting" form of heart disease examined by so many medical students that he was quite exhausted and had a bad night after it. I do not think it did him any permanent harm. But it made him suffer without benefit and without consent. It was not fair.

Every good hospital superintendent tries to prevent this abuse. He asks nurses or others who are on the spot to watch the teaching and research which is done in the wards and to report to him any excesses or perversions. If the minister is the only person on the spot when the patient complains of the students or research men, and if he is convinced that the complaint is just, he should repeat it to the superintendent.

But if a patient enters a complaint against all teaching and every piece of research on patients, he needs to have it explained to him by someone, perhaps by the minister, that medical students can never learn medicine without examining patients and that useful research cannot go on if it is done wholly on animals and never on human beings. Diagnostic research and research on treatment can often be begun on animals but must be finished on men. The differences between man and other animals cannot always be disregarded.

Conspiracy against the patient, unnecessary operations, unnecessary visits, expensive and unnecessary examinations, unauthorized experiments, may involve a group of doctors and nurses in what is truly a conspiracy against the patient's welfare. No one knows how common such rascality is, but everyone knows that fee-splitting is common and that is a conspiracy with at least two members.

If patients complain to the minister of such practices proved or suspected, the answer should be: Complain to those whom you accuse. No third person need intervene save to encourage and to advise investigation. Perhaps the doctor is unjustly accused. If not he cannot be defended but the minister has no reason to become involved in the matter.

3. *Complaints against nurses* are common in hospitals. The private nurse can be discharged if the patient does not like her. But the hospital nurse is not in his employ, and if he complains of her may take revenge on him. This has happened several times in our experience and doubtless would happen oftener were patients not too much afraid to bring it about by complaining. The commonest complaints are of:

(a) Neglect. "Will not answer the bell."
(b) Roughness or clumsiness in handling the sufferer.
(c) Blocking direct and close relation between patient and doctor, by always being present at his visits. (This also makes it difficult for the patient to complain of the nurse.)
(d) Inconsiderateness: noise, whispering or talking outside the door. Talking about disease and its fascinating horrors.

(e) Petty tyranny.

(f) Over-attention, when the patient wants to be let alone.

(g) Trying to attract the patient's attention to herself.

Each of these charges has been made without due grounds by patients of ours. The nurse cannot always answer the bell instantly, as some patients seem to expect. They have other duties and they usually come as soon as they can. They may well be clumsy and seem rough when they are doing their best. They are often in an early stage of their training and skill does not come without practice. Perhaps the nurse always attends the doctor on his visit because he has requested it. Perhaps she seems inconsiderate or noisy when her other work made noiselessness impossible. Perhaps her seeming tyranny or her overattentiveness are the result of obeying the doctor's orders. For it must be always remembered that whoever pays the nurse, she takes her orders from the doctor and from no one else, unless by his permission. Doubtless some nurses try to "vamp" their patients but some patients like it.

Complaints against nurses, like all complaints, should be made to the person accused unless there are special reasons against it. Even in a hospital where the patient is to some extent at the nurse's mercy and may fear her revenge if he complains, he will generally get better results in minor matters by speaking directly to the nurse herself *provided* he does so considerately and tactfully. Irritation breeds counterirritation and rudeness is apt to be returned in kind. A complaint should be introduced by a word or two of praise for whatever can truthfully be praised. One should assume that the matter complained of was a mistake, an accident, not an intentional injury, that the nurse desires to give good service and that she is doubtless overburdened with work. If made in this spirit complaints are often well received and promptly remedied.

If the complaint is a serious one, if there is good reason to suspect gross neglect, ignorance, or ill will, the complaint should be lodged with the doctor or with the superintendent of nurses. In relaying the message the minister may be of use. The superintendent does not *always* support the nurse. Doubtless many unfounded complaints are brought to her and she needs to be sure of the facts before taking action.

II. THE ILLUSION OF ROUTINE

When a doctor begins to examine a patient in bed he wants every organ in its standard position. Some of them change their position if the patient lies on his side. So he says, "Now lie flat on your back." But the patient is now only an inch or two away from that position. He cannot imagine that the doctor is so particular that he wants him to shift just that inch. He wants to oblige. So he turns over onto his stomach and has to be rolled back again before the examination can begin.

The first few times that this happens in a ward, the doctor and the nurse are amused. But when twenty or thirty patients have done it it grows tiresome because we begin to suffer from an illusion of routine, namely, that the same patient has made this rather irritating blunder thirty times though we have told him thirty times not to do it. Then the force of thirty slight annoyances merged in the last one is discharged in wrath upon the last offender. He innocently and rightly supposes that he has never made this mistake before, but we treat him as if he had done it every day for a month. We cannot realize that he is a brand-new blunderer who is trying hard to oblige us but is a good deal scared. So we come down on him like a thousand of brick, and all because we are fooled by an illusion of routine.

There are many such illusions in the routine of a great institution. As you are standing under a large wall-sign which reads "Tumor Clinic," a bedraggled old lady asks you if this is the X-ray department. You point politely to the X-ray sign twenty feet down the corridor and she hobbles off. But if you happen to stand rather often at that spot a dozen people may ask you the same stupid question within a week. Then a mirage arises before you and in it you see the same bedraggled old woman who first asked you that question, and you know that she, the identical female, has asked you the same question a dozen times over despite your dozen efforts to set her right. So you bark at her (though she's probably a small boy this time), "Can't you read? Look at that sign that you just passed by! Are you blind?" etc., etc.

Doctors, nurses, clerks and all who work long in a large institution are subject to this illusion and must fight if they are to get over it. What seems callousness in their behavior is often due to the real difficulty of imagining that every one of a thousand persons who tread on our mental corns is a brand-new person who never saw this institution before, and is just now going through one of the scariest crises of his life. You feel as if they could not help passing along the word to one another when one has made some ludicrous mistake. That they are strangers to one another and that each lives in a world of his own is hard to believe.

Few males can stand regular routine contacts with human beings without catching this illusion of routine. The net effect is to make them "hard-boiled," indifferent and rude. Women stand routine better. They keep their common sense longer and do not become so stupid as the average institutionalized male. But everyone, the minister included, will be mildewed with routinism before he has been many months in an institution unless he analyzes the steps of the process, sees its stupidity as well as its unkindness, and fights it in the early stages. The minister should be one of those who lead in the attack against the blight of routine.

III. "BECOMING HOSPITALIZED"

Most patients dislike hospital life and want to escape it as soon as they can, but if they stay for months in a ward some of them become dangerously content with it and with their own invalidism. Progress stops and relapse threatens. They must be sent home even if they are not physically fit to go. Any change may do them good even though their medical treatment may be less efficient outside the hospital.

Hospitalization is one of the blights of a routine existence. One acquires the habit of being helpless, of being waited on, of passive acquiescence in others' decisions and in others' efforts, until one likes it better than any life that forces one to make an effort of one's own. Even pain and insomnia become habits. We cease to fight for recovery. Then the unconscious tissues follow suit. Food ceases to nourish us. Blood corpuscles do not respond to drugs that should make them multiply. Muscles waste from disease. Will power and brain power grow flabby.

Sometimes impotent tissues spread their decay to the mind. Oftener, we believe, the mental atrophy comes first. Then it is part of the minister's job to read the riot act. The patient has forgotten what makes life worth while. The world outside the hospital has grown dim. His normal interests and affections can still be awakened if a new person not associated with the hospital routine sounds an alarm. This noise may hurt. There is pain in the wrench out of habits of passivity. We must steel ourselves to be firm when our sympathies betray us. Firmness is not cruelty but it needs some of the same negations if we are to loosen the grip of hospitalization before it forces us to send the patient home while still he needs care that he cannot get there. The will to live and to conquer disease can be roused when it has not fallen too heavily asleep. But doctors and nurses are especially impotent in this direction because they have begun themselves to lose faith in the patient's power to revive. The minister's unfamiliarity with the long chapter of failures in such a case is an asset. He starts fresh where others are jaded.

The gist of this chapter may be summed up thus:

1. Listen cautiously but sympathetically to complaints.
2. Expect and so avoid certain illusions due to routine.
3. Recognize and combat the danger of "hospitalization."

CHAPTER IV

WHAT THE DOCTOR IS LIKE

IF we were writing this book primarily for doctors we should need a chapter on what the doctor should know about the minister. As things are we shall content ourselves with a description of the doctor's point of view written for the minister, and including something of what the doctor thinks about the minister.

1. The central point in the doctor's make-up is *concentration* with its strength and its weakness. He is trained to focus on disease. Whatever the patient does or says, his looks, his voice, his gait and motions, the words he chooses, the signs of emotion or of lethargy, the way he uses his hands—such facts claim his attention while he is sizing up the patient. With these data he soon weaves in the items which he finds by examining the patient's body, his temperature, the action of his heart, the sounds heard in his lungs with a stethoscope, the evidence of good or of poor nutrition, the state of his internal organs so far as he can feel them or see them in his throat, his retina or his rectum.

Further knowledge is obtained by X-rays, by examining blood, urine, sputa, etc., and through the reports of nurses or relatives on what happens between his visits and at night. The doctor works all these facts together, in the light of his knowledge of other sick people and of his reading on disease. Reasoning on this mass of complex, disjointed, often contradictory facts, he tries to join them in a single diagnosis and then to prescribe the treatment which experience and reading have shown fit in that disease.

While he is with his patient, his mind is running out along paths of reasoning designed to fit the queer facts into one of the two hundred odd diagnoses which his medical training has taught him to look for. His diagnosis is often uncertain. Many of his cases seem unlike any disease that he knows. Even after he has made a diagnosis he is always watching for new evidence and new clues which will fit the facts better than the one which now steers his treatment.

Concentration on diagnosis absorbs him so fully when he is with the patient that he gives little thought to the patient's life, character, and interests. Much he intentionally disregards. It is none of his business, he says, because it has nothing to do with the diagnosis or the treatment of this case. What a lot there is that he does not notice, or seem to notice! Yes, but so it always is with intense work. There is a good deal that a juggler does not notice while he is doing his tricks. Think how much a fox-hunter ignores when he is jumping a fence. We approve of his narrowness of vision because we can see what he is doing, but the doctor's furious activity is largely invisible. It goes on in his head or in brief, rapid, technical language quite opaque to the patient.

The doctor's strength is in the minuteness and accuracy of his work within his own chosen field. His weakness is in the crowd of obvious facts which he disregards, often rightly. He has little idea of what is in his patient's mind. He can treat his disease without that and he has no time for it. So he thinks, and he may be right. But now and then the patient's hopes, fears, longings, sorrows, and disappointments, his interests balked by illness, his affections, his prejudices, and habits of mind, are prime facts for the diagnosis and the treatment.

To the minister these facts make up the most interesting and important part of the patient. To ignore them or to pay scanty and hurried attention to them may seem to the minister a kind of blindness. Doctors see many of these facts but have learned to disregard them because they do not contribute to the one end and aim on which the doctor has taught himself to concentrate. Like one looking through a microscope he sees that field alone, and necessarily ignores the rest of the world. It is most important that the minister shall see the doctor's great strength within his own field and also the enormous areas of human life which his work leads him to neglect. The more acute and dangerous the illness the better this medical habit of concentration works. In long slow illnesses one *must* take into account what is going on in the patient's mind and heart. There the minister finds his great chance.

The doctor's way is an economy of time and talent. He does what he is expert in. If he did not cram his time with this sort of work he could not earn his living. It is for the public good that he should concentrate on the physical-chemical side of his patients, and not try to spread his attention over mental and spiritual problems in which he has no skill. His habits rarely issue from a theory about body and soul, from any theological beliefs or disbeliefs. He is a practical man with little urge to meditate or to theorize. He leaves such things to others, certain that they are out of his line. Sometimes he is acidly skeptical about religion and has little respect for the minister. Oftener he is content to mark off spheres of interest. So long as the minister does not try to practice medicine or psychiatry he is glad to welcome what he can do for the sick.

He needs first to see that the minister does not tire or excite the patient. Fatigue and excitement check the healing of disease. The patient may greatly enjoy the minister's visit and yet be worse the next day. The doctor wants to be certain that this does not happen. Moreover the doctor wants to be sure that the minister will not alarm the patient. There is a general impression abroad that patients interpret a call from the minister as the approach of death. In our experience this is not true.[1] But such is apt to be the patient's impression if he is used to visits from his minister only in the crises of life. The doctor is right in trying to prevent the harm done by a groundless fear of death roused at sight of the minister. But if the doctor knows that the minister will not scare, tire or excite the patient, and will not discredit medical treatment, he is glad of the minister's aid, or at least is neutral.

[1] See Chapter XXII, The Dying, p. 298.

2. Few people are aware how much of the doctor's behavior is governed by his need to "play safe." He cannot do or say anything that will spread distrust of him in the community. For example, doctors are sometimes queerly anxious to get a very sick patient transferred to a hospital even though the patient and his family oppose it and even though the hospital affords no special treatment (operation, X-ray) which cannot be given as well at home. But the doctor must be on the safe side. He wants hospital treatment for the patient because he thinks that he is going to die. Every death in a patient under his care is talked about by the neighbors and counts against him, but if the death occurs in the hands of hospital physicians no one can blame him. He must avoid blame at almost any cost. How else can he live? Patients will not come to him if they often hear him blamed.

Because of his need for "safety first" it is hard to make a doctor commit himself about anything in which he may later be shown wrong. Prognosis, the probable outcome and length of an illness, is one of the hardest things to tell in advance. Doctors are therefore silent or vague about it. For a similar reason it is hard to make a doctor say clearly that there is nothing at all the matter. He may believe so. All his examinations may have shown healthy organs, but disease may be latent and may escape through the net of our closest medical test. Knowing this, the doctor fears that if any illness appears weeks or months after he has said that there is no disease, he will be blamed for having missed it and will be distrusted as one who is hasty in his examinations. So he is apt to hedge or to be vague at a time when clear-cut statements are needed. Some patients need above all things an emphatic declaration that there is no disease in them. Till they know that, they will go on feeling vague pains, sleeping and eating poorly, worrying and miserable. When really convinced that they are free of disease they will stop worrying, begin to sleep and to eat, and soon lose all their bad symptoms. Ministers must know and sometimes forgive the doctor's tendency to "play safe" even when he really ought to assume a slight risk for his patient's good. Till doctors are sure of a regular income they cannot be expected to risk the little they have.

3. The minister is apt to be surprised at the doctor's inbred habit of content with facts which he cannot explain. The minister wants to know why disease hits one child and spares his twin, why it is severe in this case, mild in that. Why does jaundice make folks glum? Why are "bleeders" always male? No answer. The doctor is so used to dealing with shut doors that he seems to have lost curiosity for what is behind them. Science asks for reasons and is not content with brute facts. Does it? Then the minister seems more scientific than the doctor, because the doctor has got used to living with crowds of "bare facts" which he cannot explain. In truth he wants to know why as much as anybody, but he has got used to a life in which he can explain only a few of the facts which he handles day after day.

He gets a little impatient sometimes with the minister's wonder at the number of *surds* in medicine. The minister seems quite ignorant of the actual world because he still hopes to find reasons for most things. The real world, as the doctor knows it, is made up mostly of brute facts utterly unexplained. So it has been for as long as he can remember. Anyone who expects it otherwise is "soft." Yet the minister is right when he refuses to be satisfied with mere facts and seeks forever for reasons. He is in line with the spirit of good scientific work. And the doctor is right too. Science talks much about the small fragments of the world which we *can* explain and is often silent about the huge percentage of unmapped yet insistent facts. Hence ministers and the general public have been led to think that we know a great deal more about the world than we do. The doctor is right that the lighted parts of nature are the rarity and the dark parts are the rule.

The "real world" that comes to us through our five senses is still mostly unexplained. Only a small corner of it has been illumined by the light of reason. It is the inner world, the world of the spirit, that contains most of what man has thus far understood. Religion, philosophy and mathematics include a great deal that we already understand. The natural sciences can seldom answer the question "Why." They still give us mostly "bare facts" and fairly probable theories. Ministers and the rest of us have been fooled by propaganda about the glories of science already attained, because our machines and our medicines work well even though we know as little about them as the average motorist knows about the engine of his car. He can drive it and that is all he wants. We can drive our data in medicine, biology, geology, chemistry, and physics without knowing them in any deep way. In music, literature, logic, ethics, and much of theology, we understand what we are dealing with even when we cannot "work it" as we work the mysterious entities of chemistry and physics.

4. Doctors hate to hear medical terms on a minister's lips. Even if he uses them correctly the doctor is apt to suspect that the minister is out of his depth. He may use a technical term rightly once and make a bad blunder the next time with the same term. A term is almost as hard to master as a golf stick. The beginner makes a perfect stroke and cannot repeat it for months. The minister should avoid the use of technical terms in his talk with a doctor, or if he uses them should put quotation marks and question marks into his voice. Terms often imply theories. The doctor fears that the minister will mix his patient up with "explanations" which give an impression different from the doctor's and so leave the sick man wondering whether anybody really knows anything about his disease.

Ministers win doctors' approval by deeds, not by words. An action that shows devotion, courage, foresight, imagination, tact, self-sacrifice, will win the doctor's admiration as soon as any one else's. The minister who listens well and learns well wins the confidence of the physician.

5. Many doctors who care little for sects and churches are themselves deeply religious. The same motives send some men into medicine, others into the ministry. The experiences of a doctor's life

are at least as often favorable to religious belief as prejudicial to it. We know men who have shifted from medicine to theology, and others who have made the opposite shift. Theology seems to deal with ideas, medicine with people. But in fact both professions deal both with ideas and with human beings.

Hints for good medical-clerical teamwork:

1. Doctors are strong on facts and means; ministers on motives and ends. Hence misunderstanding is natural *until* they come to work together for a patient's good. Then each feels the serviceability of the other when both are sincere and competent.

2. By the patient's or the family's mandate the doctor is as much the boss in illness as the minister is at a funeral. The doctor rightly does not want interference with his job or question of his authority within his field.

3. If the doctor does not want the minister or is antagonistic to him the conflict will do the patient more harm than the minister's services will do him good. In the rare case of genuine malpractice and injury to the patient by the doctor, the minister can probably work through others and not get implicated.

4. Working with the doctor with deference and under his guidance, avoids most difficulties.

5. Where the doctor is most needed, in the acute cases and in the acute phases of chronic disease, the minister is least needed. When the minister can do most, as in chronic or "hopeless" disease, and in convalescence, the doctor is most impotent.

6. Don't practice psychotherapy in any technical sense (or so that the patient or the doctor knows it). Come as a friend or as a minister and not as a healer; then you will get on well with doctors. They fear competition and interference, in church clinics or home visits.

7. Hunt the chance to do the doctor a favor in some way connected with the sick, to praise him when he deserves it, to help out in sitting up with patients and by laboring with indigent, cross-grained, hopeless, "uninteresting" cases. Then he will want you on other cases.

PART II

THE SITUATION

CHAPTER V

SPIRITUAL BACKSLIDING

OF the two campaigns which the minister undertakes for the growth of the spirit in "religious" or in "nonreligious" people, one is hard and one is relatively easy. We have mentioned the hard one first: the effort to develop character along the path of the Christian way (Chapter I). We turn now to the easier one, the attempt to keep people from sliding backwards. It is hard to help them forward, and almost no one asks us to do it. We have to go after it. But to stop sick souls from going astern is a task that jumps in our faces when we confront the problems of sickness. People go backwards in their spiritual growth when they are terrified, depressed, bitter, lonely. They come to a painful pause in forward progress when, as so often in illness, they are dreadfully bored.

Most people who have experienced both, agree that mental suffering is worse than physical pain. They welcome sharp pain as a relief to mental pain. Physical pain at its worst often brings its own relief in loss of consciousness. Mental pain has no such limit. Mental pain is harder to help than physical pain. It lies closer to the central control of a personality which another person can hardly touch. But it is the minister's business as much as anybody's, or more, and if he refuses to touch mental disease and perversions he can be of use. For the temporary backslidings which physical disease initiates he may really do something.

When he visits those whose suffering is largely physical there is in most cases much less for the clergyman to do than when there is mental suffering. But even in physical disease the sufferer wants to feel that someone knows how he suffers. If the minister can honestly say, "Yes, I understand," there is some comfort in it for many patients, though it is from the doctor or the nurse that he expects definite relief.

The effort to check spiritual backsliding is parallel to some of our medical endeavors. In pneumonia doctors try to hold up people's strength, to maintain their nutrition, to keep them from exhausting themselves in delirium or restlessness. So the minister, if he meets the patient where his immediate needs jut out, begins with attempts to fortify him against whichever of the mental poisons just mentioned he is then fighting. This is right though we know that the only long-time treatment for the ills of the spirit is to forward the spirit's own growth, not merely to check its tendency to slide backward.

We are not often vigorously urged by our medical colleagues to the campaign for growth. They want the patient to be quiet, serene, uncomplaining, unemotional; but they do not always realize that we cannot keep up such serenities merely by suppressing their opposites. Stagnation is as bad for people as restlessness, and the reiterated medical insistence on rest sometimes leads to atrophy of the spirit as it often leads to atrophy of the muscles. The good life for every organ in the body and for every capacity of the soul is a life that is moving ahead, not one which has merely ceased to explode or to wear itself out with emotion.

When we have realized that the only radical and permanent treatment of mental suffering is to nourish crescent life, then we may set ourselves to "meet the patient where he is," on the surface, where his symptoms and sufferings appeal for help. The patient who throws his food tray on the floor is given attention (but only by the nurse as a rule). When the patient sits by the window gazing out, or scowls into space, or restlessly paces his room, no one is much concerned with these signs that he is brooding or lonely. Ordinarily the patient is left to prepare himself mentally as best he can for an operation, no matter how serious that operation may be. He is seldom even asked what he thinks about it. It would often be well for the doctor to find out in various ways what his patient thinks and whether he would like to see his priest or his minister. Some doctors do that very thing.

We can do something to meet *fear* by showing that many fears are groundless. Behind many specific physical fears are often the deeper spiritual fears. The clergyman, whose faith gives him defense against the ultimate fear, will watch for it at the back of the patient's mind. By watching for it he can be ready to meet it if opportunity comes. The fear of death is far commoner than most people realize. When this is latent yet torturing, one of the clergyman's best opportunities is in sight. No matter what people think or do not think about religion, they are glad of anyone who will try to give them courage against death.

Loneliness is a foe to many a sick person, even when he has plenty of people about him, because they often fail to reach the core of his suffering. They do not know what he is lonely about, or what piece of him is lonely. Or his loneliness may have grown up because he feels useless and has nothing to do. Or perhaps he thinks that his sickness has made him so unattractive and uninteresting that people come only as a matter of duty.

Bitterness and grudge against someone who the patient thinks has treated him ill, against a particular group such as the rich, or against society as a whole, often retard convalescence.

We have something to say about five common forms of spiritual backsliding: loneliness, boredom, fear, bitterness, and the morbid obsession of guilt. The rest of this chapter will be about

I. LONELINESS

One friend of ours, a man of thirty-five and widely traveled, insists that he has never been lonely in his life except once—when he returned to his home after a long absence and found things greatly changed there. Throughout the rest of his life he remembers no loneliness. We have never known another person so nearly immune to this form of suffering. In health as well as in sickness, in childhood, in adult life, and in old age, in educated and in uneducated people, most of us are lonely sooner or later and some of us suffer bitterly from it. It is not at all peculiar to "mental disease" or "nervous disease," and does not suggest that any such trouble is coming. It is the ordinary "run of the mill" in bodily sickness. It is one of the reasons most often leading a doctor or a nurse to ask the minister's help. Loneliness is especially apt to seize the patient in a hospital when he first arrives, when the first night in the institution draws near, at visiting hour when other patients have visitors and he has none, or when he is bundled down to the operating room. But even in our own home, sickness often makes us lonely because it takes away the companionship of our daily occupations and our usual habits. It throws us back upon ourselves. Others go off and have a good time. We hear their laughter downstairs but we are out of it. No one realizes, we say to ourselves, what we are going through.

We often find loneliness in convalescent patients. As one patient expressed it, "The better I get, the less interesting I am." The further he pulls away from acute stages of illness the less medical attention he needs and the less he gets. His friends have got over being excited. Then may come the despair of feeling, "I guess I don't matter much anyway." His temperature is normal and other clinical symptoms have probably disappeared. But what of his mind and spirit? Unfortunately we have no tests to determine the clinical condition of the spirit. If we had such tests we might avoid distressing relapses at a time when medically the patient seemed to be doing well.

Loneliness comes upon a patient gradually but with determined certainty, especially when he is fearful or worried yet cannot express those concerns to his family. He may be fearful of a pending operation, yet he does not mention it because he knows that his family are themselves suffering under the strain. He may know of his impending death yet may not tell his family even though he surmises they too know. Thus protecting each other, patient and family often carry a front of courageous determination to the very end, and all to the good. One patient we knew told the minister she thought the end was near. He knew already that her family had been told this. Together the patient and the minister faced her death. The minister was interpreter not only between the patient and God, but between the patient and her family, bringing them together so that she need not bear alone the majesty and the grimness of death, and so that the family might share the noble courage which she had attained.

Recently a supervisor of nurses asked my aid (R. L. D.). "Will you see a very difficult patient for us? He says he's a Jewish minister, whatever that is." Another patient said of him, "Of all the mean men I have ever seen, he takes the prize." He turned out to be a Jewish cantor of orthodox faith, orthodox at least in form if not in belief. He was glad to see me, after he found I was not interested in converting him. "You see," he said, "I have no one to come to me. I talk to no one. These other patients dislike me because I shut them up when they make a noise at night." Some days later, upon my third call, he said, "Tell me why I should want to get well. I am fifty-three. I have no one in the world, no family, no friends, no money, and I am a wanderer. I make my living by traveling, and I do not like to travel." He reached for a towel to wipe away his tears. "Pardon me for putting you in an embarrassing position. . . . I have no ambition. You are young. Life is before you. But I am different. I think love is the greatest thing in the world. I am a great sentimentalist. I love animals, a horse, cows, but not mice. Only mice and cats I do not like. And dogs, some dogs I like. But they are not useful. All other animals I like." He dried his eyes and continued, "I have a family and friends but I do not care to know where they are. I do not care for them, even as much as I do for these." He swept his hand around the ward and his expression indicated that his liking was not at all strong. "But I have no one. There is no reason for my living. The afterlife, I do not believe in. I live for the present. Why should I go on living?" It was a hard question.

This singer had been isolated long before he was sick. Illness merely revealed the fact and made it cut. "Did you feel this way before you were sick?" He said, "No. Just since I have been in the hospital." His busy life had left him no time to be lonely. Loneliness comes stalking upon us when we are ill because there are so many long idle hours in which to brood. The world seems to be going by, and what of ourselves? We wait, wait, wait, and for what? Is it any wonder that many, whose lives are not very full at best, find no value in life when they become ill? They despair not only of the value of their existence in illness, but of the whole purpose of life.

Some patients blame others for their loneliness. In health they may be very resourceful, but in illness they are hopelessly lost, because nothing happens to keep any interest alive. A patient mentioned elsewhere [1] had many friends in health but did not want to see them during his illness because of their curiosity. Yet he was lonely and that made him bitter. So he said as he looked back on the experience later. His bitterness took the form of blaming God. "I thought God had handed me a backhanded slap. Few people came to see me last year, and those who did were chiefly curious about my disease."

Another patient asked to see a minister because of his loneliness. This loneliness made him bitter against his friends, but not against God. He said with determination, "I know One who will not forget me."

There are two groups who suffer because of loneliness when they are ill. There is a tragic group of patients who have no family, no friends, and no money. When we question them we usually find that they do have families somewhere, but have never cared for them or do not now desire to establish contact with the past. They prefer to die as they have lived. Perhaps their decision is more considerate for all concerned. They are usually above the fifty-year mark. They have treasure neither in gold nor in memories. Illness brings enforced reflection for them as it does for others more fortunate. They search for a last ray of hope in religion but usually reject it as

[1] D. N., p. 345.

they have throughout their lives. To relieve loneliness for these people one would have to erase the impressions and the thought-habits of a lifetime. Who can approach such a task with anything less than the whole of heaven's hosts behind him?

But we can do something for the great number of patients who are lonely in illness but not in health. This is the average person who has lived the average life. He is neither a pauper nor a rich man; he has a family to whom he is fairly devoted and on whom he is dependent; he has a few friends and some ambition. This group includes many a laboring man; he has worked most of his life, he reads the daily newspaper and listens to the radio. He becomes excited about the World Series and knows the names of all the leaders in the sports world. He is a member of a church, which he attends for the sake of the children and the wife more than for himself. This group includes also the average woman. She is dependent upon her husband but her pride and joy is in John who has just made the football team. She prefers that John shall not play football, but the fact of his having made the team is one of the first things she tells you. She is sick, "has been poorly for some months," and she wonders how they will get along at home without her. Church to her means the Ladies' Aid Society. She recalls her pastor's mannerisms more easily than she recalls his virtues.

These people are not lonely until they are sick. They include also the young boy whose mother brings him fruit every day at the hospital and will hover over his every need when he returns home. He has never been sick before, is somewhat embarrassed by hospital routine, but soon comes to enjoy having his life ordered by the nurse. At home "the fellows" come in to see him and he passes the time reading Western stories. There he is seldom lonely, more inclined to be bored. But in the hospital nothing happens except his mother's visit.

So much for the disease loneliness. What more specifically of its treatment?

The clergyman can perhaps help more than others because he studies more accurately the nature of the patient's loneliness. As an outsider he may be quicker than others to catch its flavor, and so by giving companionship and affection he may effectively palliate the symptom. But, as with fears, it is always quite possible that behind the obvious signs of loneliness there is a deeper loneliness, a sense that no human being can ever understand what he cares for most, that his real home is not on this earth at all; in short, the religious loneliness which has been the beginning of religious faith in many of us. To be ready to recognize this, to see slight dawning symptoms of it, and to be ready to respond the instant he does see them, is another of the clergyman's best opportunities.

Loneliness is homesickness; but "home" is not always to be found in one's own dwelling. It has to be found elsewhere and it is the minister's business more than any one else's to help people find it. Like much of the minister's work with the sick this task has two phases: immediate help and long-time education, water and living water. Experience seems to show that when we are lonely we can be most swiftly relieved by the assurance of someone's interest and by being given something to do, especially something which holds attention and is of some use to other people. To see one's own people, to feel their affection and to talk with them of the familiar home affairs is often impossible. Then it may be a great relief to the lonesome even to see someone who knows one's people, who has been in one's town and can call off the names of its familiar streets and buildings. This may be possible if the minister is a widely traveled person.

Samuel M. Crothers, for many years the deeply loved minister of the First Church in Cambridge, Massachusetts, had the habit, so Mrs. Crothers tells us, of reading up in an encyclopedia or elsewhere, the details of the home town of anyone whom he knew to be homesick, and so preparing himself to talk intelligently and almost familiarly about it. This seems to us to illustrate the way in which a minister's devotion to the sick might well differ from that of people belonging to other occupations. If it is one's business and not merely one's occasional occupation to minister to human beings, one has the right and often the duty to prepare himself to do one's best by such means as reading up on a patient's home town or on his other interests.

Another friend of ours, not a minister but a nurse, was interested in an Armenian Jew sick in a hospital and especially homesick during the Christmas season because he had so little part in the celebration which included the other patients in the ward. Some time before this his kindly nurse had discovered that he was by trade a mender of oriental rugs. She then read up the subject of oriental rugs sufficiently to talk with him about it. When the Christmas celebration so depressed him she turned her new information to use. He was delighted and began very cheerfully to chatter with her, first about the technicalities of rug-mending and then about oriental rugs in general.

The same worker, finding a lonely Italian in her ward, began to practice on him her stray scraps of Italian and then set him to teaching her more of the language. This set in motion two home-favoring drives—the use of the home language and the use of skill in which he was at home and through which he could instruct another, which makes almost any of us feel more adequate, more placed, and so less homesick.

When these connections cannot be made it may still be possible to get something like them in spirit. One is at home not only in certain places but in certain ideas, on certain topics, in certain interests. A woman talking of her children feels herself for the moment at home with them, and a good listener may encourage her to talk about them in so much detail that for the moment her homesickness is relieved. Most men are "at home" in the technicalities of their profession. Get a gardener talking of flowers, a farmer of farming, a musician of music, a politician of politics, and you banish his loneliness for the time, and often for days.

Heroic souls keep loneliness at a distance by looking after others perhaps lonelier. Twenty years ago an Irish Catholic sewing-woman from a remote town in Canada conquered her fear and decided to come to the Massachusetts General Hospital for a disease that would probably require amputation of her leg. She saved little by little the necessary money, made the journey, had the operation, and settled down for a long slow convalescence in a surgical ward. Then the doctors and nurses of that ward began to notice a marked improvement in its morale. The little Canadian sewing-woman had brought her sewing along with her and after her operation she occupied herself happily with her old trade. But more than that she interested the other patients in the ward in sewing till she had them contentedly busy and imbued with enthusiasm for making something good out of their illness.

The success of her efforts in that ward was a turning point in her life. It gave her the idea that she could direct a sewing and dress-making establishment where all the work was to be done by cripples like herself. By the time she had got this started she had lost her other leg by amputation (below the knee), but none of her enthusiasm had been lost. Now for over twenty years she has taught and supervised sewing by a group of cripples and other handicapped persons, first in a little shop of her own, later in a Catholic Home. Part of her success comes because she is constantly overflowing with happiness, affection, and with gratitude to God and to man. This was always in her make-up but it emerged most signally after her first experience in the Massachusetts General Hospital:

"My intention," she wrote, "is the sanctification of incurables. We will gather up their pain and sufferings and present them to God. He will teach us to suffer in union with Him. I wish the sick were organized into one great body of prayerful sufferers. We have so many petty shackles that we might dispense with and find greater things to fill our minds. Well, we must leave it all at the feet of our Heavenly Physician.

"Sometimes I wonder if anyone is happier than I am. This (May) is such a lovely season, when new life is pouring into all creatures. The very air seems full of new life and I am glad to be able to breathe it. Oh, let us coin the precious time that is given us to do big things for God. No matter how small or trivial they are, if done for Him they will be big.

"Religion to me is like a wonderful flower garden where every flower of every shade and perfume grows, and where each of us can enter at will and taste of its fullness. Please do not overestimate my work. I am just trying to catch a glimpse of the lovely spirit of Christ."

Had any minister visited her at that time he would have learned living religion from a saint. He could also have forwarded her new mission in life and spread to others the influence of her spiritual life. To be in at the birth of a new enterprise like this, to feel the nascent spirit emerging and to assist it to grow, must always be one of the hopes of a clergyman's life. We believe that there is more chance of its fulfillment in the uprooting and transforming experiences of hospital life than in any part of the clergyman's work. In such moments, while the iron is hot and malleable, while character is in turmoil, new vistas may be opened and the minister should have a hand in opening them. At such a moment character may take a new set for evil or for good. In this transformation the minister's influence may be decisive—all the more so because he is himself getting a revelation. His own life currents are running faster than usual and there is more chance that he can transfuse the Christian spirit into the new enterprise.

The opposite of loneliness is something like cosiness, a close, warm, familiar texture of response such as a baby feels with its mother. Flowers are homelike and friendly to those who care for them. Pictures that tell a familiar story are exactly what people want when the world seems cheerless. In a lonely hour Jessie Wilcox Smith's pictures of children are the next best thing to the children themselves.

It makes a great difference to the lonely invalid where his bed is and what he can see from it, whether noises come to him or are shut away, whether his favorite colors, tastes and individualities are expressed around his bed or are forgotten in a cheerless hygienic propriety. The iron chair so often seen in hospitals is easily sterilized and wears well, but it is an abomination to put one near the bed of any patient of delicate sensibility. Nothing is lonelier or more depressing.

Here as in all that we do for the sick, palliation is easier than cure. We can banish the more strident injuries to the sense of beauty, but it is hard to hang up beauty permanently upon the walls of people's minds. We can do something through music and through the other art to which most Americans are sensitive—the art of humor. It sometimes seems as if humor and good humor were the American's only window into the world of spiritual values. Laughter lifts us for the moment above the wounding surface of our road. It is the nearest that some of us come to the praise of God, and if we cannot help a man to pray it is some comfort to help him laugh.

Not all of us are gifted with a keen sense of humor but all of us can increase by training whatever sense we have. We believe that it is as much a clergyman's duty to train his sense of humor as it is to train his voice. By watching experts at the game of joke-seeing and joke-making anyone can catch on to it more firmly. Anyone can accumulate a stock of amusing stories and add new ones as the old are worn out. Most people have a small deposit of them laid away. It is the minister's business to have an unusually large bank account of humor because he needs to give away so much of it, especially to the sick.

Not to all the sick. Some patients swallow jokes like a bitter medicine, and many find them tasteless. But to most of the long-time sufferers, that is to most of those who especially need the minister, jokes are better than flowers and almost as necessary as food. Not all who appreciate fun want it in chunks of side-splitting merriment. Dry humor, humorous twists to a sentence or to an expression, refresh the shut-in. They lead him to show what he can do in that line himself and you have done him a service, and not a wholly transient one. A good joke may linger long in the patient's mind and rise up again and again when he thinks of it. He turns it over in his mind, sees new jokes branch out of it and stores up some of them to tell you at your next visit. We once saw a skillful humorist establish between himself and an invalid a sort of *chronic joke* which was revitalized again and again by scraps of village news, by headlines in the newspaper, and even by the whims of the family cat. So the joke grew, branched, sprouted leaves, struck its roots deep into the sufferer's life and put out fruit on which quite a portion of his life was sustained. He went back to it as some do to their Bible. He depended on it almost as he did upon his wife.

Next to humor the beauty now most nutritious to the American soul is music. With the help of radio and especially of phonographic records the clergyman can help sick people to permanent spiritual property in the world of music. For music, even more than humor, lasts beyond the moment, comes back to us in the night, and through tedious hours stands between us and vacancy. More than humor it weaves itself into our growth. One can go on and on for a lifetime exploring the literature of choral music, of orchestral music, of chamber music, of music for piano, for violin, and for the solo voice. And if one picks out the best specimens in each of these six fields, one can progressively deepen one's understanding as one hears them again and again. Only a small fraction of what one ultimately learns to hear in a great piece like Bach's *B-minor Mass* or Wagner's *Parsifal* comes out in the first hearing even though it delights us so much that it seems complete.

If the clergyman has not the talent to conduct this sort of spiritual education, he may be able to find others who have, and who will be glad to find someone with whom they can share their enthusiasm and their knowledge. From such enthusiasts and sometimes from the patient himself the minister can learn more of musical appreciation. To learn from a sick man is to do him lasting service.

Beauty in literature, distinguished from the interest of reading for information or for amusement, has been a godsend to many sick people. To learn by heart poetry that one cares for gives one a resource that is at hand in the arid stretches of time which confront the tuberculous and some of the sufferers from heart trouble, in the darkness of a wakeful night, and in moods of depression. Passages from the Psalms and from the Gospels, from the religious poetry of the Orient, from the writings of Milton, Browning, Emerson, and many more, mean more to us, whether we are sick or well, if we put work into them until they become part of us, circulating in the mysterious lifeblood of the memory. It is an insult to great literature to turn away from it after the brief and partial contact that we call "reading it." We break away in the middle of its first greetings when we might so easily ask greatness to live closer to us than breathing, nearer than hands and feet. Perhaps the healthy man can afford to treat great literature so rudely but certainly the sick man cannot. He must learn it by heart.

This it is the minister's privilege to make credible to sick people, not only by precept but by example. If he knows much poetry and much of scripture by heart it will be natural for him sometimes to repeat it and for the patient to absorb it. This starts the patient on the road to learning it both because he has begun to be familiar with it and because he sees that another finds it worth while to possess it in memory.

CHAPTER VI

SPIRITUAL BACKSLIDING (*Continued*)

2. FEAR

FEAR is like some dreaded skin disease. It starts as a small rough spot; it spreads slowly or rapidly, but spread it does until it covers the whole, consuming whatever smooth surface it finds. Minor fears like minor skin diseases may not be serious in and of themselves, but unless they are checked they suck our vitality into themselves. We are not here writing of serious and chronic states of panic or of anxiety with which the psychiatrists now deal. A person who shows unexplained restlessness and anxiety should see a doctor. If the doctor then desires to use the minister as a resource in the patient's treatment, the minister may co-operate, but it will be understood that the doctor is responsible for the patient's well-being. The fears of which we are writing in this chapter are those that appear in patients already under the care of a doctor for some organic disease.

Certain fears occur again and again in illness. There is that vague dread which one observes in patients when they first enter a hospital, and the more acute alarm before an operation. We are convinced that no patient in full possession of his senses ever went to the operating room without a certain amount of apprehension. We may go even further and say that no person ever watched an operation for the first time without a certain amount of fear. This may do no harm. A more rapid blood flow and respiration are desirable in order that the organism may have fuel, just as the athlete needs more oxygen during a race.

A patient with an intestinal obstruction was called to our attention. By an operation the obstruction could be removed and the patient's life saved; otherwise he would surely die. The patient refused to have the operation. One of our theological students went to see him. The patient, a boy of twenty-two, said he was afraid he would die if he submitted to the operation. But in fact he was dying anyway, and had had two blood transfusions already. For three days the doctors had been trying to convince him of the necessity of an operation. The student, after letting the patient know that he was a minister, as he had been ordained before coming to the hospital, said, "Suppose you do die: what is there in death that you fear?" He thus centered the boy's attention on death rather than on the fact of dying. After some thought along this line he agreed to have the operation. We discovered later that it was not death but the anesthetic which he feared; by centering attention beyond the operation he was helped to see this.

This instance illustrates both skill and understanding on the part of the minister, plus confidence in the face of death, which probably was as responsible as anything else in helping this boy to face his ordeal.

A second common type of fear in the sickroom is worry. One hears a thousand insignificant concerns and complaints over conditions at home, if the patient is in the hospital. If at home it takes the form of brooding, irritation, and nagging. These worries may cover up apprehension over the outcome of the illness or the dread of facing the world with a handicap. A fear of the years ahead or a fear of repeated illness may haunt him.

After being told that I (R.L.D.) must face the possibility of loss of an arm, I wanted to do two things. I wanted to tell someone of what I was facing, and then I wanted to be alone with the idea. The next day I sat for several hours (fortunately it was a beautiful, sunny day) with the idea squarely in front of me. I had had a bad experience once before with an anesthetic. I faced the experience in detail, passing through it bit by bit. Gradually I gained that element of quietness of which we write in Chapter XV. I had accepted the future. From that time on I never looked back.

Fear of the dark, which seriously handicaps many children and sometimes lasts into adult life, exemplifies a characteristic of many fears. *It is the unknown that terrifies us* because our imagination peoples it with fearful possibilities. Turn on the light and show what is there, fear vanishes, though it may recur as soon as the light is turned off again. Many children should be allowed a night light in their sleeping room. It does not increase or prolong fear of the dark. It banishes it until by the child's normal development darkness ceases to be fearful.

Akin to fear of the dark are the vaguely imagined possibilities of a new country, a new job, of disease, of death. The vaguely pictured unknown makes a large part of the terror. To know the worst and know it clearly is often a relief. The fear of fainting, of taking an anesthetic, or of undergoing an operation, can often be greatly diminished by a literal description of what can and cannot be expected.

Fear of physical pain becomes more and more groundless as medicine elaborates more and more ways to quench it. To dread losing consciousness in a faint, under an anesthetic, in disease, and death, is to fear something as familiar and harmless as going to sleep. Who's there when we go to sleep? God is there and will look after our souls. To fear extinction is to distrust God, to doubt the rationality and continuity of the universe which are the foundations of scientific effort and of logical thinking.

In a hospital there are special opportunities for the minister because there are special terrors there, for example those at the gates of "admission." A patient comes to the hospital for an operation. He is ordered to bed by the straightforward, business-like nurse whose concern is to do a routine duty, not to consider the sensitive feelings of patients. If the patient is an ordinary human being he will be tremendously afraid of the surgery which may be done to him tomorrow or the next day. If his is "an acute case" and he is faced with emergency treatment he will be all the more "upset," but he has the advantage of having "it" quickly over. If he is not an acute case and must await further diagnosis and assignment, he will spend the ensuing hours brooding over the outcome of his illness. Yet the hours before he goes to the operating room should be spent in mental and physical relaxation, conserving energy and storing confidence. It may be his confidence and not that of the doctor which will turn the tide. Some may say that it is not essential for a newly admitted patient to relax and cease brooding over himself, but none would deny its desirability. I (R.L.D.) have tried both. I have brooded before an operation and I have relaxed. When I relaxed the lessened severity of the post-operative suffering was astonishing, both to myself and to my doctor.

There is chagrin on the part of men patients when attempting to accustom themselves to hospital clothes and routine. A patient next to me was restless and miserable for hours, when he should have been quiet, because he was too embarrassed to ask for a urinal. A boy scheduled for surgery was told, by another patient, that he would be given an enema the next morning. He worried more over that than he did over the operation. Insignificant details, yes, and yet details that build up an obstacle to the main job of recovering health. Details, however insignificant, cannot be overlooked where every ounce of energy is needed. Life may hang by a hair and yet be preserved; but if two hairs can be stretched over the chasm the chances of recovery are increased one hundred per cent.

Which fears are within the minister's province? It is for the doctor to say whether the patient's fears have so strong a physical or chemical connection to his disease that only by fighting his disease can any impression be made on them. There are fears against which talk, reasoning, and reassurance are as useless as they would be against ocean waves. In such cases the minister may wear himself out and waste his time. Insane fears and the terrors of the delirious are usually of this sort. A sedative or a cool bath may then be our best weapon.

But if the doctor can assure us that this is not the case, if he is neutral on the subject or if he is glad of the minister's assistance, the campaign against the patient's fears may be undertaken upon the following principles:

1. *General reinvigoration.* There is a group of measures to be

undertaken against any sort of emotional disturbance, against boredom, irritability, depression, loneliness, and bitterness, as well as
against fear. All these forms of suffering are apt to be helped by
the familiar and essential foods of body and spirit; getting rested,
getting nourished, getting affection, companionship, appreciation,
work, distraction, hope, prayer. These should be our first though
not our strongest line of attack on any form of emotional suffering.

2. *Explanation*. Because the fears that cause most suffering are
groundless and because this suffering can often be banished by a
knowledge of the actual facts, one should watch carefully for slight
signs that any notoriously common fear is burdening a person. For
example, people fear a surgical operation, heart disease, paralysis,
cancer or insanity, when in fact there is not the slightest sign of their
presence. Only a doctor's examination and reassurance can quiet
such fears, but the minister may do a valuable service by discovering
the source of fear and getting the tortured person to see a doctor.

One of the most effective fear cures in the minister's outfit is this:
face the dreadful facts and see for yourself that they are not terrifying when clearly understood. If they still remain fearful try to fill
your life full of whatever best makes you forget them. This is the
least satisfactory way to deal with them, and before you come to it
you can perhaps realize how inclusive is the formula: "See the truth
and escape fear."

3. *Concentration*. The sufferer should be himself in the campaign
for success. If he understands his own need to build up immunity
by increasing doses of success he will be able to go after his medicine
now and then and to recognize its effects when he takes it. As a
small boy I (R.C.C.) was sometimes sent with a message to my
uncle's house a mile away. I was terrified as I passed through a
grove of hemlocks. In their rustling shadows huge wild beasts
might be crouching. But I was ashamed to confess my fear and so
I carried my message with a dry mouth, a pounding heart and shaky
legs. One evening I had been playing on my violin up to the
moment when I was sent on my errand. The theme of Mozart
which I had been playing still ran in my head as I started. To my

surprise I found that I was not frightened. The tune seemed to keep out the fear. After that I tried putting a familiar tune in my head when I had to go somewhere in the dark. If it held my attention I was not scared. It was the old principle of "whistling to keep one's courage up." A full mind holds fear at arm's length.

4. *Cheering others* still more fearful helps to overcome one's fears. Fear-tortured mothers encouraging their children against fear get more confidence themselves. Fearful patients in a hospital may be asked by a nurse or by a minister to help others still more terrified, for action, especially action directed to help others, obscures "self-consciousness" and with it fear-consciousness.

5. *Religion*. Intellectually fear rests upon a philosophical outlook. Emotionally it is believed to rest upon painful experience in the past. Insofar as fear represents a lack of confidence, it becomes a concern of religion. Patients often use interchangeably the words, confidence, courage, faith. A lady recently told us of having been "in the depths of black despair for eight weeks," while in the hospital. She said, "I thought my religion was strong, but it had never been tested before."

Jesus himself not only believed, taught, and healed fearlessly, but he chose a course of action so dangerous that in the outcome it cost him his life and the lives of most of his followers. Apprehension, perhaps strong misgivings, came upon him as he faced his death. "If it be possible let this cup pass from me." Yet Jesus' confidence was such that he did not hesitate. His confidence was so strong that his followers caught it. They faltered for a time but after his death some of them likewise became leaders of men. Their message spread so effectively that today, centuries later, the whole world takes account of a Nazarene called Jesus.

The keynote of his life, his teaching, and his influence is confidence in God. Whatever else he was he was not fearful. Whatever else he became he is worshiped today because of his ability to overcome the world. Today those who have come most under his influence are most capable of facing with serenity severe tests of the spirit. Apprehensive, yes, concerned, perhaps stricken, but confident also. To fight fear thus becomes one of the central tasks of the Christian religion, for fear is one of religion's strongest opponents. Of this we can be sure: wherever we find great fear, not merely apprehension but panic, we may know that religion has gone astray. Fears are signs of lack of confidence in God.

Religious truth defends many of us. It is a fact that "underneath are the everlasting arms." It is a fact that when we pray with our whole heart God answers prayer for strength against fear. That God is caring for all of us so as to supplement all our sincere efforts, that whenever we do our best He will help us in the way that His infinite love and wisdom knows that we need most—this is our strongest defense against fear.

A heroic woman once said to me (R.C.C.), "If in nervous illness we've fought off demoralization as long and as hard as we possibly can, and at last it swamps us and we go under, then I think it must be in God's plan that we should actually be demoralized and get the humility which comes from it. In such a gulf it is a comfort to know that if we *really can't* control ourselves God must intend us to be humbled by that experience so that we shall know that we are ordinarily self-controlled not by virtue of ours alone but by what the universe gives us of vital, neural, mental strength which is not ours always to control."

3. BITTERNESS AND GRUDGE

Bitterness rarely looks itself in the face. A person does not keep on being deliberately bitter, knowing that he is so. His mind is focussed not on what he is doing but on his enemy and on his own wrongs. He is hardly conscious of what he himself is *doing,* only of what he is unjustly *suffering.* If he can be made to face the facts about himself he will probably decide ruefully that, as he can do nothing to help himself, he had better think about something else. But unless his mood is a rare and superficial one, he will not be able to get rid of it merely by deciding that his grudges do not pay or by laughing at them. By some longer road he has to come round not to forgetting his injuries but to forgiving whomever or whatever he blames. Here the minister ought to be able to help him. Perhaps some wrong can be righted, some reparation made, some reform accomplished. But not often.

In our experience the righting of its "cause" does not often cure bitterness, and this for two reasons. First, because other similar "causes" are apt to arise in the life of anyone prone to feel bitter. Injustice great or small comes again and again to most of us. When we right it here it is pretty sure to break out there. The crucial question is, how do we take it? The person who has taken it with such a prolonged and acrid sense of bitterness that his sufferings come to the clergyman's attention is generally one who has built up a habit of taking things in that way. It has become his ingrained way of defending himself against ill fortune.

The other reason why bitterness is seldom if ever cured by removing its "cause" is that this relief cannot wipe away the past. The weight of injuries accumulated through months or years still remains and cannot be forgotten. There is no way to get rid of it permanently except to forgive.

We know a young college athlete who was injured in an automobile accident. After two operations it was found that nothing could be done for his broken spinal cord. The best he could expect was to be up in braces supporting his paralyzed legs. The weeks dragged on. He repulsed the efforts of the librarian and the occupational therapist. He welcomed no one, but sat brooding hour after hour. He could not reconcile himself to what he faced and his bitterness gnawed at the vitals of his personality.

A sixteen-year-old, attractive Swedish boy was brought to the hospital suffering from a brain tumor. After opening the boy's skull the doctors found he had a highly malignant tumor which could not be removed. When the father was told of the boy's condition he said little. Later, as the father talked with a minister, he burst out, "There is no God. There could not be if this is true. I have been a fool to believe there was."

Often there is little we can do about such bitterness as these men felt. It is our hope that through our devotion to a sufferer, he may be led to convince himself that his bitterness does not help but harms him and at the same time hurts those who care for him. One patient said to me (R.L.D.), after many months during which time he had blamed others for his suffering, "You never agreed with me, but you were wise enough not to disagree. I knew you could not agree as that would not have helped me, for my bitterness helped no one." A patient suffering from bitterness must discover that you stand by him even though he may curse many things dear to you. If you directly oppose him or are led into argument he may transfer his bitterness to you; you thus add fuel to the fire of his hatred.

Out of your affection for him and out of his knowledge of the forces which send you to him he may reconcile himself to that which has injured him and in consequence may renew his zest for life.[1]

4. THE SENSE OF GUILT

Illness often brings humility, for illness is a time of helplessness. We know a man who dates the time of his fondness for people from the day a nurse turned his head to one side, and placed a basin under his cheek, so that he might not strangle in his vomit following an operation. He remembers also that she wiped his perspiring forehead and that she did not indicate either by comment or action that the task was distasteful. He was a complete stranger to her yet in his helplessness she helped him. The fact that the nurse was merely doing her job made little difference to him. He said to himself again and again, "How fortunate that there are nurses and doctors, and that one has friends who go out of their way to see one when one cannot go to them." During this experience he came to appreciate people, not because they were different from what they were at any other time but because of his own greater helplessness.

Helplessness and prolonged suffering in illness bring reflection and often humble strong pride. Many who have traded upon the mercy of God suffer from a stricken conscience even while they

[1] See Chapters XVI, Prayer, p. 215; and XVII, Scripture, p. 234.

suffer physical pain. "Why does God punish me?" said a forty-two-year-old woman after five months in the hospital, during which time she had had repeated operations. One had but to know her history to guess why she might think she was being punished.[2]

Our attention was called to a man who was uncommunicative and unresponsive to those around him. We found he was brooding over an injury his son had suffered while working in a machine shop. A few months before, a splinter of steel had hit the boy in his eye, causing him to lose the sight of that eye. Our patient held himself responsible for his son's injury because he had forced the boy to take the job. His own long idleness had given time for reflection, and brought to his mind the more clearly his own part in his son's suffering.

With some there is a striving toward humility in illness, but a lifetime of pride and partial indifference makes the accomplishment practically impossible. We say partial indifference, for if it is complete indifference no sense of guilt will appear. One patient said, "You can't get well as long as there is hatred in you." The minister asked, "Whom don't you like?" She responded immediately, "I hate that doctor." Two days later she asked, "What are you going to do to help me with my hatred?" She had set her feet upon the road of humility but her returning health brought back her pride. She passed her hatred over to the minister as if to let him do the worrying about it. He might answer, "What are *you* going to do about it?" He could not say, as did the confessor of Baron von Hugel, *"On your knees!"* Yet anything less is unsatisfactory with such people. They see the way dimly but their eyes are so overgrown with cataracts of self-conceit and self-deceit that the minister stands helpless before them.

Bitterness often hangs on a sense of guilt. Patients blame some other person or blame God for their suffering. They do not say what they mean and they do not mean what they say. Their utterances are clouded by a hot mist and there is little light present. One may have to listen weeks or even months before this mist clears

[2] Chapter XVI, Prayer, p. 227.

away to reveal, not blame of some one else, but blame of self. Reasoned answers to bitterness usually do not help; the sufferer knows that you attack not the cause but a symptom.

We recall a forty-year-old man whose daughter ran away to get married. He told a theological student, "If she wants to act that way I'm through with her." Since he made this statement his nineteen-year-old son has gone also. The son left a note saying, "Have gone to look for a better job. Don't try to find me." The patient is sick, without funds, and loaded down with bitterness. He will never be well, so the doctors think. Why do both his children run away from home? This man may well feel guilty because he has been such a poor father. Yet his attitude is not one of humility but of bitterness and revenge.

Often the cause of bitterness cannot be removed. A childless woman brought up in luxury and opposed on principle to divorce finds that her husband can never earn more than three thousand dollars a year and that she is condemned to live in the small town where his job is. She consults a physician for advice about obstinate insomnia. He finds her entrenched behind walls of bitterness. Its "cause" cannot be removed though its deeper reason in her own nature would vanish if she chose to take her marriage seriously and to make it good, which she probably cannot do without help from a physician or from a minister.

What should be done for these people? We cannot leave them to their own mental and spiritual resources. We often hear them complain only by chance. We say by chance, because we seldom listen for complaints. We often say with a touch of contempt, "You're pretty lucky to be alive." Of all possible remarks we think that is the worst. If the patient says it about himself he expresses his appreciation, but if we say it we express nothing. It is easy for us who have two good feet and breathe with two good lungs to speak thus to those who do not. We may hold up to the patient President Franklin D. Roosevelt and E. Stanley Jones, or Dr. Trudeau as examples in overcoming handicaps. But when we do so it is seldom with a consciousness of what we are doing to the sufferer whom we face. One patient was asked how he felt when someone cited to him cases of patients "worse off" than he is. He said, "I grit my teeth, close my ears, and curse them for saying that to me!" We believe that is the result with most of the sick.

To persuade the resentful man that someone sincerely cares for him is the minister's first task. That is often hard because the guilty and bitter person shows himself in an unfavorable light. He is not lovable until we can get to feel, beneath the surface of his words and looks, first how very miserable he is and then how natural it is that he should feel so. He hates someone or something, or he hates the arrangements of this world as he sees them. He is denied the outlet of action and so he can do nothing but gloom and fume. He has worn out the affection of his friends and even of his family. He has hidden his lovable qualities under so deep a layer of prickles that people keep their distance. He does not know that he is lonely and that this is one of the seeds of his bitterness. But this comes almost inevitably to be the fact. He has formed the habit of repelling not only the enemies whom he hates but many others whom he would like to have as friends.

We can never force and never rightly pretend affection, but through compassion, understanding, and faith we can prepare a soil where affection is almost certain to spring up of itself. The battle is not yet won. Liking that gradually warms into affection is essential to success, but it is still far from its goal. If we like him there is a chance that he will like us. He sees that we are on his side. He sees there is some decency in the world. Then one fine day we are surprised to hear such a remark as, "Did I tell you I have forgiven Tom?"

We assume throughout this discussion that to forgive and to be forgiven is the only lasting cure for guilt and for the bitterness that often hides it. The attempt to forget without forgiving will not work. But once forgiveness is at work, not only in a single act but as a temper, forgetting comes to our aid in the guise of a shift of emphasis. A new set of mental habits makes us forget much of our bitterness by leaving it behind.

Both in and out of the sickroom two pitfalls must be remembered in dealing with a sense of guilt: First, too easy an affirmation that the sufferer's problem is not so important as he conceives it to be, once he has recognized it as a problem. One works from the patient's point of view toward that which the minister knows to be more desirable. A patient told me (R.L.D.) the story of his struggle to free himself from the habit of masturbation. I attempted to minimize his worry about it, and thus help him toward gaining his self-control and self-respect. To my surprise he pointed out that I took it all too lightly and did not really understand his difficulty. Recognizing my mistake I suggested that he might like to discuss it with one of the doctors, which he did. At the surface it seemed to be a physical problem, yet it was essentially a moral one. I gave too little attention to the physical side and so, though I rightly directed his attention to the real root of the trouble, I failed.[3]

Secondly, one must not give too much attention to the details of an act from which a patient is suffering a sense of guilt, lest the patient suspect the minister of being curious. A patient who was suffering more from pain than from a sense of guilt spoke to a minister of his extramarital sexual relations. In an effort to discover what his real attitude was, the minister inquired as to the frequency of such acts and where they were carried out. The patient failed to see the reasons for such inquiry and forthwith refused to discuss the subject further.

The minister must never expect to find a patient suffering from a sense of guilt without other spiritual burdens as well. He may face such a situation in his study but never in illness. There is always pain and guilt, or fear and guilt, or loneliness and guilt, or bitterness and guilt. One can seldom be treated alone although one may be worked through to reach the other.[4]

[3] See Chapter XIII, Start with the Patient.   [4] See Chapter XIV, Listening.

5. BOREDOM

Many more affecting titles might be given to this state. Some call it "world weariness," painful monotony, or a "vacant life," but we prefer the plainer word. The most active practical peoples, for instance the English, seem to be those most subject to being "fed up" when deprived of the support and impetus of their muscular habits. In 1917 I (R.C.C.) was working with the medical division of an English regiment in the line near Amiens. The officers with whom I messed were more hopelessly bored than any set of human beings that I have ever seen. Every possible topic of conversation had long since been drained dry. Nothing ever happened that had not happened endless times before during the three years since they entered France with the "Expeditionary Force." None of them cared to read or to write. Every evening at 5:30 the Germans attacked with airplanes the observation balloon which hung over our heads. The antiaircraft guns fired a few shots and then until 5:30 next day there was nothing to do but polish the leather of puttees and Sam Browne belts and wait for the next period of "leave" in England. Mentally these men were as flat as a broken automobile tire.

We hear less of boredom in Orientals and in primitive peoples like the American Indians. Perhaps this is because they are less articulate or more used to it. Perhaps they are sleepier. A more adequate reason seems to be that the more highly *specialized* a person's habits are, the more easily he is bored when illness, war or poverty throws him out of his usual routine. One can hardly imagine a great "generalist" like Alfred N. Whitehead being bored. He would find interests wherever he was. Contrast him with a day laborer out of work. Lacking his habitual work he can turn his hand to nothing else.

Men are oftener bored than women in sickness, because men are naturally more restless and because they do not know "how to be sick." They do not easily learn the rules and satisfactions of this new game. They want contact with impersonal events, tools, and plans. There is advantage as well as deprivation in this. A friend of ours tied to bed and a plaster jacket for the slow years needed to heal his spinal tuberculosis, carried on his business by telephone, letter, and conversation with his subordinates. Such a grip on events is more essential to men than to women in illness.

Time with nothing in it, space entirely empty, are primal horrors or ultimate bores. This sick man's day hangs heavy on him because so little happens. Meals, the doctor's visits, and the coming of night are welcome reliefs, but they are spaced too far apart. He needs more punctuation between these diversions, more variety and more purpose. He is helped by whatever divides the long stretches of his day into manageable lengths so that each hour leads up to something else.

The healthy man at work is at home in his life. The sick man is in mid-ocean, drifting nowhere. He is not strong enough to keep on long at any single bit of work, play or talk. The surprises of chance events are too few to distract him. If he could watch the waves on a beach, or sit in a chimney corner and watch children play he might be content for a while. But this elemental beauty is just what it is hardest to bring into a sickroom. Things do not happen naturally there and let him watch them. He is out of the current of events. We must help him to generate a current and to find ends and beginnings that have life in them.

Boredom is quite different from acute physical suffering and from other forms of mental suffering, though it may accompany them. It is the internal gnawing of a hungry mind which finds no food to munch. The bored patient can neither stop his mind nor fasten it on any interest. Hence he preys upon himself like an empty stomach. He gets temporary relief from the company of someone who is *not* bored, especially if the visitor chances to do or say anything surprising. For surprise is what the bored person most craves. As time goes on, however, it takes more and more to surprise him and the relief from cheerful company becomes rarer because the cheerful person has a life elsewhere.

Occupation is obviously the most effective relief for boredom and our first problem in ministering to the bored patient is to seek, within the limitations imposed by his illness, something that will keep him busy for more than a few minutes at a time. Presumably he would not be bored if he had his regular job and his usual amusements, but these his illness excludes. Usually he has no habits of reading; readers are seldom bored. In his sickroom there is nothing for him to watch that he cares to watch, and nothing for him to do that he cares to do. The papers, the card games that he can play alone, the few remarks that he can exchange with doctors and nurses too busy to attend to him, or with other patients as bored as he is, serve to kill time for only a small fraction of his day.

Patients are less bored in an open ward than in a private room. The ward has something going on in it. One can watch, however listlessly, the doings of doctors, nurses, scrub-maids, and ward tenders. There are occasional visits of students, social workers, of the librarian and the occupational therapist. For this entertainment one may sacrifice the seclusion and quiet which a private room affords. Sometimes the balance of privacy *versus* loneliness is delicate.

Something to see out of one's window is a help. A patient of ours watched the hospital baker mixing, rolling, and cutting his dough. Another watched nurses prepare and sterilize dressings and passed the time of day with wheel-chair patients as they were rolled out into the sun and rolled back at noon.

Something enjoyable on the walls of one's sickroom is usually forbidden by the economics of housekeeping in hospitals, but at home we can be less barbaric. We can change the pictures frequently. We can move the patient's bed to the window or to a different window.

Besides aiding so far as he can in supplying occupation and variety in the bored patient's day, the minister should make at least an effort to prevent his being bored. The appetite for being frequently roused, thrilled or excited by surprising events goes to morbid extremes with the prevailing American temperament. The happiest lives are not full of jerks and leaps. Compared to the life of the person easily bored they run along on a smoother level of satisfaction. Delightful events are found by them in places that would seem to him quite arid. The capacity to find small satisfactions in our daily experiences most people can cultivate more or less successfully as they get toward middle life. It is perhaps only a few times each year, not a few times each day, that one gets the excitement of an upheaving experience. The sum total of exhilarating moments is far greater when it is added up from a multitude of small pleasures accessible to all. R. L. Stevenson, who was sick most of his life, learned to enjoy even the firm resistance of the ground under his feet and the tightening of his leg muscles as he walked. Not everyone can do this, but many people certainly reject a vast number of invitations to enjoyment because they are looking for "bigger game" and disdain or ignore the insignificant. The habit of finding significance and so interest in a great many common occurrences is one that can be cultivated and is in fact cultivated by many.

What leads anyone to make the effort? We believe the commonest energizer is the affection that one receives and the affection that one feels for others. That heightens interests, sharpens perceptions, makes common events pleasant. Affection, as we have elsewhere said, can often be increased by understanding. The minister can help the patient and his family to understand each other better and so to like or to love each other better. He does this by liking them himself, by emphasizing the good points of each as he talks with the others, by helping to untangle misunderstandings and by suggesting ways in which they can work or play together.

Another aid to the development of affection is to say what you feel. In a family group the habit of expressing affection is often lost or never developed. We think it is a safe rule that people should be thanked for whatever they can honestly be thanked for, and praised for whatever deserves praise. Thanks, praise, and slight services build up the fire of affection so that it will burn steadily. The materials must be there and there must be some heat in them. One cannot start a fire merely by laying wood and paper in good position. But many families are not so cold as that. They are like a wood fire when its sticks have fallen somewhat too far apart so that they do not reinforce or consume each other's heat. The minister can bring the still glowing sticks and coals together.

But without a draft they will not burn. What the draft does for a wood fire, gratitude to life and to the Author of life does for the feeble affections of men and for sick people in danger of chronic boredom. People must have some gladness in existence or they will not go on living. Can one keep on loving life when physical and fortunate reasons for exuberance are gone? To few of us are they in evidence perpetually. When dullness threatens we must find something to be glad of in the very build of the world and of society, in the dimly seen plan of the whole, which is God. If we are to keep on loving the people whom we love, we must learn to see them, and ourselves, as servants of something as great as spiritual development or the incarnation of beauty which find their best example in the life of Jesus Christ and in the Spirit by Whom he lived.

The prevention of boredom comes back to religion. That gives zest and permanence to our affections and through them to our daily experiences as they can be rearranged and enriched under the minister's advice.

CHAPTER VII

PAIN .

(a) Physical Pain.

The differential diagnosis of suffering can rarely be made in one visit. Each patient's individuality tinges his fears, his boredom or his despair with a color that is unique. His pains, mental, emotional, physical, are flavored by the life he has lived, and the future to which he looks forward. The furniture of his universe modifies his suffering. Simple people have more massive and inarticulate misery. National, racial, and cultural groups, Jews, Negroes, Yankees, suffer each in their own way. The Slav's rooted distrust of any lasting success in this world inclines him to give up at once with an "I-told-you-so" expression when illness strikes him. It proves his theory that the world is a trap or an illusion. The Yankee fights suffering like a malignant enemy, the Negro accepts it like bad weather. The intellectual watches and describes it with zest or with fury.[1]

So it may take as long to grasp what a man is suffering, physically and mentally, as to understand his character. The minister must keep at his task, visit after visit, making as few false moves as he can, correcting his impressions as errors appear. *But he can see only that which his previous experience has taught him to look for.* If he has never known irritable weakness, dumb misery, disappointed love, remorseful sorrow after the death of a neglected parent, his power to see that another suffers these experiences is slight. Yet if he has something of the novelist's temperament, he will catch the whole of an experience from a hint of it shown in a companion. His imagination may enable him to fill up the defects of his sympathy. The visitor who can look for only two or three kinds of pain or of

[1] In *The Journal of a Disappointed Man* by W. N. P. Barbellion (G. H. Doran Co., 1919), the writer enjoys making brilliant phrases for his suffering, like, "I feel like a sloppy tadpole," "like a jellyfish on stilts," etc.

87

soul-sickness, because he has himself felt but two or three, is like the doctor who can diagnose only two or three of the two hundred and fifteen or more diseases recognized by medical science. He will inevitably call everything fever, fits, or fractures. The minister need not have a name for every variety of human suffering that he recognizes, but neither must he put everyone's miseries into so few pigeonholes that the patient feels himself radically misunderstood.

We think it important that the minister should be as familiar as he can, not only with mental suffering but with the different varieties of physical suffering, even though it is not his business but the doctor's to treat them. Primitive people do not name and can hardly distinguish more than two or three types of physical discomfort, but most of the sick whom the minister will see, recognize many more than this. The minister needs to distinguish them too, because he wants to be abreast of the sick man's total experience, conversant with all that he is suffering, not merely with his mental, emotional or spiritual distress.

We have therefore made a list of the main varieties of suffering.[2]

1. *Pure pain* may be rhythmically recurrent as it is in intestinal "colic," or rhythmically accentuated with each heartbeat ("jumping toothache"). For the severest kinds of pain patients use such phrases as "tearing," "cutting," "stabbing," "wrenching." Milder types they call "aching," "dull," or "nagging." Most sufferers distinguish pain which engulfs them from pain which they can sit off and look at. We may suffer mildly from an awareness that the weather is hot, or we may feel as if we were burning up. Medical science has as yet no way to measure the intensity of anyone's pain. The best we can do is to notice whether the patient seems to forget it when his attention is diverted, whether he cries out, writhes, sweats, or turns pale, whether it disturbs his sleep and appetite, and whether he goes about his daily tasks in spite of it. These are coarse and vague tests, but we have no better.

---

[2] Physical sufferings relate themselves to some area of the body or to the whole body. Mental sufferings are not localized. They are often linked with physical pain but there may be no such association.

Some people and some races are more sensitive to pain than others. A moderately bad sunburn, bruise or cut, the pulling of a tooth, a subcutaneous injection, objectively the same, seem to cause a good deal more pain to some than to others. We have seen a horse cropping the grass at the roadside in apparent content, though his leg had just been hideously gashed in an accident. Perhaps certain individuals are nearly as insensitive as this. We hear this said of the Chinese. We know definitely that a standard insult, say the bite of a mosquito, gives us more suffering when we are "keyed up," when we are "on edge" or worn out by lack of sleep, than when we are in full health. In view of this well-proven fact, doctors often labor not only to quench the pain which a patient now feels but to build up his general condition, so that future shocks, from within him or from without, will give him less pain. A person may be so "keyed up" that the slamming of a door gives him acute distress. After rest, food, and a quiet mind have been secured for him, the door may slam again as hard as ever, but he does not mind it. In his effort to get this quiet mind for his patient the doctor often needs help which the minister can give.

People who have suffered for a long time, for example from chronic rheumatism, sometimes say that they "get used to having pain," though they are positive that its intensity is no less. This is a well-established fact though it is hard for us to picture just what it means. Perhaps they have learned to set up a mental barrier between the pain and the rest of their experience, so that each goes on independently. The pain is there, but they do not mind it very much. Ordinarily the greatest curse of pain is that this distinction cannot be made. The pain engulfs personality, blots out thought, sympathy, all that takes us out of ourselves and most that makes our fellows dear to us. It centers us in itself. When it is severe we *are* the pain and hardly anything more. The rest of personality is for the time gone. If such suffering lasts for years it wears down our resistance and we become selfish, fractious or cruel. Then we need help if anyone on earth does. But sometimes no one can give it except the doctor—with a narcotic.

The word *"tenderness"* or "soreness" is used by physicians to mean pain that comes only on motion or when someone presses on the spot. The joints in acute rheumatism may be so tender that the patient dreads to have people come near his bed because he fears that they will joggle it and set his pain going. Ordinarily and without a dread like this, tenderness is far more easily bearable than pain.

2. *Itching* is generally a mere annoyance, but may become a torture, especially when it lasts so long that the sufferer's nerves are set on edge by loss of sleep and poor nutrition. Itching is generally worse at night. One of the discomforts of a plaster cast, and one often ignored by surgeons, is the itching that springs up underneath the cast. Most causes of itching are aggravated by scratching, a few are relieved by it. Distraction of attention is generally possible and helpful.

3. *Burning.* A bad sunburn gives most of us an experience of this. Sometimes it is combined with "pure pain" or with itching. Some persons and some races seem to suffer a sense of burning from injuries or disease which give most people "pure pain." A striking proportion of Jewish patients complain that *"es brennt mir"* in diseases which make the Gentile say, "It hurts."

4. The *sense of pressure* or crowding is a relatively mild and bearable discomfort which may gradually increase, as in headache, toothache, or in heart disease, to "pure pain."

5. *Prickling* is the sense of "pins and needles" such as one feels when one's foot has been asleep. It often needlessly alarms elderly people who believe that it is the precursor of paralysis. In the vast majority of cases nothing serious follows it. In itself, attended by no fear of worse to come, it is usually but a mild annoyance.

6. *Chilliness* and *shivering* are often a sign of fever; sometimes they are due merely to nervousness or fatigue.

Sharply distinguishable from all these types of suffering are:

7. *Nausea.* This is sometimes joined to faintness.

8. *Faintness* is often combined with *dizziness* (vertigo). Sights and sounds grow dim. One's muscles give way and, at the extreme, consciousness is lost. To some it is a horrible sensation be-

cause they fear to fall or because, dimly or vividly, they fear death. To others, more experienced in it, fainting may be only an inconvenience or even a luxury. This happens when an extreme degree of loneliness and of the consequent desire to get attention or to arouse someone's interest at any price, leads adolescents or younger children to "faint" voluntarily. Sometimes this is used, half-consciously, to escape some test like an examination or a reprimand. Perhaps the opportune fainting of heroines in eighteenth-century novels had some resemblance to what we are here describing. When in children we encounter this type of "hysterical fainting" the best immediate treatment is to ignore it. When no attention is paid to it children soon give it up.

The underlying sense of inferiority and of loneliness in these cases is pitifully great and deserves all the long-time help that we can give. To make such a child successful at something and to convince him that someone really cares for him is the duty of any parent, teacher or friend who knows what it feels like to be lonely.

9. *The sense of weakness,* muscular as well as mental, is sometimes very distressing though clearly distinguished from pain of any sort. It is often combined with *irritability,* "irritable weakness."

10. In *the sense of fatigue* or exhaustion an element of pain, soreness and heaviness is mingled with weakness. It is not always distressing. There is a comfortable fatigue when work is over and sleep near at hand. But when it lasts long it soon begins to be worrying, irritating, depressing, and so passes over into some of the forms of suffering described in Chapters V and VI.

So far as our own experience goes, physical pain is almost pure evil, something which God intends us to get rid of by better medical work. But not everyone sees it so. The following paragraphs were written for us by a friend who knows physical pain by long experience and perhaps more truly than we do:

"1. *Pain jerks you out of comfortable and dangerous contentment, false certainty, and complacency.* You think yourself master—till it comes. Then it masters you, even temporarily engulfs you. You are compelled to discover that you are subject to something greater than yourself. God may not have willed this particular pain. Yet He permits Pain, in general, as a discipline to mankind. We submit to Divine necessity in submitting to pain. It is an experience that may make definitely for humility. It may call one back to the consciousness of God.

2. *Very intense pain isolates the spirit from much that has entangled or surrounded it. You are alone with pain.* You and it wrestle together in a void. When the pain subsides, that aloneness stays with you for a little while. Your spirit is freed temporarily from its usual preoccupations, and so, in that first blessed moment of relief you are unusually able to drink in the goodness of God. This is a time very open to the processes of growth.

3. *If one is forced to suffer pain over a long time, one may learn to build up a technique of bearing it,* which must have value in the progressive self-mastery involved in growth. Up to a certain point it is possible, by a determined focus of attention elsewhere, to cut down the quantity or intensity of painful sensations which push through the gate of consciousness ("raising the threshold of sensitiveness to pain," the psychologists call it). I know from experience that this can be done. Dentists and doctors comment on the way I can bear pain. It all goes back to this voluntarily erected barrier, not to any Spartan courage. Of course, some pain is too great for this technique. It bursts through the barriers and engulfs us. But I am speaking of the lesser pains which still materially lessen efficiency.

I believe that this kind of mastery, resting on concentration, is transferable to other fields of endeavor. It supplies moral or psychological calisthenics to strengthen character.

4. *There is also the well-known value in pain that it trains imagination and sympathy,* to feel and to aid the sufferings of others. To know that another person has suffered as you have suffered is a bond of union between sufferers. Anything that makes for compassionate good will and fellowship is not without value. A mother after the pangs of her first labor spoke to me of her new fellow feeling for all the animals who bear their young in lonely pain.

These points may not apply to the majority of sufferers, who perhaps have not been disciplined into a thoughtful attitude toward their pain, but that such values can be wrested from physical pain I do emphatically affirm. I should count myself poorer if I had suffered one bit less.

There are four mental habits which help us to escape bitterness and a loss of faith in time of painful crisis:

1. *Get beyond blame.* Our childish impulse is to place *personal blame* on some person or object for every difficulty or hurt. A child turns around and hits the chair over which he has just fallen. Grown people still tend to do this. When a definite person cannot be pointed out as meriting blame, they blame God or Fate or whatever they have looked to as the power behind their lives.

The mature attitude is that of an impersonal search for causes, an effort to understand. This involves neither praise nor blame. We have no feeling that evil is directed vindictively at us. We see certain laws, operating in a large sphere, in which we happen to be involved. If we can bring ourselves to this point of view we see light. We still may not understand pain, yet we are not tempted to blame anything or anybody for it. We develop an attitude of humorous detachment from individuals and their stupid blunders.

Perhaps we none of us get quite beyond the habit of blaming, but the more nearly we escape it the less our faith will suffer in time of crisis.

2. *Learn to see that nothing happens to you as a unique experience leveled at you alone by some special design.* Thousands are tasting thoughtlessly just this sort of joy, just this sort of pain. If we have gradually built up a more thoughtful attitude, then, when a crisis of suffering comes we are better able to keep our perspective and not go to pieces. I remember learning gradually, when I could not sleep at night because of pain or discomfort, to pray not for myself but for all those who, all over the world, were unable to sleep. This helps me to avoid tension and self-pity. I try to imagine the myriad kinds of suffering, physical and mental, that are keeping men and

women from sleep. I try to let my prayer reach out to all of them. My own suffering dwindles in importance. When the mind turns away from self, relaxation comes and one holds pity rather than self-pity at the center of one's thought. One gets to thinking of oneself as a private in a vast human army fighting a cosmic battle against pain.

3. *Learn, after each experience of pain, to sum it up and discover what value you can wrest from it.* Of these three habits of mind, this third was the one that I developed first. Before I had ever been called upon to bear any great pain or disappointment, I had built up the habit of looking back and discovering gains in seemingly disadvantageous happenings. I had begun already to learn that all things can be made "to work together for good," because I could see what I had learned from this or that small pain or grief. When the greater pains or disappointments came, I was ready because of my own previous experience, to believe that somehow, some time, I could wrest good from this too, and I set about to do so with a determination built on faith.

4. *Learn how evanescent pain is,* and look beyond the present agony to the time when that agony will have dwindled to a dim memory.

None of these four habits is definitely religious. The Stoic as well as the Christian could develop them. But if we have gradually built up a faith that the universe ultimately means *good* and that God loves all that He has made, that faith becomes more nearly impregnable in time of stress in case it has been buttressed by these habits. It was by habits such as these, rather than by consideration of the place of pain in a divine plan, that I strengthened my defenses when I came to meet suffering. I had long since attained the conception of a God-centered universe. I built it chiefly out of a reverence for beauty, particularly beauty in nature. Because of the four habits just described I was able to carry over that conception into other experiences.

None of these habits came suddenly or separately. There was a curious reciprocal action in their growth. What I had built up in the way of faith helped me to bear a small pain or a small disappointment. Then the fact that my faith had stood that strain strengthened my reliance on it when a greater strain came. It was in this way that my faith came to be actually enriched by suffering."

(b) Mental Suffering.

For the more thoughtful and spiritually minded person physical pain may be an ally and a teacher, but to most of those whom we have seen suffer it is mostly evil, a destructive not an educative experience. Mental sufferings on the other hand, though they overwhelm a few, seem to us to develop character in most of those who bear them. In other words, mental pain, sorrow, disappointment, humiliation, teaches us what we need to learn—that growth is our prime business on this planet. We are ready enough to admit this when we are thinking chiefly of exciting novelties, but it looks less inviting when we know that it implies pain.

To keep us moving and to kill our conceit, mental pain keeps breaking the protective shell of habit which our laziness builds up again and again in the hope of settling down in comfort. In business we are painfully hounded by competitors, inventions, and substitutes, such as oil and electricity for coal and wood. Just as we settle down in a warm swaddling of affection death robs us. We please the public by our writings and the royalties pile up. Then the public tires of our little menu and we must move on or be neglected. Or perhaps a worse fate befalls us. The public does *not* get tired of us and we go on successfully repeating ourselves. Then complacency settles down on us and we are robbed not of money but of worth.

This inner punishment is automatic and self-enforcing though the outer visible penalty often fails. When our refusal to grow takes the form of dishonesty we often "get away with it" for years unpunished. Honesty is not always the best policy though it is always in the line of growth, a statement which we shall not try to prove here. But dishonesty is punished invariably by loss of self-respect.

It kills a portion of the self that can be respected. We no longer wince at our own rascality.

"For we have this treasure in earthen vessels," always easily broken, "that the excellency of the power may be of God and not of us." God who is reality has to be faced, obeyed, and assimilated again and again. It is by painfully piercing the surface of things and not by our own interior wisdom that we get the power to do anything original in business, in music, or in conversation. "Lean on your subject," said George Herbert Palmer to his students in the art of writing fresh and original English. He meant that originality and growth come by swallowing and reshaping realities which seem at first quite foreign to us, as beef and beans are foreign to the human tissues into which they are changed after digestion.

The metaphor of eating God in the Catholic Mass is none too violent. We eat a bit of the Creator's manifestations in nature every time that we sit down to a meal, but it has to be transformed within us before it can be assimilated. That is the second step. The first is when we acknowledge our dependence on God by eating a part of His creation. Omit that act. Then we are helpless within a few hours and dead within a few days.

Our spiritual life is no less helpless without its food, but our spiritual death is hidden. People do not find it out for years, perhaps never. We may not recognize it ourselves, but it is as inevitable and invariable as the death of a body without food and drink. The only power that keeps our souls alive is the power of God absorbed when we "take in," as we say, something new. We are not passive. We have to set our seal upon the new realities which we take in, just as the body does after it has broken up or "digested" the structure of roast beef into its original "building stones." The individual artistry of the body rebuilds them into the cellular architecture of human muscle. The "power," the fresh energy, is not of ourselves but of God, the Creator of our food.

In this process of growth, mental pain is an unrivaled schoolmaster. It hounds us on to claim again and again our sustenance out of reality by learning something new and by breaking the shell of easy happiness which keeps new insight away from us. We grow by fits and starts, with intervals of slow and often happy regression. Our fits and starts are forced out of us most often by pain. The public criticizes us by buying of our competitors. God criticizes us when we make death a disaster and an ostracism instead of a love-deepening sorrow. Friends criticize us when they endure our apparently ineradicable shortcomings and cease to give us the honor of blame. They no longer challenge us by expecting the best of us. They expect only the continuance of our old habits.

Because success is one of our gravest dangers, pain is one of our best defenses. The talker who succeeds in rousing a laugh by his *bon mot* repeats it again and again. His savior is the friend who hurts his feelings by telling him to stop. Such a friend saves him not only from boring other friends but from the slow corrosive of complacency. Such a friend gives him pain and may be resented like a stroke of ill fortune, like the loss of money or the loss of a job. The worse we feel, the less we are apt to go on relying on what theologians call "our own strength," our own old jokes and witticisms, the more we are forced to rely on what is eternally reliable.

Absolutely reliable is the habit of searching daily experience, which is God's face, for new facts, for new meanings in old facts, for new ways to be of use, for new beauty, new humor, new lovableness in our friends and even in our enemies.

Ossification is hateful to all. Pain cracks the thin shell of bone which begins to stiffen us in our ease and soon is thick enough to immobilize us in our habits. In sober fact new bone is always forming in our joints and in our arteries after our twentieth year. Stiffness is the very spirit of old age, visible in our tissues, metaphorical though no less demonstrable in our minds. But we have far more power to arrest or to destroy ossification in our habits than in our joints. We can fight it successfully with sheer will power aided by "psychic brakes and tractors." [3] But the writers of this book have found the blows of ill fortune still more skillful in rousing us to

[3] See *The Meaning of Right and Wrong*, Richard C. Cabot (New York, Macmillan Company 1933). Chapter XX.

fight ossification. Such a blow of pain Emerson described in his "Each and All." [4] He had been squatting beside a rocky pool on the seashore, fascinated by the iridescence of wet shells.

> "The delicate shells lay on the shore.
> The bubbles of the latest wave
> Fresh pearls from their enamel gave,
> And the bellowing of the savage sea
> Greeted their safe escape to me.
> I wiped away the weeds and foam,
> And fetched my sea-born treasures home;"

Then pain the schoolmaster took him in hand:

> "But the poor unsightly noisome things
> Had left their beauty on the shore
> With the sun and the sand and the wild uproar."

Emerson's pain was like the ache of trying to recover the past, to get back to our childhood home, to recapture the ecstasy of first love. Like Emerson's shells these joys were glorious, but only *in* their setting.

> "All are needed by each one;
> Nothing is fair or good alone."

Growth has now called us on and we are punished for trying to hold back. William Blake reinforces Emerson:

> "He who bends to himself a Joy
> Doth the wingèd thing destroy.
> But he who kisses the Joy as it flies
> Lives in Eternity's sunrise." [5]

The mental sufferings of sick people usually express painful shrinking from the challenge to growth. Their treasures, like every-

---

[4] R. W. Emerson, *Poems* (Boston, Munroe & Co., 1847), p. 14.
[5] *Selected Poems by William Blake,* (Oxford University Press, 1927), "Eternity," p. 121.

one's, are in earthen vessels or left thoughtlessly where moth, rust, and thieves destroy. They have read the warnings of the New Testament but they have never believed them. They must learn by painful experience or reject the experience and suffer only the pain. Neither pain nor any other experience can teach us if we refuse to learn. God gives us free choice: go to the school of experience, or stay outside. Even He cannot compel us to learn. On this side of death some of us are apparently unteachable. When we reflect on this we do not want it otherwise. Compulsory, automatic learning would leave us dead machines. Huxley said he would welcome this, but it is hard to believe that he realized what he was saying.[6]

We are not so foolish as to maintain that *all* mental suffering promotes spiritual growth. We maintain that, unlike physical pain, it often offers us a good and rarely an evil, because it gives us a chance to get our eyes opened and to see the next steps in our development. We see no way to tell except by trial how much mental suffering can be turned to good by any particular person. It is the severest pains that revive us most signally. What is beyond our capacity to respond to, is often beyond our power to feel. We notice it as little as an idiot in an asylum notices his mother's death.

God does not pick our mental pain and send it to us. He has planned a world in which pain seems inevitable for growing beings. He permits pain as He does ignorance and sin because unless these challenge us we do not grow. Unless we accept growth as the absolute good, unless we value joy, ease, and rest because they wake us up, mental pain is a blot on the universe. God plans an order which contains pain as stimulus, challenge, teacher, and guide. We co-operate in the process of our growth by accepting painful experience, and learning its lesson, or we refuse to face reality and so degenerate.

The minister can help patients to cultivate a new sensation, the *sense of growth*. When a man has made up his mind that growth

---

[6] "I protest that if some great power would agree to make me always think what is true and do what is right, on condition of being turned into a sort of clock and wound up every morning, I would instantly close with the offer."—T. H. Huxley, *Lay Sermons*, (New York, D. Appleton, 1870), p. 340.

is the only thing on earth that he needs, he gradually becomes aware of *growth-tension*—an experience not accurately described either as pleasure or as pain. German poets have tried to suggest this tension by linking these opposites: *selige-schmerzen*. Royce writes of the "dear sorrow" that is inseparable from the love of any creature except God. We suggest that this complex awareness is in fact *a sense that we are growing*. It is not a pleasure or a pain, but a richer experience that includes them both and something more. There is nothing super-refined about it. It is like the pleasure of carrying a painfully heavy canoe, when we are fresh for it. There is both pleasure and pain at the start of a race. Our eagerness gets its drive both from present uneasiness and from anticipated fulfillment, but feels beyond pleasure or pain the climbing of desire up the rungs of fulfillment. A mountain climber does not dissect his progress into pain and pleasure. His desire is being fulfilled. His child is being born or will be if he minds his business and sticks to the path. Those who play any game with zest, combine bitter and sweet with many other items of planning and steering, and bite into them all at once like a club sandwich.

There is simultaneous pleasure and pain for the doctor who finds an error in his diagnosis—pain in his blunder, pleasure in the new knowledge that will guide him and others next time. Messages from past, present, and future, positive and negative, are included in a sense of growth. We had better call it that and not try to split its elements apart. We feel a stir out of desire into realization. We feel the process of growth and, if we are wise, we help it on, like a good obstetrician, ignoring the pain and the pleasure, but sensing the growth.

We fool ourselves badly when we focus attention on success and failure, on good fortune or ill fortune. Our eyes are upon our own sensations when we think in these hackneyed terms. Success and failure are not there unless we invite them with sidelong glances. The sensations called up by these words are important only as guides to the next step or as glimpses of the whole which will never live unless we stop dissecting it.

The will, like the heart's muscle, has no power unless it has resistance to push against. To feel this resistance when we grow is more than pain or pleasure. It is evil, it is good, and it is something more vital than either; more vital because pain and pleasure are often narcotics. They are always narcotics unless they fertilize growth and die or live in it. *The sense of success and the sense of failure are signs that we are off the path of the growth process.* Regret for failure is close to self-pity and so to self-destruction; content with success melts into self-indulgence and self-annihilation. When we learn to feel neither regret nor complacency in the fortunes that meet us in sickness, in poverty, and death, we carry our boat round two dangerous cataracts, success and failure, and hold our road unchecked.

It would be strange if man, stamped by his Creator with one decisive mark, the need to grow, could not *sense* his growth when it comes. We believe that he does sense it and that he has no more important task than to make himself more sensitive to it. The locomotive engineer saves and forwards the lives in the train behind him because, for the time of his run, he lives by his awareness of red and green. The soul of man lives by its awareness of growth, steering toward it and away from what checks it as an animal steers for its food. "This is my meat," says the soul as it senses a crescent idea, a nascent beauty, a dawning power. Then pain and pleasure, the awareness of success or of failure, die down to subordinate notes in the theme of growth. If we pause or are stricken to stop on one note, bitter or sweet, growth stops. If we carry each note along upon a single breath creation goes forward and God is content.

Chapter VIII

EVIL

I. THE PROBLEM OF JOB

THE problem of evil becomes urgent when ministers see the accumulation of misery in hospitals and slums. They are forced to doubt whether there is more pleasure than pain in the world. They are carried on to question whether there is more good than evil in it, and so to wonder about God. The problem is especially urgent for those who have not nailed the flag of growth to the masthead as the absolute good. The mystery of evil hits us hardest when we are on the road leading from the idea that God plans pleasant fortunes to the belief that He plans spiritual training.

Philosophical discussion rarely if ever helps a patient who is in Job's situation. It is highly improbable that Job ever so mastered his sufferings as to pour out the passionate eloquence with which the writers of the Book of Job make him confront his uncomforting opponents. It is still more improbable that he would have had more than a passing impulse to dispute with them. Such arguments are dust and ashes to the sick man. Their value is for the healthy and inquisitive student. Their proper place is in the college, in the theological school, and in the "clinical year." [1]

Yet it is easy to forget this when a sick man challenges you to debate Job's problem, and asks with desperate earnestness, "Why does this horrible sickness come to *me? I* have lived a good life. Where is the justice of it?" [2] It seems heartless not to answer such an outcry with the best reasoning that we can muster. But though

[1] Richard C. Cabot, *Adventures on the Borderlands of Ethics,* (New York, Harper & Bros., 1926), Chapter I, A plea for a clinical year in the course of theological study.
[2] See Chapter VI, Guilt, and Chapter XVI, Prayer.

the patient implores you to reason with him, it is his pain and not his reason that speaks. He wants relief not argument. He needs bread and you give him a stone, excusably enough because he has asked for the stone. He wants firm conviction and peace but not the means to them—hard thinking. He is not strong enough for that.

We write this out of bitter experience. We have often been lured into arguments that brought in the end no comfort but only fatigue and disappointment. Clear, prolonged thinking about Job's problem is impossible for the sick man. But we believe that the minister will be in better condition to serve the sick if he himself reviews in the atmosphere of the sickroom the arguments about this problem which he studied in the theological seminary. Intellectual clarity makes him firmer and more comforting in his dealings with illness, even though he never argues. Like the underpinning of a house, solid theological convictions can be serviceable though never displayed. If the minister is solidly convinced, the sick man sees it and his doubts are more bearable even though he never discusses them. Conviction is contagious, especially when well founded. Postpone discussion of the problem of evil, then, until the patient is well, but be everlastingly sure that you postpone it because of the patient's weakness and not because of your own.

Sooner or later it is a minister's business to recapitulate and to test out by reason and experience what has been said by philosophers and theologians about God, about immortality, and about evil, since men first recorded their struggles with these problems. The minister's resources of conviction about evil will include the following:

1. *Some men suffer for their sins.* They have broken the rules of health and now they are sick. They have broken the laws of ethics and so they are sick of themselves. They have broken the law of the country and so the community is sick of them.

Only a small percentage of illness can be thus explained. Much of it comes from no fault of the sufferer's. Most of the sufferers whom we have tried to serve could say with Job that they see no connection between their sickness and the way that they have lived. Their doctors would back them up.

The drunkard, the libertine, the recklessly imprudent stonecutter, has to admit that he knew how to avoid disease and did not. But he is apt to remind you that many others have been as reckless, yet escaped injury. The wide differences in men's natural immunity to disease spoil the strict working of what we loosely call cause and effect. Many break the law of the land and the laws of ethics yet escape obvious penalty. Job said so and he was right. The same is true of health. Physical penalties seem to be capriciously imposed, hitting this man and sparing that. It is still true, however, that many men take a chance that they know they have no right to take. They gamble what they cannot afford to lose. Some are getting what they deserve and will frankly say so. But not all.

2. *Some men suffer because of other people's carelessness or stupidity.* Automobile accidents make this dreadfully familiar. Hereditary syphilis is a rarer and more lasting blight. But it is only fair to remember that much of the good that comes to us in affection, amusement, beauty, and comfort results not from our own deeds but from our links to other people who benefit us without intention on their part or merit on ours.

We do not complain of congenital intelligence and sympathy. They are as "unjust" as syphilis. Syphilitic children are miserable by no fault of their own? Yes, and we are prosperous and happy by no virtue of our own. God sends his rain on the just and on the unjust. He joins us each to each by heredity and by environment so that we share each other's weal . . . *and* woe.

Can we imagine a world so constructed that others could give us all the good and none of the evil that now flares across the boundaries of personality? If we quarantine ourselves against evil from others we shut out most of the good that makes life rich. We cannot be both open and shut, and we have no right to complain of undeserved evil from others so long as we gladly accept so much unmerited good. Rearrange the world; keep the good of automobiles without the harm of them, abolish them altogether, or cease complaining about the cruel world that contains them.

3. *We are roused by pain to stop pain.* In the human body the pain of brain disease, lung disease, bone disease, leads the physician to the spot where help can be applied. If we are anesthetic, as a patient with spinal cord disease may be, we do not feel the pain of appendicitis and the surgeon does not get to it in time to prevent peritonitis and death. Pain rouses help!

Deaths from typhoid fever rouse us to purify our water supplies. Children's deaths from diphtheria and hydrophobia rouse some cities to abolish those terrible diseases by prevention. Our enormous laziness needs sharp goads to stir it into action.

In such cases [3] the bodily sufferer must be conceived as one who suffers mainly for others, human or nonhuman, not often for himself or for his own growth. One man suffers from cancer that others may be roused to prevent or cure it. His suffering cries out for experiment and ingenuity to free man from this curse. Perhaps no one hears the cry, but we cannot be sure of that. The soul is free to be roused far beyond its usual apathy or dullness. Like the copious pleasures that are showered on us with the chance of rousing us to grow, copious sufferings beat like cries on the dull ears which at last *may* hear them effectually. No one can prove that impossible, and when it happens we suffer that others may live.

During the World War there was, in the merchant marine, a master mariner, Captain Charles Martell. He was an officer on the S.S. *New York* when she was mined in 1918 near Liverpool, with Admiral Sims and his staff on board. During his service he developed pains in his bones and began to lose in height. After the Armistice he was treated in various hospitals under various diagnoses until in 1926 it was recognized in a New York hospital not only that he had a bone disease but that some of the chemical changes in his excreta were like those noticed at the Massachusetts General Hospital in patients who were receiving an extract of the

[3] See Chapter VII, Evil, pages 104 to 107.

parathyroid glands. From this hint a tentative diagnosis of tumor of a parathyroid gland was made, and the Captain was sent from New York to the Massachusetts General Hospital in Boston, where the diagnosis was confirmed. Operation was advised and performed. *No tumor was found.* A second operation was likewise unsuccessful.

Several years went by, while the Captain's disease was held in check by other methods. The news of his case spread, however, and other patients in other hospitals were successfully operated upon for this newly recognized disease. Tumors of the parathyroid gland were found and removed; cures were made.

In 1932 the problem was again taken up at the Massachusetts General Hospital. Several more patients with the same disease were found and their tumors removed. The Captain was brought back from New York, where he had had one more unsuccessful operation. Meantime his disease had grown worse. He was now bedridden. Three more operations were performed on him at the Massachusetts General Hospital, but still no tumor could be found. His situation seemed desperate, though the diagnosis seemed certain. Everyone but the Captain was discouraged. He said, "Keep on operating." It was finally decided, after long study, that his parathyroid tumor must be in some unusual place, probably in the chest instead of in the neck, where the parathyroid glands are normally found. Another attempt was made. At this, the seventh operation, the tumor was found deep in his chest and was removed.

The Captain stood the operation well. His bones began to improve. A month later he was able to stand. Then one day a kidney stone that had formed as a by-product of parathyroid disease, became lodged in his ureter. For this he had to have an eighth operation, which was followed by a series of complications and death. Then came the autopsy for which Captain Martell had years before arranged, and which added to our knowledge of this new disease.

One week later, another patient, with similar symptoms, was operated upon. No tumor was found in his neck. The new insight obtained in the Captain's case suggested that the tumor might be found in the chest. It was. The patient recovered rapidly. At the

close of 1932 there had been eight such tumors removed in this
hospital, about one-fifth of the total cases on record in the world.

At least fifty people co-operated in the discovery of this disease
and of the cure for it—physicians, general surgeons, genitourinary
surgeons, dentists, pathologists, chemists, dietitians, nurses, and last
but not least the patients themselves. The largest contributor was
Captain Martell of the merchant marine, of whom it might be said
that he charted unknown seas and died that others might live.[4]

We think the Catholic theologians are right that, in a good world-
plan, suffering which does not test or stimulate the sufferer must be
good for some one else. To say that in our pain we are working for
"souls in Purgatory," is a good phrase to hold our gains until we
can see more. These souls in Purgatory represent "someone bene-
fited," not the sufferer, or humanity, or any known creature on
earth. Give us more knowledge and we might choose such suffering
and death as the hero and martyr do,—knowing their good cause.
Only our ignorance separates us from this bit of God's will. Some
day we shall know more.

4. *Mental pain is often our best guide to what has blocked our
growth.* It is not always punishment for sin. It shows up the
stupidity that we need especially to recognize and so to conquer.
Hurt feelings, disappointed hopes, the anguish of seeing a loved
one suffer, the prospect of death for ourselves, train us in spiritual
detachment. We can still fight the physical causes of these blows,
illness, bankruptcy, political corruption, while we see that for our
own spiritual growth they have been godsends.

The fact that a person not ill is bored in surroundings that he
must live in and that others enjoy, gives him a sharp warning. It
says: Develop your resources; don't be so narrow. Fear of failure
does not plague the mathematician, the astronomer, the honest and
devoted statesman. They are quite apt to fail but not to fear failure.
Such fear has no poison for the man who is doing his best. Humilia-

---

[4] Condensed from the *Report of the Massachusetts General Hospital,* 1933, pp.
18-20.

tion at failure does not occur in good scientific work. Failure does; but the psychical result of it is not humiliation. Social, political or artistic failure brings humiliation to him whose treasures are accessible to moths, to rust, and to the sting of social disapproval. But any man whose face is set steadily toward growth welcomes humiliation so long as it has power to live in him. It is grist to his spiritual mill; it is money in his pocket. He "welcomes each rebuff" *of this kind*—not physical disaster but moral pain.

5. *If we were built for happiness no one could defend the Creator for making us so sensitive to pain. But we are not so built.* A conscious stone would be far happier than a man, exposed to a thousand wounds through his sensitiveness. Built for growth through experience, we have nerves, senses, and a brain that could not know delight unless it knew suffering. Pain stirs us out of the original sin of laziness, itself inseparable from our physical make-up and from our capacity to grow. The oases of civilization on our largely uncivilized planet are situated where cold and hunger stir men to work. Primitive men wandered widely. Some settled in the tropics and stayed there because it was easy to live there without exertion. Others settled in temperate zones. They are "the elect" in the sense that their persistence in a hard, challenging climate has produced the best that we know in civilization. Primitive races often seem happier than civilized races. We see no reason to doubt it or to regret that the growing peoples find much pain mixed with their growth.

Much of the pain that we know seems to have been the stimulus needed to prevent people's settling into stagnant happiness and so into a slow degeneration. Comfort is as great an enemy to growth as we know. Growing pains are therefore no special theological puzzle except to those who assume that man was created for ease and happiness. Pain seems to be necessary to growth because it is painful to be stirred out of fixed habits and fixed habits contradict growth. We do not mean that every case of suffering favors development. Most of the suffering in insanity has no good result so far as we can see. We have faith that in some way not visible to us, and so long as we have done our best against it, it serves a good end. In this belief we only echo in another key the fundamental faith of science.

Particular pains are no more mysterious than the particular shapes, colors, weights, and tensions in the world around us. Many of these mysteries delight us like the colors of the sunset. Yet they certainly were not made merely for man's delight. They were here presumably for millions of years before man or any other creature noticed them. They are as inexplicable as any pain and as certain to be *somehow* a part of the divine plan. Our delight in natural beauty ought not to blind us to the fact that most of it is as mysterious and seems as fortuitous as suffering. The universe is not arranged for pain or for pleasure. Most of it is insensitive to either, and most of our physical functions produce neither pleasure nor pain, neither happiness nor unhappiness. Man's fortunes are planned to make him grow.

II. IGNORANCE, FUTURITY, AND EVIL

One of the difficulties in the problem of evil is this: we seem to be in a contradictory frame of mind about it. We justify its presence in the world; yet we seek to abolish every particular evil. We blow hot and then we blow cold. How can we defend Evil with a capital letter when we hate and destroy every evil that is written with a small *e*?

The answer is clearest in the case of ignorance. We want to wipe out every item of ignorance that we find blocking our way. By education we slay as many ignorances as we can, yet life would be terrible if it had no ignorance in it. We could learn nothing. There would be no surprises, no discovery, invention, progress, in short nothing new. We want Ignorance because it is necessary for Growth, but we want to abolish every bit of ignorance that we become aware of as we grow. New areas of it come in sight with every step in our progress and we never want to stop.

This paradox seems to be nothing worse than our plight in relation to time. Life without a future would be death. We look forward into an unknown abyss from which come freshness, variety, surprise, and the delight that is in them, but we learn to predict bits of this future, and by predicting them we kill their futurity. Time still flows on but we have denatured it so far as we know its future contents. When we grasp and manipulate the future as if it were present, it differs from the present in no essential.

We must have a Future, then, else growth would be meaningless, but we abolish every partial futurity as fast as we can. We make ourselves snug and secure by pinning down the future through science, but if we could pin it all down so that nothing came unexpectedly, life would be a terrific bore. The monotonous life is one whose future is so like the present and the past that the difference amounts to nothing. It might as well be the past. Unless we hanker to destroy the future we cannot wish to destroy all evils, such as ignorance. But any particular future, any particular evil or ignorance we want to destroy as quickly as we can by knowing it and so mastering it.

We need to find the world full of exasperating, enraging opacities, full of futures that no one can know save by creative growth. We need to find the world's interweaving so variegated and so profuse that we are sure some time to be caught unprepared by an evil that challenges us—earthquake, temptation, cancer. It is someone's task to meet and kill this dragon, but St. George is not always on the job. My unfaithfulness to what I now see brings disaster to you whom I never heard of. Tragedy? Yes, but we need the world's stage so set that this tragedy can occur. We need a world with plenty of surprises in it; and my surprise is sometimes your disaster. We are built for a world that develops us by challenges, but the challenge which you welcome overwhelms me in defeat. We welcome a life where mysteries strike us like hail in the fact, but cold that stimulates one freezes another. Your courage-generating fear is paralyzing terror to me.

Cosmic Evil then is as essential to our growth as the flow of time is. We are bound to destroy every conquerable evil as fast as we find how to do it. We need to pull every penetrable future into the present and so to destroy its futurity, but we need the evil and the future to grow by.

We need a *Future* shrouded in mysteries because the known and mastered present is its fellow member in the life of growth, but in the process of our development we destroy every particular mystery in it as fast as we can.

We need *Evil* because good is inseparable from it, but we must destroy every recognized evil as soon as we can.

How much evil, ignorance, mysterious futurity, do we need in our lives? As much as our growth requires. How much do we need of attained virtue, of completed knowledge, of a future de-natured by scientific prediction? As much as our growth requires. Temptation is an evil when we succumb to it, a good when it is resisted with effort and with enlightenment which increases our stature. To sit down contented before our ignorance makes it an evil. To be stimulated by it to learn something makes it a good. There is no fortune good or evil but behavior makes it so.

If evil were a temporary, outgrowable thing it would be an unpardonable blemish on the universe. It is good to have it in the world, so long as we fight and kill all we can of it, but only because it can never be eliminated or diminished. A goal of perfection *slowly approached* through the ages would be an outrage if we could ever get there. A lazy, cruel World Plan it would be that started us off so far from an attainable goal and moved us toward it as slowly as man has developed through his millions of years on this planet. We are not on a transient pilgrimage endured as we go through a bad world for the sake of heaven. Our pilgrimage is the very pick of life; not a means to something better but the best we know.

How long, O Lord, how long, shall we be at it? Forever; not in this stage of it, but in the struggle with some sort of evil. On this basis evil cannot be *mere* evil if we are to call the world good. Yet it is not a negation or an illusion either. Good—success, happi-ness—becomes another evil if we are not stimulated by it to get beyond it. Conscious virtue is vice. Money, leisure, easy climate, contentment, peace, even knowledge are evils to some of us. They are bad unless we take them as steps in growth as well as blessings in the instant. Each good is an evil the instant it checks progress. The instant it is gloated over, indulged in, hung on to, basked in, it becomes a curse. Thus goods easily turn into evils. Unless we grow through them they poison us.

So with evils. They become goods when they are welcomed as challenges needed to arouse the best in us. Sin is not thus good. Temptation is. Sin is a challenge refused.

III. THE PROBLEM OF JOY

Why does joy come to me? Have I deserved all that I get? That question is as hard to answer for good as it is for evil, for pleasure as for pain.

We are *"body"* (rhythmic repetition, stagnation, laziness) *and* *"soul"* (growth, new experience, cumulation). The "goods" or pleasures of the body have no obvious relation to growth. They are the sign that one of the body's jobs, say eating, is being carried on as usual. The body stands still or repeats itself. This stagnation is the body's health. Sometimes we are aware of the stagnation; then we have a balance-sense, a maintenance-sense, or, more generally, a homeostatic-sense.[5] That is bodily pleasure. Sometimes health (or homeostasis) gives no pleasure. It is quite unconscious. Sometimes heightened bodily functions become conscious. That is pleasure. Sometimes we are painfully aware of them as we are in the palpitation of a normal heart.

When beauty, love, and suffering arouse us, they are the call to body and soul to do their job. We respond by action or by lethargy. Both are right in their place, but we must not misplace them. To respond with homeostatic sense and habitual action when crescentic sense and growth are the need, is to degenerate. The morally lazy man is one who makes a "body-response" when a

[5] See Walter B. Cannon, *The Wisdom of the Body,* (New York, W. W. Norton & Company, 1932).

"soul-response" is due. He answers with a maintenance-reflex when crescentic-response is called for.

In sickness, the mind should often rest, relax, or "be lazy." Then it is like the normal body which attains its health by stagnation. In some phases of illness, our minds as well as our bodies ought to be lazy, to "adjust" themselves, to favor self-maintenance and defense. So it is with the life of the savage or the feeble-minded. They are infantile or "resting" stages of humanity. Like resting plants or sleeping men their growth is in abeyance. Perhaps savages, like sleepers, are building up a reserve for future growth. If so they are right to be not mentally active or growing, but bodily active or homeostatic.

The free good gifts which we receive from God in beauty and friendship are signs of His exuberant love. In these gifts He offers us body-food and soul-food far beyond any finite plan of ours. He offers us copious maintenance-material and growth-material. We take it or ignore it. If we are ready to make poetry or invention out of it we get growth. If not God still pursues us, as the Hound of Heaven, with maintenance-material and with material for growth. Beautiful weather may benefit our health only, or it may also stimulate us to work, to sacrifice, and to appreciation of man and God. Then its crescentic-material meets a creative response.

I (R. C. C.) find the wealth of unassimilable beauties painful sometimes because I cannot respond to them nor penetrate them. Why do we get so much more good than we deserve or assimilate? Because we are free, as in Emerson's "Days," [6] to take far better

[6] *Daughters of Time, the hypocritic Days,*
Muffled and dumb like barefoot dervishes,
And marching single in an endless file,
Bring diadems and fagots in their hands.
To each they offer gifts after his will,
Bread, kingdoms, stars, and sky that holds them all.
I, in my pleached garden, watched the pomp,
Forgot my morning wishes, hastily
Took a few herbs and apples, and the Day
Turned and departed silent. I, too late,
Under her solemn fillet saw the scorn.
—*Poems* by Ralph Waldo Emerson (Boston, Houghton Mifflin Co., 1904), p. 228.

gifts than we do. God offers us myriad temptations to rightdoing, to invention, creation, reform, and discovery. He treats us as if we were capable of anything or, rather, He sets no limit to our free will and so to our capability for crescentic life. He calls out to all our powers, to many more than now answer, because there is no wisdom even in God to limit what we *might* take. He loves us all so infinitely that He offers excess to all. So our huge bill of fare always contains infinitely more than most men eat.

The profusion of opportunity around us looks like waste when we realize that we are not merely blind to much beauty and joy but actually narcotized by some of it, as primitive people are by an easy climate, as many are by money, marriage, admiration, and success. The pleasures that seem hardest to understand if we believe that we are planned for growth are not moral but esthetic. When we hear the chime of a beautiful bell we come to rest. We want nothing but the continuance of this delight. We are dumb, motionless, useless. Tolstoi faced this fact and declared courageously that beauty was often an evil.[7] He was right. Beauty like pleasure is morally neutral. Sometimes it makes us say *"Lass mich sterben,"* like the lovers in Wagner's *Tristan*. Then it is a delicious narcotic poison, no less poisonous for its deliciousness. It poises us like a locomotive's wheel at a dead point, in a trance that is deathlike. Pain does the same by causing us to faint.

That we like the swooning pleasure of moveless beauty is no reason to call it good. We like to be lazy. All the healthy juices in the body urge us that way when they swim up into consciousness unmodified by the growth-impulse. Beauty is not only "pleasure objectified," as Santayana says.[8] It is also a call to our growing life. It calls to us to play up to what delights us, to be both content and restless, both satisfied and unsatisfied. Otherwise it is a soporific. The *narcotizing beauty* of which Wagner, following Schopenhauer, was not ashamed, must be driven out by the *challenging beauty* of Brahms and Plato.

[7] L. Tolstoi, *What is Art?* (London, Oxford University Press, 1932).
[8] George Santayana, *The Sense of Beauty,* (New York, Charles Scribner's Sons 1896).

"A hunger for pain and difficulty emerges from worship," says W. E. Hocking. Yes, and from the bath of beauty too. "In worthy joy," says James Hinton,[9] "there is latent an element of pain. The only happiness God can bestow bears martyrdom within it." Any Philistine of us may be waked, suddenly or gradually, by the bombardment of good and evil in the midst of which we choose our path. Being free to grow is more than being free to choose between right and wrong. It is being open to the invitations of infinite light and strength at each stage of our growth. Even God does not know what each of us will take from the Daughters of Time. So He permits exuberant, copious streams of unperceived sensation and undeserved love to pour upon us. Much of it seems wasted. He permits the waste in order to tempt us with every possible test.

It is the same with the mental sufferings (evils) which He allows us to feel. They too are invitations to growth. They may crush us. He cannot tell how much of them we shall use, since, despite its sins, the will is free, free for a long time, anyway, before it is paralyzed and dead. Do we get more suffering than we have deserved? More than we can transmute? How can even He tell that without depriving man of freedom? He permits the waste of invitations to growth-through-suffering in order to be sure that there is enough, and with the certainty of another chance after death if we fail.

All this applies to mental ills, disappointments, betrayals, sorrows of bereavement, to cramping poverty, illness (aside from pain and anemia), to remorse, worry, and depression, but seldom to insanity. Insanity and many bodily evils, such as severe pain, paralysis, anesthesia, nausea, convulsions, coma, are rarely invitations to the sufferer's growth. In most people they stop it. Yet we must believe that bodily ills are suffered in a good cause though we do not see it, except when they rouse us to research and to the ministering tenderness and patience of faith. None of these rewards the soul that suffers. This sort of pain ought to be abolished, root and branch. Plenty of stimulus will be left for us still.

[9] James Hinton, The Mystery of Pain, quoted by F. von Hügel, *Essays and Addresses*, (London and Toronto, J. M. Dent & Sons Ltd., 1926), Second Series. pp. 168-169.

What is the divine plan about the bacteria which live and thrive on our sufferings? We do not know. Presumably we ought to work out ways to *live and let live* in our relation to them as to all the other life on our planet. At present the problem, How many ought to be born? seems as insoluble for bacteria, cats, bisons, egrets, as it is for men. We do not even know how to approach it. But one thing is clear: He who suffers agony because we cannot cure his disease is getting no adequate good out of life in this world. In a just world his turn for that good must come later. Others—bacteria, animals or men—are now having their chance in his pain. Presumably God's plan will provide other chances for them when we have abolished disease.

Strength to bear the tragedies and to explain the absurdities of daily life comes in part from a fighting faith. We wager our lives that there *is* an explanation for much that we cannot explain. This faith differs from superstition because we make the leap after reflection and not before it. When we make afresh the ancient effort to think out why people suffer we see so much reasonableness that when our sight gives out we are ready to move on by faith in the same direction. We use the same assumptions which push along the work of the doctor, the physicist, and the chemist. None of these worthies would hustle so hard as he does for new discoveries if he did not assume that all intelligent questions have an answer. Inductive reasoning cannot prove this. There are as many defeats as victories for the questioning mind. Yet the energy of scientific work still issues from the dogged faith that the universe is reasonable provided we put our questions to it intelligently.

A world lucid to us throughout would be cheap. We want it to go beyond our present comprehension. We need to find it so built that it will always leave us more to know. Meantime it *is* opaque to us in much, perhaps most, that meets the eye, in blessings as well as in evils. The religious man knows no more than any one else about particular evils. He says they must have some meaning because the inexplicable is nonsense and because he recalls examples where patient faith has been rewarded by ultimate comprehension.

All this rests on the certainty that God permeates *all* with His good plan. Of this plan we get glimpses by worship, by meditation, by revelation, through beautiful outbursts of the divine in man or in other creatures, or, lastly, by philosophy. The universe must be under a plan, and that plan could not be bad else it would contradict itself, as it seems to do in evil, and so be no plan at all.

Chapter IX

VIS MEDICATRIX DEI

I (R. C. C.) went into medicine in the hope of helping people. I found that I could help vastly less than I hoped. I was not wise enough to help as I wanted to. But though I could give a great deal less, there was a great deal more for me to receive. There was more for me to learn and to be inspired by as I watched the behavior of this extraordinary creation that we call the human body. I have been more and more amazed at the intelligence, not of the human brain but of the other organs of the human body. I think every minister can share this amazement and ought to do so.

The minister, I take it, is a person who arms himself adequately before he goes into action. The minister's preparation is as special as his job. When he visits the sick he takes along a special set of ideas, chiefly a mental picture of the patient whom he is to see, and of his own plans for that patient. But besides this the minister should revive in his mind a picture of what God is actually doing in the body of the sick man. The ordinary phrase for this is "the healing power of nature" (*vis medicatrix naturae*). Every physician recognizes and relies on this like a tried and trusted friend when he makes his prediction of the length and outcome of the disease in any patient under his care. His forecast is based on two elements: (1) what his medical or surgical treatment can accomplish and (2) what nature will do. Experience with disease in his student days, during his internship and through the years of his practice has packed his mind with examples of what "nature" does to heal disease. The minister cannot draw upon so rich a fund of experiences but we think it essential that he should get the best substitute that he can. Dr. Walter B. Cannon's book on *The Wisdom of the*

Body gives the best account known to us of what "nature," or as we believe, God, does to keep the body sound despite the strains which challenge its strength in health as well as in disease. That book is a series of examples of what he calls the "homeostatic" power of the body. As a ship rights herself after a squall has heeled her over, so that body rights itself after the minor "squalls," chemical and physical, that strike it daily in health and after the tempests of disease. The body's power to right itself when something tends to upset it is what Dr. Cannon calls "homeostasis" or "standing the same."

In this chapter I (R. C. C.) shall give first a number of examples of this power and then explain why, though some call it homeo-stasis, we call it God. The examples which follow are familiar to all educated physicians but are not known to the public so widely as they should be. We divide the examples of "homeostasis" into four groups:

1. Reserve.
2. Balance.
3. Compensation.
4. Defense.

In one sense they are all defenses against attack present or threatened.

1. *Reserve.* In the chief organs of the human body we recognize an extra supply that can be called upon in need, like the reserve of a bank. When a man suffers from tuberculosis of the lungs, a certain portion of the lung is destroyed, but he has a great deal more lung tissue than he needs. He can call upon his reserve and get along, as the great Dr. Trudeau did at Saranac for nearly forty years of hard work, though he had only a part of one lung still healthy.

Experiments have shown that one can remove more than two-fifths of the human liver and still the remaining three-fifths will carry on the work of the organ, so far as one can see, just as well as before.

When we see a surgeon cut and tie thirty or forty blood vessels in the course of an operation, we may wonder what is to become of the blood that should circulate through them. The answer is that we have many more than we need. We can sacrifice a great many and still get on perfectly well with what are left.

Each of us has about twenty-two feet of intestine. By reason of disease a portion of it may have to be removed. One can lose three or four feet and hardly miss it at all.

2. *Balance*. In the laboratories where physiological and bacteriological work is carried on we use an instrument called a thermostat, that is, an instrument which keeps the temperature stable. In growing bacteria we have to arrange that the temperature around them shall not vary more than a few degrees. If it rises or falls more than that the bacteria that we are trying to study die. A thermostat is a difficult instrument to manage. It seldom works perfectly, and it never works nearly so well as that extraordinary instrument, the human body.

Most of us know that if our temperature is taken with a clinical thermometer it is approximately 98.6° Fahrenheit, varying only a few tenths of a degree during the twenty-four hours. But we do not realize perhaps that when a person goes into a temperature of 40° below zero, or when, as used to be the case with the stokers in steamships, he has to live minutes or hours in temperatures of 130° to 150° Fahrenheit, still his body keeps its temperature the same. A piece of metal and most substances that can become heated or chilled, will respond to the temperature around them. The human body has the extraordinary capacity to keep its balance in terms of heat. Unless that were the case death would occur whenever one went into a cold temperature or into a hot temperature. This balance may be lost under a very hot sun, and then "sunstroke" occurs. The body's temperature runs up to 110° or 115°, which it cannot sustain for many minutes and still live.

By a number of ingenious devices the body ordinarily preserves its temperature at a point between 98° and 99° Fahrenheit. These devices are not familiar to everyone. For instance, if we are cold w often shiver, and we think of shivering, perhaps, as an inevitable misfortune. As a matter of fact, by shivering we keep ourselves warmer than we should be if we did not shiver. Shivering is a muscular action, and the action of any muscle tends to create warmth.

There are many other ways, which we shall not stop to describe, by which our body preserves its own temperature as it must if life is to go on. Our brains do practically nothing about this; it is beyond our conscious powers; it is part of the intelligent action of the body itself.

A second example of this intelligence is the *balance of moisture* in the body. The human body is about four-fifths water, and it must preserve nearly that proportion of water, or life cannot go on. We are giving out water and taking in water all the time, and yet the body by its own intelligent arrangements preserves almost exactly the same proportion of water in itself at all times.

Most of us, most of the time, preserve the balance of our weight. Some people tend to get too heavy and others to get too thin, but on the whole it is amazing how seldom this happens, in spite of the fact that we are putting bulky substances into our tissues all the time and losing pounds and pounds of weight in every violent exertion. A football player sometimes loses ten or twelve pounds in one game. Nevertheless we hold our weight, most of us, within a pound or two, year after year.

The most delicate of all these balances is our chemical balance. Most of us have heard of the common chemical terms, acidity and alkalinity. Most substances that enter or leave the body can be classified as either acid or alkaline. When a substance is in chemical balance between the two we call it neutral. The body has to be held very close to this neutral point. If it varies as much as a few parts in a thousand we become unconscious. But every act that we do, every muscular motion, every strong feeling, every deep breath, would change the chemical reaction of the body toward acidity unless the body balanced it by a change in the opposite direction. Every meal that we take pushes the body's reaction toward the alkaline side. And yet, although acid is being taken into the body or made in the body in great quantities, in irregular quantities, and at irregular times from moment to moment, the healthy body still preserves almost unchanged this delicate balance of acid and alkali.

It is hard to bring this miracle vividly before ourselves. Imagine a bank with its receiving and paying tellers; imagine that thousands and thousands of dollars are being poured into that bank in various amounts, large and small, and at various times of the day, without any rule or order. Then at the same time imagine that large amounts or small amounts are being taken out of the bank by depositors. This is what is usually going on in fact. Now imagine what, of course, never happens, that the balance of money in that bank is preserved within a few dollars of the same amount at all times. Imagine that if the balance in the bank varied more than a few dollars the bank would break. Then you have a picture of what is actually going on at the present moment in your body and the bodies of all human beings. It seems too strange to be true, but it is true.

3. *Compensation.* We all know that if a person is unable to use one arm and as a result uses the other constantly, the arm which is used for two gains something like the strength of two. In the School for Crippled Children at Canton, Massachusetts, I saw a few years ago a little boy who as the result of infantile paralysis had lost altogether the power of his legs. He had been at home without treatment for a long time, and there he had learned to walk on his hands. When he wanted to walk he folded up his useless legs, pushed them out of the way over his head, stood up on his hands and walked on them. He could walk upstairs and downstairs. Of course, his arms were enormously developed. That is "compensatory hypertrophy," or enlargement of the muscles in response to need and use. It is familiar to most of us in muscles. It is not so familiar, perhaps, inside the body.

When heart disease takes the form of valvular inflammation and deforms the valve, the situation is like what would happen if one of the doors of a room were stuck halfway open, so that it would neither open nor close fully. That is what happens to the heart valve when the germ of rheumatism attacks it. The individual could not live if it were not that, as the deformity gradually occurs in the valve, the heart gradually thickens and so strengthens its own muscle. A heart that is ordinarily the size of an individual's fist will become as big as two or three or even four fists, because it must. In no other way can it push the blood along hard enough to maintain the circulation when the openings into the heart and out of it are narrowed. The circulation must go on about as fast as it normally does. The compensatory growth of the heart muscle makes this possible.

With automobile accidents as common as they are today, there are a great many cases in which children are run over by a wheel in such a way that the kidney is broken or cut. The surgeon, when he operates on such a case, tries to repair the damage and in some cases he can. But in many cases he cannot do so and in order to stop the bleeding he has to remove the kidney altogether. How can he possibly have the temerity to do such a thing as to remove a human kidney? Because experience has shown that as soon as one kidney is removed the other begins to grow, and in a very short time doubles its size so that it is as big as the two were before, and does the work exactly as well.

The work of the kidney seems to us one of the most wonderful things to be found anywhere on earth. In any pair of healthy human kidneys there are many miles of tubes, and within those tubes all sorts of processes are always going on. When the solitary kidney gets twice as big, something very complicated is rebuilt or enlarged. All the details are rebuilt so as to leave the patient in the end not merely somewhere near as good, but exactly as good as he was before. The architecture of a kidney is far more complicated and differentiated than the architecture of any ordinary building. In a house we build a cellar, kitchen, sleeping rooms, attic, closets, and so forth, for different purposes. The kidney has as many different parts. It has its own chemical laboratory in which analytic and synthetic, dissolving and combining processes are done. Some of these chemical processes are new. On occasion they make substances which so far as we know have never been manufactured in that kidney before. They are made in response to a need for an antidote for a special poison.

We said just now that we have more blood vessels, tubes which carry blood, than we need. One of the reasons that we get along so well when a number of vessels are cut or destroyed is that some of those that are left become enlarged. One of the common diseases of the liver is called "cirrhosis" or the "gin-drinker's liver." That means that alcohol or some other substance taken in with the liquor circulates through the liver, hardens it and blocks it so that the blood which should go through it from the intestine cannot pass. Yet people sometimes live with this disease for many years and never find out that they have it, because detours, such as we provide when a street is blocked, are arranged by the wisdom of the body. The blood goes through a new set of blood vessels, partly newly formed and partly old ones enlarged. In this way we sometimes get such perfect compensation for the cirrhosis that the individual feels entirely well for years and finally dies of something else.

When one goes into a high altitude and lives above 5,000 feet, the air which one breathes is rarified so that less oxygen is taken in at each breath. No one would be able to live at this altitude were it not that the red corpuscles, which carry the oxygen from the lungs to all parts of the body, begin to grow in number as soon as the air becomes notably thinned, and soon increase to an extraordinary degree.

In every cubic millimeter of blood (which means a drop about the size of a large pinhead) we have five millions of red corpuscles. After a person has spent a few weeks in a high altitude he has six million, and if he goes to a higher altitude he has seven million. I (R. C. C.) have seen a person who had gone to so high an altitude and lived there so long that he had nine million red corpuscles to a cubic millimeter of blood. This was a compensatory change. He used the diminished supply of oxygen which came into his lungs in that high altitude so effectively and so rapidly that he was perfectly well. When he came down to a low altitude the extra red corpuscles were destroyed and put out of the body and he throve on five million, as he did before.

4. *Defense.* Rest is defense. If you sprain your wrist it becomes swollen and stiff. Nature says, "You had better rest that wrist." Even before the doctor comes, "nature" splints the wrist by making it so sore that you hesitate to move it, and so stiff that you cannot easily move it. The doctor reinforces nature's splint with an artificial one.

If a patient is strained emotionally or physically beyond a certain point by exertion or terror, nature says, "Take a rest," and he faints. Soreness and stiffness in a wrist, fainting after a hard race or in an accident, seem like something hostile to our welfare, something to be fought against. But the truth is that they are evidence of a power working on our side to do us service.

What we do in the treatment of an injured joint is to imitate nature and to supplement nature. What we do in most branches of medicine is to imitate and supplement nature. We imitate by means of a stomach tube one of the body's natural defenses: vomiting. When poison is swallowed the stomach usually rejects it before the physician with his stomach tube can get there to help in the emptying. The body rejects poisons through several channels; it throws out alcohol through the lungs so that we smell it in the drinker's breath. The body also puts out poisons by the bowels and sometimes by the blood. Nosebleeds in persons with kidney trouble help to get poisons out of the body. Any competent physician knows that when a person with kidney trouble has nosebleed it is one of the best things that can happen. By bleeding him nature is unpoisoning him and lowering his blood pressure at the same time.

The body also defends itself against poisons by neutralizing them. The most familiar example of this is in the germ diseases, from which we suffer because bacteria invade our bodies and form poisons or "toxins." These must be neutralized or we die. The body itself forms antitoxins which are specific, unique substances, each different from each and hostile only to the poison of the disease for which it is formed.

Before we had the remedy which we now call "antitoxin" for diphtheria the mortality was about forty per cent, which meant that in about sixty per cent of the cases nature formed enough antitoxin in the child to cure it, but that in forty per cent the body did not make enough antitoxin. To supplement it we make outside the body an artificial "diphtheria antitoxin," imitating nature as nearly as we can. We build up in the blood of another animal, ordinarily a horse, an antitoxin like that which the human body itself builds up against diphtheria, but which it does not always build in sufficient quantity. We put into the veins of a healthy horse a small amount of diphtheria poison. The horse eats a little less hay for a day or two and then he is all right. Then we put in double that dose. Again he may be a little under the weather but in a few days he is all right. So we go on step by step to build up in this animal the neutralizing substance opposite to this particular poison. His blood will not neutralize the toxin of any other disease except diphtheria. The new-formed antitoxin is a specific and unique substance.

Then we draw off from the jugular vein of the horse a certain amount of his blood, not enough seriously to incapacitate him but enough to be of use to many human beings. We drain off the corpuscles, put in a preservative, and the result is a yellow fluid which we call diphtheria antitoxin. That is what we put into the child's body to aid the antitoxin which the body has already made there after the disease began. In this way the mortality of diphtheria has been reduced to six or seven per cent, and with the protective injections which are now being carried out in every intelligent community we are reducing diphtheria to zero. Many of us now alive may see diphtheria wiped out altogether, as smallpox is in places intelligent enough to down the antivaccinationists and enforce vaccination laws.

We have described how the body neutralizes poisons of the

kind produced in infectious diseases by bacteria. But the body neutralizes poisons in many other ways. A suicidal unfortunate swallows a strong acid. Then the body manufactures enormous quantities of alkali, far more than it was making before for any other purpose, and so neutralizes the poisonous acid. When one recovers from certain kinds of poisoning it is nine-tenths by reason of what the body does by way of neutralization and one-tenth what the doctor does to imitate and to supplement nature.

Consider now another of the body's self-defenses. If you wound your finger with a splinter of wood or with anything else that is apt to be dirty, there often occurs the process that we call *festering*. What we call "pus" appears round the splinter. We do not stop to think what this means. To me it is one of the most dramatic and one of the most wonderful things that happens in the human body. What is this stuff called "matter" or "pus"? It is the dead bodies of leucocytes, that is, of white corpuscles from the blood, which have come to the spot, have fought upon our side against the bacteria, have died in the fight and have piled up their bodies to make a wall of defense between the attacking bacteria on the one side and the free circulation on the other. If this wall were broken down and the bacteria got into the blood we should have blood poisoning and probably die. Every dirty splinter that we get into our hands might be fatal were it not for the fight put up for us by these little creatures called leucocytes.

The human body is built up of cells, just as houses are built up of bricks. Among these cells most are as fixed as the bricks in a wall, but there is one race of free, lively and intelligent cells, the leucocytes in the blood, which in response to a need for them, travel to any part of the human body and there fight, destroy many bacteria, and are themselves often killed in the fight. They conquer in the vast majority of cases because they build up the protecting wall just described. Almost every case of appendicitis would be fatal if this wall of leucocytes were not built by "nature" around the diseased appendix. What doctors call "walling off" the disease happens without any surgeon and before the surgeon gets there, in the majority of cases. The bodies of the leucocytes shut in the inflammation until the surgeon gets there to remove it.

In my medical work I (R. C. C.) have had the chance to examine dead bodies of persons who had died in spite of the best we could do at the Massachusetts General Hospital, where I have worked for nearly forty years. Nothing sounds more sordid and more discouraging than the job of examining dead bodies. There we see the failures of nature's healing, the defeats of the human body in its struggle against disease. Yet the study of these bodies has been one of the most inspiring experiences that has ever come to me. For we see at an autopsy not merely the defeat that has resulted in death, but the whole history of that body's earlier victories written in its tissues. Here we see the battlefields on which the body has conquered disease years ago, without even letting the brain know that the disease was going on.

When we cut into a lung at autopsy we often find evidence of a healed tuberculosis which during his life the person never knew he had. The knife with which we cut may be broken across a stone, a mass of lime deposited there by the blood so as to wall in a group of tubercle bacilli, as in the Middle Ages they sometimes walled in a human being in the wall of a castle and left him to die. So the healing powers of the body, wall in the tubercle bacilli in the lung so that they are harmless. We cut through this stone and sometimes find the tubercle bacilli still alive but harmless, because they are shut off from the lung. Till recently the majority of all the bodies which we examined showed some signs of a healed tuberculosis.

Then comes the fact that on the whole has impressed me most. Knowing as I often do the histories of these people, including all that they knew about themselves during their lives, I know that they were never conscious of any illness corresponding to this tuberculosis which we found after death. Tuberculosis often "cures itself," as we say, without producing any symptoms, because of the healing power of nature, which even our great-grandfathers knew about and honored, and which any man who faces disease as I have faced it all my life comes more and more to honor and to admire.

Nature also makes mistakes; nature fails, else we should never die. There is no good, so far as we know, in the human appendix. It is of no possible use to us. No one knows why we have cancer. We have made no progress to speak of in the understanding of it and not very much in the war against it. Failures of the healing power of nature are with us. We must look them squarely in the face, and gather our forces to fight them. Perhaps human beings could in no other way be challenged effectively enough to get over their ignorance about disease, to get over their laziness in fighting it. Perhaps we need the presence of these diseases which, in spite of all that nature does for us, force us to fight, to imitate nature and to supplement nature as physicians and public health workers are now trying to do.

Summing up this chapter I will describe one individual whose face comes before me as I write about him. An elderly man, sixty-four years of age, with a ruddy, fresh complexion and white hair, stepped off the corner of a street without looking where he was going, was struck by an automobile and fatally injured. He was brought to the Massachusetts General Hospital and died within an hour. His wife came soon after, and when we asked her about him, she declared that he had never been sick in his life. He was a bartender, a local politician, a most active person both in mind and body. I was present at the autopsy on his body, and this is what we found: (1) Healed tuberculosis of both lungs. (2) Cirrhosis of the liver, with all the blood going around by a new set of roads above and below his liver. (3) Chronic kidney trouble, but with enough reserve kidney tissue to carry on the kidneys' function perfectly despite the destruction of a large portion of one and a small portion of the other kidney. (4) Hardening of the arteries and compensatory enlargement of his heart. No doubt he had had high blood pressure for a long time. All this he never knew. In other words, here was a perfectly well man with four fatal diseases inside of him, none of which had done him any harm!

When part of a vessel is injured in a storm, they rig up something to take the place of it. A "jury mast" is rigged up for a broken mast, or a "jury rudder" for a broken rudder. This man's body was full of "jury" arrangements. Four vital organs had these compensatory defenses, *but he was a going concern.* He could do what he wanted to do and felt no inconvenience, because of the intelligence of the human body exerted in his defense.

The facts are before us. Every doctor knows them. There is nothing new or doubtful about them. The conclusions are for each to draw for himself. The conclusion which I draw is a greater confidence in life. However we may fall short, a gigantic healing power fights on our side. Matthew Arnold defined God as the power not ourselves that makes for righteousness. The thing I am speaking of here is that great power in ourselves that makes for health, and that works day and night, when we are asleep and when we are awake, when we are good and when we are bad. Its beneficence falls like rain upon the just and upon the unjust.

To me that means the goodness of God—*vis medicatrix Dei.* It means that the powers which carry on the work of our body are not neutral in the battle between us and the enemies of our health. A great healing power fights on our side and wins most of our battles for us. When we look around at "nature" in the mountains, the forests, the plains or the sea, we see no evidence of powers that care about us. Nature seems indifferent to our welfare. But if we look at that portion of nature which concerns us most, our own bodies, we see no indifference, no neutrality, but an extraordinary bias in our favor. On the basis of these healing powers our intelligence and our will get their opportunity.

The facts of this chapter, which came to me unexpectedly in a profession where I thought I was going not to learn but to teach, not to be strengthened but to try to strengthen others, are one of the great reasons for believing in the goodness of God. He is the plan of this world. Our bodies have been built up in evolution as part of that plan. They show us that plan, never slumbering, watching over us when we sleep, exerting in our bodies an intelligence which we try to imitate and to reinforce by our medical and our surgical work. God does not do all our work for us. He leaves undone enough to challenge our intensest energy. He helps those who help themselves and some who do not, but He is never neutral in our life struggle. He offers us a model of healing work and does most of the healing Himself.

His plan also includes enemies to our welfare, bacteria, wild beasts, earthquake, famine, torrid heat and freezing cold. He intends that we shall have plenty of enemies to fight. But in our fight against disease we have a prodigiously ingenious and powerful force always at work on our side. The minister needs to realize this force and to trust it as the doctor does, not to replace but to reinforce and to stimulate our best efforts.

CHAPTER X

SPECIAL POINTS ON A FEW COMMON DISEASES

1. Acute fevers (pneumonia, grippe, scarlet fever, etc.)

Many patients are too drowsy or too uncomfortable to care for anything but good nursing: frequent cool bathing, well and frequently made bed, frequent tempting meals beautifully served. Some like to be read to. They should move as little as possible, to conserve strength. In convalescence they sometimes see the world with new eyes and find it far more glorious than before the illness. Visits and reading are often welcome then, but the awareness of returning strength is usually all the comfort and encouragement they need.

Contagion: Much that was believed by the medical profession about the ways to catch and to carry disease is now obsolete though still in practice here and there. The clergyman should follow the medical ritual current in the hospital or in the town where he works. Gowns at operations and in visiting possibly contagious patients (scarlet fever, measles, meningitis, diphtheria), washing one's hands after a visit, are practices still clung to in a good many places just as fumigation is. The minister should fall in with all such local customs.

Contagion by breath and by cough is almost the only one that is well established scientifically. To keep six feet or more away from the patient, to avoid coughs and coughing, and in some cases (for instance pneumonic plague) to cover one's mouth and nose with a gauze bandage, are the points of importance when contagion is seriously to be feared.

Some physicians adopt precautions in pneumonia, erysipelas and even in infantile paralysis as if we knew how they are conveyed.

The minister should follow the ritual, though there is no scientific basis for it. Washing one's hands after visiting a typhoid patient is sensible because nurses have often caught this disease from their patients.

2. *Pulmonary tuberculosis.*

In the incipient stages when condemned to long rest in bed at a time when he does not feel sick, the patient is often greatly depressed. His life hopes are broken, he finds the time terribly slow in passing, he fears that he will not recover or that if he does he will never be good for anything. Absolutely rigid routine is usually the easiest as well as the safest way to get through the months. So far as the doctor allows it, and doctors differ on this, visits, reading, pictures, radio, may be a godsend.

In the advanced, usually "hopeless," stages of the disease the consumptive is often optimistic and cheerful, confident of recovery when every one else has given up hope. In fact no case is hopeless. Patients have recovered against all expectation and despite advanced disease in both lungs.

Hemorrhage from the lungs in the early stages of the disease is almost never a serious symptom. Later it may or may not be.

Consumption is one of the few diseases in which as death approaches (after the optimistic stage is past), the patient faces it clearly for some days and may be terrified at the prospect. Ministry to those who know, or believe, that they are dying has here one of its greatest opportunities.

Contagion from the tuberculous patient is a special danger to children, who are extremely susceptible to it and should rarely be allowed close contact with a consumptive. Yet even for them, and for others more clearly, it is true that there is no danger if all that the patient coughs up is burnt and if he learns *never* to cough without covering his mouth and nose with a piece of cotton, gauze or paper. The danger, especially for children, is that the patient may forget this rule or bungle in carrying it out. Tubercle bacilli are thrown into the air for a distance of five or six feet when a patient past the incipient stage of the disease coughs without covering his mouth and nose. These bacilli may be directly inhaled by anyone near the patient. One often sees a doctor dodge if his patient coughs unguardedly while his chest is being examined. If not immediately inhaled the bacilli thus coughed out may settle in the dust of the room and later be inhaled with that dust.

The danger from kissing a consumptive patient is less serious, but should nevertheless be avoided by all who do not choose to take some risk. Infection from table silver or from dishes used by the patient is also rare but sufficient to necessitate a separate set for the patient's use.

Of course no one and especially no child should sleep in the same bed with a tuberculous patient, though in France this essential precaution is often neglected.

No clergyman, in my opinion, should ever be deterred from visiting a tuberculous patient by the slight and quite avoidable risk involved. If the patient by any chance neglects to cover his mouth and nose when he coughs, the clergyman can cover his own.

Tuberculosis of the hip-joint or of the spine is usually a disease of children though it may attack people at any age. There is no danger of contagion. Its treatment may demand prolonged immobility of the affected bones. Often the patient must lie still for one, two or three years, sometimes for more. There is usually little or no pain, but the tedium of lying still day after day calls for all the help that a minister can bring. It is a long campaign and must be carefully planned as I have tried to suggest in Chapter XX.

3. *Heart disease.*

(a) Occupation. As in tuberculosis pain is not the enemy. There is no pain in most forms and in most phases of heart trouble. But when it attacks children, as it often does, they have to keep quiet—in bed or in a chair—for a number of months, usually not quite so long as sufferers from pulmonary or osseous tuberculosis, but still long enough to be a heavy burden for an active child. In many homes it is practically impossible to make him stay quiet unless a succession of occupations, puzzles, jobs of various kinds, can be planned for him, and unless by personal influence and teaching he can be trained into the habit of keeping busy in bed.

(b) With heart disease in children the task of occupying them shades into that of *training them* or getting them trained for some job which they can carry out when they grow up without any severe muscular efforts of lifting, carrying, climbing, etc. A person with heart disease can often live out his life in comfort and prosperity provided he can earn his living with his hands and with his wits but without heavy labor. It is tragedy when we find heart disease in a person past his youth who has no means of livelihood except heavy work. He is headed for death if he works and for deterioration if others support him.

(c) Children with heart disease often have to be kept out of school, and though this eases the strain upon their damaged hearts it does their nerves and their characters (and so indirectly their hearts) almost as much harm as it would do them to go to school. Parents, brothers and sisters, friends, everyone whom the sick child sees, must be banded together in a plan to keep him from pitying himself and worrying about himself. This is easier written than done but it has been done, it can be done and, under the doctor's direction, it may well be the minister's job to take the lead in seeing that it *is* done. For we are dealing here with a set of mental and moral factors in their bearings on a child's physical condition. We must try to keep the child so busy and so happy that he has no time to think about himself and his deprivations, yet obviously we must not overwork him. The doctor must constantly check up and supervise all that is done, but he cannot do it all himself and he will welcome help in seeing that his directions are carried out.

(d) Limitations. When heart disease shows itself first in a person past middle life, it often advances slowly or not at all *provided* the patient can learn just how much he can do and how fast he can go without getting out of breath or bringing on a pain in his breast bone. Such a patient must live on the ground floor, avoid stairs so far as possible or crawl up them at a snail's pace when they must be climbed. He must not live on a hill which he has to climb whenever he comes home. He must learn to start every walk slowly, not to walk or exert himself soon after a meal or soon after he gets up in the morning. He must learn that he can do more on certain days and at certain times of day than on other days and at other times, and that he must flexibly adjust himself day by day and hour by hour to *what he finds that he just then can do* without getting out of breath or producing pain. By absolute fidelity to this rule he can add years to his life.

Cold winds and winter cold, especially with snow on the ground, are serious dangers for him.

In all this the minister, reinforcing the doctor's directions, can help the patient, for it is a training of his will and a reorganization of his habits that is needed. For this the minister is as competent as the doctor, who has often less inclination for it and usually considers himself to have less time. Carrying out the doctor's general specifications, then, and going beyond them in the cultivation of spiritual life, the minister can help the patient reshape his life so as to get the most out of it and to give the most to others.

It is well for the minister to remember that heart disease is often wrongly diagnosed. Tuberculosis is often overlooked in a person, even by fairly competent physicians. It should often be suspected before it is proved. Heart disease, on the other hand, is often diagnosed, even by fairly competent physicians, when it is not there at all, and this may be almost as great a misfortune to the person who is thus burdened with the fears and by the restrictions following on this mistake as it is for a tuberculous patient to drag himself about with his disease undiscovered.

To establish the diagnosis of these two diseases once for all and at the outset is the proper work of an expert on them. Once that is done and the plan of life marked out, it usually does not need an expert to carry on the patient's care through the months and years that follow. But it is a shame for a person to start out on the long journey of adapting his life to the "fact" of a damaged heart when in fact the heart is not damaged at all.

4. *High blood pressure.*

Many people are too much alarmed by the fact that their blood pressure has been found, perhaps by a life-insurance examiner, to be too high. To be refused life insurance (which of course is necessary sometimes in a business which must be conducted under a system of averages as a guide) does not usually mean the presence of severe or crippling disease. Many people get on very well for years, even for decades, with a blood pressure which in others produces severe symptoms. It is very much an individual matter. The patient and his doctor together must find out by actual experience how far this person's disease differs from the average, how much he must give in to it. He is all the better for carrying on as much of his usual activities as he can without demonstrable harm. His doctor must judge of this, watching him with that individualizing eye which is essential to good medical work.

The minister, well instructed by the doctor, can help the patient to carry out the way of life prescribed for him. As in other forms of heart trouble there are two evils to be avoided—exhaustion from doing too much, and especially from worrying too much, and hypochondria from becoming "self-centered." There is quite as much harm in "babying oneself" all day long as in overdoing. It is not so much overwork as worry, alcoholism, short sleep, overeating, lack of exercise, sexual incontinence, quarreling and boredom that break down the man or woman with high blood pressure and other forms of heart disease. Right living is a very large part of the proper care of any malady and especially of circulatory disease.

5. *Cancer.*

It is for the medical profession and those concerned with public health to urge continuously and effectively upon the public the now accepted truth that the only cure for cancer is early operation. The only exception to this is cancer on the skin or in some other position where it can be reached by radium or X-ray without going through other tissue on the way to the cancer. A clergyman, like any other good citizen, can merely reinforce the medical teaching on this subject.

The word cancer has more power to discourage and to prostrate than any other word in the language. It is the doctor's business to explain to the patient what ails him and to do this at the right time and in the right way. In the inoperable cases which make up the great majority, the clergyman's task is to assist the patient to bear his pain and to face death.

6. Stomach Trouble.

Aside from cancer, to which I have already referred, stomach trouble means either peptic ulcer or nervous dyspepsia. In both of these troubles emotion is one of the most important factors. It plays a part both in causing peptic ulcer and in preventing it from healing. What is ordinarily called nervous dyspepsia should be called emotional dyspepsia. The stomach is perfectly normal but works badly because it is so intimately related to the mind and to the emotions. The cure of such trouble rests, therefore, upon the patient's ability to learn, with whatever help the minister or others may give him, the control of emotion. This does not mean an attempt to abolish emotion, which would mean substantially the death of the soul. Emotion is controlled when it works itself out either into thought or into action in line with the person's proper growth. The emotions which upset us physically are those which do not develop into any practical, systematized, unified life, but explode or tantalize their possessor. To manage them is no less a problem than the whole conduct of life, and anyone who makes progress in that direction improves not only his digestion but his family life, his business efficiency, and his capacity to enjoy himself. If the minister is naturally devoted to the study of character and to attempts at its remaking, he may be of assistance to anyone with whom he is or becomes intimate. In stomach troubles as in every other disease he will be much more effective if he can manage to work in close co-operation with the physician.

7. *Thyroid Disease.*

One of the few illnesses that can be cured by a drug is that due to lack of thyroid secretion and known to the medical profession as *myxoedema*. Because it is so brilliantly curable and because if untreated it can do such terrible damage, the minister like every other intelligent person should know that persons, especially women after middle life, who begin to show unwonted sluggishness, increased sensitivity to cold, dry rough skin, falling hair, and increasing weight, may be absolutely cured if a physician gets the opportunity to recognize and to treat their disease.

The opposite malady, due to an oversecretion or perverted secretion of the thyroid gland, is sometimes mistaken in its early stages for nervousness or excitability. Since this disease too can be greatly relieved or cured, every educated person should be on the watch for it in those who show, in addition to the symptoms just mentioned, a fine tremor of the hands, an extreme tendency to flushing and to perspiration, a rapid pulse, prominent eyes and a loss of weight despite excellent appetite and digestion.

8. *Malaria.*

In southern parts of the United States malaria is so common and so devastating that certain facts about it should be familiar to ministers. There is no such thing as malaria without frequent or occasional attacks of fever. In the absence of these the supposed malarial patient is the victim of a wrong diagnosis. Of course there are many other diseases, such as tuberculosis and the slower forms of blood poisoning, which produce fevers easily mistaken for malaria. But if there is no fever there is no malaria.

Much has been written of late about the prevention of malaria through antimosquito campaigns. In very dry regions such as Palestine these campaigns are effective. In wet, rainy climates they are almost useless. It is likewise practically impossible to prevent people from being bitten by mosquitoes containing the malarial parasite. The only method of prevention which is effective on a large scale is the discovery and treatment of every malarial case within a district. No one can get malaria, no matter how often he is bitten by the malarial species of mosquito, unless that mosquito has previously bitten a patient with malaria. We cannot abolish mosquitoes or mosquito bites. But through the giving of quinine we can kill the malarial parasite in every case of malaria within a given district, say a township or a county.

This means that a great deal of free medical care and free medicine must be paid for by municipal or county expenditure. It comes therefore within the duties of any public-spirited person to advocate such measures as a way of increasing the physical, and therefore the spiritual, vitality of the community.

9. *Chronic Rheumatism.*

Usually in elderly people but occasionally in the young or middle-aged, a stiffening occurs in one or in many joints so that the patient is partially or totally crippled. If the disease is confined to the hip-joint, as in elderly persons it often is, the limitation is chiefly in walking and there is often but little pain. If it extends to the back, knees, and shoulders almost every motion may be difficult and painful. Fortunately rare are the cases in which the disease, starting in the hands, extends gradually to almost every joint in the body until the patient is nearly rigid throughout. These cases usually begin in early life and may last for a great many years.

There is some difference of opinion among the physicians about how much is to be accomplished by medicine, by surgery or by hygiene for chronic rheumatism. I personally believe that at the present time we have very little power over the disease and that medical and surgical treatments as often do harm as good. The harm that they are most apt to do is by keeping the patient's whole time occupied in fruitless attempts at cure, when he might have made himself useful and happy in exercising the limited powers still left him in work, in recreation, and the other activities of normal life. As I see it, the task for the chronic rheumatic patient is to keep going, that is, to give up as little as he can, though as much as he must, of his ordinary activities. If he is to do this he will need all the encouragement that can be given him. Along with family and friends the clergyman may be a valuable encourager in this direction. His ingenuity as well as his cheerfulness will be taxed, especially when patients have no interests or resources except those that demand active muscular movement. Radio is a great resource in rheumatism as in all other conditions which keep people partially or totally disabled. Rheumatic patients often live a long time and tire out the patience and the ingenuity of their families. A ritual of the sickroom[1] should be instituted whenever patients are confined, or mostly confined to one room. To arrange through friends or kindly strangers that the patient may get a motor ride now and then and to help with the process of getting the patient into the motor and out again, is one of the simple manual tasks in which the minister should be eager to share so far as his other work allows.

10. Paralysis.

In elderly people most cases of paralysis are due to disease in the arteries of the brain, and the symptoms are therefore intertwined with the other signs of this form of brain trouble. As they grow older many persons fear such paralysis merely because they feel numbness or prickling in their hands or in their feet, or because one or both arms may "go to sleep" in the course of the night. None of these symptoms mean that paralysis is approaching. Indeed there are no precursors of paralysis. Till the muscles themselves fail to work we know nothing of its presence, latent or evident.

In elderly people one arm and one leg on the same side are most apt to be affected, and the paralysis is seldom complete. Pasteur had it at the age of fifty-six, and did much of his best work after that time, though it made him somewhat unskillful in the use of the affected hand. On the other hand, in most cases the arterial brain trouble which causes the first "stroke of paralysis" later

[1] See Chapter XX.

causes other and more serious strokes, one of which is fatal. After the first attack, and sometimes after subsequent ones, the workings of the mind may be altogether unimpaired. But in the majority of cases there is some weakening, perhaps slight, perhaps considerable. Memory and judgment are most apt to be lessened, self-control is often impaired, power of attention is less keen. Occasionally there are distressing moral lapses or mental twists.

Paralysis in a child or a young adult is apt to be due to polio-myelitis, the germ disease ordinarily called *infantile paralysis*. It leaves the brain unaffected and in most cases paralyzes only a limited group of muscles, leaving many others still serviceable. But whatever damage is done is permanent.

Paralysis appearing in middle-aged persons has many causes, of which syphilis is perhaps the commonest. This type affects both legs predominantly and leads to an unsteady gait often accompanied by severe shooting pains in the legs. It is somewhat relieved by effective treatment for the underlying syphilis.

In all forms of paralysis the most important thing that a wise friend can do is to encourage the patient to use all that he has left both of muscular, mental and moral powers. He is apt to give up not merely the powers that he has actually lost but many others which are still left. He still can make a good life of it in the majority of cases.

11. Alcoholism.

The first thing to be clearly understood about alcoholism is that it is rarely if ever due to a "taste for liquor." Most of the alcoholics whom I have known had no fondness for the taste of liquor. It is not a physical craving but a mental and moral disease. *People drink in order to escape something.* Most often, perhaps, they drink to escape boredom or the sense of failure, sometimes to escape grief, physical pain, remorse, domestic unhappiness, financial worry or a general vague uneasiness about the future. One wholly cured alcoholic recently said to me, "So long as he is more interested in the relief or the kick that he gets out of liquor than he is in anything else, the alcoholic will go on drinking. Some stronger interest has to drive alcohol out or it will never go."

The description just given makes it clear what we have to accomplish if we are to help the alcoholic, and how gigantic a task it is. It is very easy to suggest that new interests be developed or that old ones be strengthened, but it is almost impossible to accomplish it. The vast majority of people who get over alcoholism cure themselves. Ex-President Eliot of Harvard used to say that of all the men whom he had known drink too much in college, the only ones who persisted in it so as to cripple their lives after graduation were those with a strong hereditary taint, not necessarily alcoholism itself. This means, I think, that most of the men who get to drinking, either for what are called "social reasons" or to fill up the vacuum of an unsatisfied life, find something more interesting and more important to do after they have graduated from college, and give up drink because it interferes with what they care most for.

Rarely there is some removable and relatively external cause, such as physical pain, a nagging relative or an unsatisfactory job. But, especially with the two last mentioned, there is almost always a confederate within the alcoholic himself. He is of the type to find most jobs unsatisfactory or to be the natural target of the nagger.

Rarely can the patient be put permanently in a place where he cannot get alcohol. For more persons than the public likes today to admit, prohibition was the solution of the alcohol problem because it made liquor expensive and difficult to get. Now that the community refuses to support a prohibitory law, there is no way to keep alcohol away from an alcoholic except to shut him up in prison or in an institution. Under our present laws this is a very temporary remedy.

There is, in my opinion, no cure for the alcoholic, through making him dislike the taste of liquor or by any medicinal advice. All that can be done in an institution or clinic is to take away the liquor, enable him thoroughly to sober up, and then to face with mind unclouded by alcohol the problem of his own future. Under these conditions a minority will reshape their lives and develop interests capable of driving out the habit. These are persons of unusual moral stamina or obstinacy. They refuse to take the easiest way out, that provided by alcohol.

To sign a pledge publicly or privately is but a temporary help in the great majority of cases. When it does help it leads immediately not only to other resolves but to undertakings which hold the man up by the engagements they involve and by the interests which they develop.

If the clergyman is a good friend of the alcoholic and does not have to become so during the period of treatment, he may be of substantial help in shaping the new plans of work, recreation, personal associations, and religious observance which will enable the alcoholic to beat his old enemy. I have very little faith in the value of sudden religious conversion as a cure for alcoholism unless it is simply the first step in a line of systematic endeavor followed up and assisted by those to whom the conversion is due, or by others. Religious feeling and religious resolves which do not develop at once into action aimed to remake the terribly tough structure called "habit," have in our experience no value here or anywhere else.

It is not worth while to waste one's time with attempts to help people who have no other substantial interest in life except drink. We must face the fact that drink is a very substantial interest and that a good many of our fellow citizens have no other.

12. *Morphinism.*

Those who become habituated to morphine or to other narcotic drugs can be roughly divided into two groups, (1) people who prior to their morphinism had some strong interest and the regular habits that result from it; (2) those who had no such interest or who are members of the underworld.

In the first group fall a good many physicians, nurses, and others who began to take a narcotic for the relief of pain but who have an interesting professional life to go back to when they give up the drug. For members of this group it is well worth while to go to an institution, be freed from their drug, and start life over again.

Many have successfully accomplished this. For the other group there is little or nothing to be done. Bellevue Hospital, in New York, had at one time several social workers who gave their whole time to the attempt to help morphinists, but the attempt has now been abandoned because it was found that nothing permanent was accomplished. This is because most of those who enter the wards of Bellevue Hospital for morphinism have no other substantial interest in life.

The connection between morphine and crime deserves a few words of further explanation. Many a morphinist needs at least ten dollars a day to supply his daily dose of the drug. He cannot earn this in any honorable way. He steals or commits other crimes, therefore, in order to keep himself going.

The clergyman's possible usefulness in relation to cases of morphinism is limited to members of the first group distinguished above, and the line of his endeavors has already been suggested in what I wrote about alcoholism. The only lifesaver for a morphinist, as for an alcoholic, is the chance to do something that he enjoys more and finds better worth while than his drug. It is the hardest of all gifts to extend to another. It is like trying to give him a bodily organ. It has to grow up from within. All that we can do is to favor the conditions of growth. To be hopeful for more would be to deny the freedom of the will.

13. Syphilis.

Patients catch the germ in the vast majority of cases through sexual intercourse with prostitutes. The moral stigma attached to the disease is to this extent justified. Many innocent wives are infected by their husbands and many children are born with the disease (congenital syphilis). Occasionally a surgeon acquires it during an operation on a syphilitic patient. A person with a cracked lip may catch the disease through the kiss of a syphilitic or by smoking the pipe of a syphilitic. These exceptional cases make it unfair to call syphilis a venereal disease. It is a contagious disease usually contracted in extramarital intercourse. But the injustice of a moral stigma on syphilitic patients arises chiefly from the fact that so many unstigmatized people visit prostitutes yet are lucky enough not to catch the disease. The syphilitic knows that from many of his fellows he is distinguished not by his morals but by his ill luck. Unless the moral side of the problem is brought up by the patient himself the minister has no good reason to raise it.

The danger of contagion from a syphilitic is practically *nil* unless one has bodily contact with him. It is wise not to use the knives, forks, and spoons of a syphilitic, for syphilitic sores in the mouth are common and infect the saliva. Syphilis of the brain and spinal cord produce the diseases called tabes, locomotor ataxia, paresis or general paralysis. These maladies are noncontagious.

The disease can generally be cured by efficient treatment begun early and continued for many months. But some patients never find out that they have the disease until it is too late to cure it. Others grow tired of their treatment and give it up before its good effects are assured. It is the duty of anyone who has influence with a syphilitic patient to urge him in the most forcible way to persevere in treatment, for the ultimate results of unchecked syphilis are terrible.

Starting with a small, hard sore on the genitals, the germ is carried by the blood first to the skin where it produces various eruptions and then to most of the body's organs, especially to the heart, the brain and spinal cord, the bones and the liver. Through heart disease and brain disease it often causes death.

When a woman acquires it during or before pregnancy, persistent treatment will usually cure her and prevent the disease from infecting her unborn child. If the child is born with the disease it shows itself first on the skin and in the nose ("snuffles"), later in the teeth, eyes, and shinbones. Even at this stage it can be arrested and blindness prevented by persistent treatment. But the eye symptoms are at first so slight that the child does not mind them and parents neglect the doctor's warnings until it is too late to prevent blindness.

In hospital clinics for syphilitics patients are urged, often with success, to bring in for treatment the person who has infected them. Two-thirds of the women who have syphilis get it from their husbands. Syphilis is acknowledged by about ten per cent of the men who are examined for any reason in a free hospital.

14. Gonorrhea.

Men often refer to this disease as "the clap." It is about three times as common as syphilis and is acquired in the same way, but it is far less serious. In men it is only a local inflammation affecting, in the great majority of cases, the tube by which urine is passed. It lasts a few weeks and often gets well of itself. In women it may spread through the womb to the Fallopian tubes on each side of it and set up a troublesome, sometimes a serious peritonitis. It is a common cause of sterility and of invalidism in women, though rarely a cause of death. In men it may cause sterility. It may also narrow the urinary passage producing "stricture," so that it is difficult or impossible for the patient to pass urine. The consequences of this are often troublesome, occasionally serious.

Newborn babies often catch gonorrhea in their eyes, acquiring it at the moment of birth from their mothers. This is ophthalmia neonatorum, or babies' "sore eyes." It gives little trouble at first but later often causes blindness. It can be prevented if a few drops of an antiseptic are put into the baby's eyes immediately after birth. *The doctor should do this to every baby as a matter of routine.* In Massachusetts blindness from this cause has almost disappeared since physicians have learned to be conscientious about this matter.

15. Broken Bones.

A broken leg, especially if there is splintering of the bones or if a piece of bone has come out through the skin at the moment of the accident ("compound fracture"), may be very slow to heal. Though the broken bones themselves may have united firmly in six weeks, the period of limbering up the stiffened joints and getting the wasted muscles back to work is much longer. It is then that the patient is very apt to get discouraged. His "healed" leg seems of very little use to him and the gain from day to day may be so slow and attended by so much pain that, after the surgeon has ceased his visits and the patient is supposedly well, the hardest trials are still to come.

There are certain general principles agreed to by most physicians, nurses, and masseurs who have often had to do with the protracted convalescence after fracture of a large bone.

(a) The patient must *push his way through periods of pain to make a gain in capacity* to use the limb effectively. There are often several of these periods as he advances toward complete recovery.

(b) *What the patient does for himself* is generally more effective than what can be done for him by others through massage and passive motion. These have their place as encouragements and as supplements to what the patient does by the use of his own muscles. But it is *using the injured part that does it most good* (after the bones are united), though the motions that do the most good are often painful.

(c) *A motion that accomplishes something useful* for the patient or for others will do his muscles more good than any sort of gymnastics or special exercises. Here as everywhere else reality wins.

The surgeon speaks of these painful and tedious tasks as "limbering up" stiffened joints, tendons, and muscle sheaths. While the broken bone was held fixed by splints, scar tissue, called "adhesions," has formed between and around the parts. These adhesions have to be stretched and this is painful, but stretching by exercise is usually the only way to get them back to normal. To break the adhesions, under an anesthetic, sounds as if it would be a swifter way to get rid of them. But in most cases they quickly reform after such a procedure and may then be worse than ever.

Besides the limbering up of joints just referred to, *wasted muscles have to be rebuilt* by using the little that is left of them. In this the main difficulty is to persuade the patient that he can do it. We must show him that many others as badly off as he or worse have attained perfectly strong muscles in the end. No one can reassure the sufferer so effectively as one who has himself gone through the mill and come out as good as new. It is worth while for someone (why not the minister?) to go to considerable trouble if that is necessary so as to find a patient who will come to "testify" in this way in the presence of a discouraged and skeptical sufferer. To see as well as to hear such a living proof that one can recover completely from the effects of a broken bone, may be the turning point in the patient's long struggle. If he is steadily and genuinely to believe that the effort is worth while, he must see convincing proof that others have succeeded in it. Moreover, anyone who has recently been through the different stages and maneuvers in recovery from a serious fracture can generally give the patient a good many small but useful points which the doctor may not have thought to mention.

Successful and complete recovery from fractures is often delayed or prevented by the mistaken sympathy of the patient's friends and relations. Especially if the bone has been broken in an accident for which some other person or corporation—a railway, a streetcar company or a manufacturing concern—is to blame, the hope of getting damages blends with "righteous indignation" against those actually or supposedly at fault, and with discouragement at the slowness of one's improvement. These three causes unite to prevent the patient from fighting with all his own resources for his own recovery. He may even lose the desire for complete recovery and come to believe that "the world owes him a living" for the rest of his days. The more injured he can prove himself to be, the less he is able to do for himself, the more damages he will succeed in getting. Thus, to gain as much and as fast as he can in power to use his injured limb comes to seem really against his interests.

Reinforcing this quite natural tendency in the patient there are often other and less excusable forces. The lawyer who has charge of his case is interested to have the injuries as serious as possible at the time when the case appears in court, and to encourage the patient's belief that it is some one else's business, not his, to pay for his misfortunes.

If the "law's delay" plays its usual part and postpones for weeks or months the hearing of the case in court, the effect may be to make the patient postpone vigorous efforts to limber his joints and to re-build his muscles until it is too late to get the best attainable results. Then his adhesions get firmer, and his muscles weaker, with every month. Worse still, the "habit of incapacity" gets more and more firmly fixed in his mind as well as in his limbs.

Meantime the family and friends tell him with sympathetic reiterations that it is a shame, that it is too bad, that the company should be made to pay and that he should be supported for the rest of his life. If this is so, of course he has far less reason to work hard for his own recovery and especially to work at his own occupation, which is what his injured limb most needs.

Deeper and more dangerous still is the patient's own laziness. Almost every son of Adam has in him somewhere, latent or patent, a vein of laziness. Illness encourages it and the enforced rest and degeneration due to injury is prolonged and increased by the natural tendency of his family, who urge him to take things easy and not to tire himself.

In view of all these facts, recovery from a severe fracture of the arm or of the leg is more a matter of *morals and morale* than it is of medical or surgical treatment. The surgeon's indispensable serv-ice is in the initial setting and splinting of the fracture and in its subsequent progress until the splints are removed and the patient is told to exercise the limb. Long after that the best guide to the patient's convalescence is still the surgeon, provided he has the interest, the special knowledge, and the patience to continue in charge of the case. No one can take his place if he can and will take it himself. But in most cases this is too expensive for the patient and the surgeon is too busy with other and greater needs for his skill. The nurse, the masseur, or the members of the family to whom the management of convalescence may then be left, are apt to be concerned almost exclusively with the physical procedures which the surgeon has advised. They are seldom as energetic or as resourceful as they need to be in maintaining the patient's morale. Under their care it is quite possible for the patient to gain physical comfort and lose his own soul—or a large piece of it. He may get large "damages" but be ruined morally by his victory and by what has led up to it. When this disaster occurs it is often because his friends know no better way to cheer him up than to offer him a drink. Alcoholism develops because he is bored and discouraged and because the sympathy of his friends is so stupidly expressed.

Therefore, aside from the encouragement and reinforcement which the patient needs in his struggles to get back power and flexibility in his injured limb, the minister can often do him an essential service by keeping his mind occupied and his will braced during the hours when there is nothing to be done for the fracture itself. Here the minister's opportunity is not essentially different from that which he enjoys in combating boredom, lassitude, and discouragement from any other cause. We shall not repeat, therefore, what has already been said on these subjects.

Amputations. As discouraging as the fracture of a large bone is the course of convalescence and rehabilitation after amputation of the leg. The stump is slow in healing and often painful. The fitting of an artificial leg is a hard and disappointing business. The stump adjusts itself very slowly. Even the simplest apparatus is expensive. To keep up morale and to prevent the patient from giving up the determination to get back to work needs all the help that the minister can give. The patient's morale is often upset by anxiety about damages to be obtained by law from the person or the company that employed him or from those who injured him. The law's delay keeps patients on tenterhooks for months or years and prevents them from focussing their energy on the task of getting well. They get the habit of idleness and of dependence on others. It is hard to face life with an arm or a leg gone. Jobs are not easy to get even for those with two arms and two legs. Unless the firm in whose service the patient was hurt makes a place for him, he may never find one. In fact the moral problems are as great as the physical and far harder to treat.

16. *Childbirth.*

Whatever requires the services of a physician may be called a disease, though some people would object to my including childbirth under that heading. The minister's opportunity comes after the child is born. Whether the parents are believers in the importance of baptism or not, they face, when a child is born to them, one of the moments when, if they are ever to be open to spiritual influences and to the chance to make a new start in life, the opportunity is at hand. A minister who knows that one of his parishioners is expecting a child should make every effort to help the parents realize, after the child has come, what the event means or can be made to mean for the future of their lives and so for the child himself. This to my mind is the significance of the baptismal ceremony. If people do not care for that ceremony they must find some other way to accomplish the same beneficent aim.

17. Obesity.

Though I do not suppose that the clergyman is likely ever to be consulted on the subject of this disease I think he should know that it is largely a moral problem. Rather few people choose to control their appetites. Most fat people eat too much and see no sufficient reason for eating any less despite their burden of fat. Under a doctor's directions the great majority of the obese can reduce themselves to normal proportions, but the doctor's prescription alone will not do it. The patient must see some sufficient reason to abide by what he knows he ought to do if he is to reduce. It is useless for the obese person to omit any one food such as bread, potatoes, sugar or cream. He simply satisfies his appetite with some other food and remains as fat as ever. There are drugs which will assist in reducing flesh but they should never be taken except under a doctor's directions. Death or blindness may otherwise result.

18. Diabetes.

The treatment is diet and insulin. Both are expensive. Diet involves a degree of self-control which many patients lack. Sometimes it leaves the patient always hungry and therefore irritable. If these difficulties are abolished by insulin the cost of illness often becomes a burden. There is not much that the minister can do for these difficulties but it is well that he should appreciate them.

19. Feeble-mindedness.

One in every twenty-two of the children entering the public schools of Massachusetts has been found by recent psychological examinations to be feeble-minded. Among well-to-do people the proportion is probably somewhat smaller, but the problem is still a huge one, not to be abolished by any cheap popular nostrum such as sterilization and birth control, because only about half the cases of feeble-mindedness are hereditary. The community's task—and I say the community's task because it goes far beyond the province of the doctor or the psychiatrist—is to educate the feeble-minded industrially and socially, so that they can use to their full effect the powers they still have. They cannot do much with books or schools of the ordinary type, but they can be taught a great deal about manners and about manual tasks, so that they can in some cases earn their living and in many cases live peaceably and comfortably at home. A minority have to be segregated for life to prevent disaster in the field of sex.

20. The Disturbances of Adolescence.

I suppose few pass through the period of adolescence without difficulties physical or moral, for which the clergyman might be of service. There are relatively few who will seek his advice at such a time. Any minister who is consulted by such young people or by their parents about them should be familiar with Stanley Hall's monumental work on *Adolescence*. Though it is a disorderly book and contains chapters of very unequal value, its different parts contain almost everything that is known about the physiology and psychology of adolescence. Anyone who reads it with common sense and selective judgment can get great benefit from it.

The most important fact about adolescence is that there is almost no degree of mental, moral or physical dilapidation, instability or explosiveness which may not pass by and disappear with the end of the adolescent period, even when nothing of importance is done by anybody to help the suffering youth. The "passage of time" and the experiences which it brings can work wonders. One ought, therefore, never to be discouraged about the future of any individual who gets into trouble at that period. What we call "nature" works prodigiously hard on the side of health and stability and in the vast majority of cases brings about unaided a cure.

Beyond this what most adolescents need is, first, affection, second, understanding, and third, patience. They are self-distrustful to an almost unbelievable degree and need therefore the ceaseless reassurance which affection can give. They are often most bottled up about what they need most to share with a wise friend, and even the most complete sharing may accomplish little until a certain number of months or years have done their work. Parents who have been intimate with their children before the period of adolescence have the best chance of being able to continue this intimacy and to give it a healing quality when the storm comes. To advise parents, and sometimes to advise the adolescent himself is a great opportunity for one with the spiritual and moral resources of the minister.

In spite of what I have said as to the gigantic tendency to self-healing inherent in the adolescent it must be recognized that serious mental diseases, schizophrenia and manic-depressive psychoses, may begin at that period.

21. *Insanity.*

It is very tempting nowadays for the minister to study psychiatry, which he understands to be the diseases of the mind. Since his province includes the mind and its disabilities, whether he distinguishes this faculty from the soul or not, he naturally asks himself what right he has to desert any member of his flock in mental and spiritual distress. Especially today when the emphasis of the psychiatrist tends to be on the emotions and their perversions, the minister, who knows emotion as an integral part of religion, finds it hard to stand aside while others treat emotional disturbances.

But first of all the minister should realize that insanity includes disease of the body as well as of the mind, and cannot be thoroughly understood except by one who has studied medicine. Though a good deal of mental treatment including psychoanalysis is now done by ministers, they do it at the peril not only of their patients but of their own position in the community. We strongly advise ministers, therefore, to make no attempt to treat mental disease. When they know or suspect that it is present they should urge that a psychiatrist be consulted; at any rate they should take no responsibility themselves.

Nevertheless, about insanity, as about other common diseases, the minister should have somewhat more than the average intelligent person's understanding. He should know, first of all, that insanity is not a single disease but a group of diseases, some of them due to known degeneration in the tissues of the brain, some to known chemical changes in the blood, and in the brain which it nourishes, some to causes altogether unknown at the present time.

When should a minister suspect insanity?

(a) When a person at or near college age begins to show profound and prolonged depression associated with self-reproach and the slowing up of muscular and mental action.

(b) When a person of the same age begins to show a degree of excitement, volubility and restlessness quite unlike his ordinary behavior.

(c) When a person of this age or a little older becomes increasingly indifferent, apathetic, silly, unable to apply himself to his usual tasks, prone to talk to himself and to live in a world of his own.

(d) When a person of any age begins to see visions, hear voices, and have other hallucinations of touch, smell or taste. A perfectly healthy person such as Joan of Arc may see visions and hear voices. It would still be right that insanity should be *suspected* in such a case. It can be disproved only by the whole tenor of the person's behavior.

(e) When a person concludes that he is the victim of a conspiracy in which many enemies are co-operating to persecute him, to deprive him of opportunities, to slander him or to despise him. It is the element of conspiracy and co-operation which makes such a story unlikely to be true. No one has either the time or the ability nowadays to engage in such complicated operations as patients with this type believe in.

(f) When a person of any age, especially an elderly person, becomes increasingly forgetful, obstinate, impatient, and subject to obvious delusions, as, for example, that he is not in his own house, that some one is taking his property away from him or is otherwise maltreating him.

(g) When a person of any age, especially a young person, suffers from groundless and unescapable terror or anxiety.

When the minister suspects insanity he should communicate his fears to the family in case they are not already aware of the facts, and should urge them to consult a psychiatrist or family physician, even though the patient himself is unwilling to see one. If the patient at any time becomes violent or seems in danger of injuring himself or any one else, the police can be called into the situation at once and can usually be trusted to act wisely.

It is important that the minister should realize that a large minority, perhaps forty per cent, of insane patients get well, though a considerable part of this number have recurrent attacks. When insanity occurs before or after childbirth or when it occurs during or immediately after an acute febrile disease, the attack is often brief, recovery follows, *and no relapse occurs*. On the other hand cases beginning with delusions of persecution or with increasing apathy and silliness seldom recover.

For all of us who have to deal with the insane the most important things is to treat them so far as possible like normal people. In a large per cent of cases they respond to this by behaving surprisingly well. It is especially important to tell no lies to anyone believed to be insane. He is apt to be lied to in the process of getting him to an asylum or other institution. If he is deceived by those of his own family, by those whom he knows and trusts, it will be difficult for his physicians later to gain his confidence and so to give him their best aid.

Always the minister works in co-operation with the physician and public health authorities. Most doctors are eager for an intelligent ally.

PART III
PRIMARY NEEDS IN THE MINISTER'S ART

CHAPTER XI

THE MINISTER'S KIT-BAG

A MINISTER, like a doctor or a lawyer, needs a bag. Among those whom he visits there are some whom he will see many times. His bag represents the continuity of his relation to these long-time sufferers. At his last visit he noticed perhaps a lack in the supply of raw materials or in the tools of the patient's manual occupation. Or he has promised to bring a book, a magazine, a game, a photograph, a phonographic record, or some old letters. He needs a place to accumulate these as soon as he has thought of them, so that they are ready and sure to be remembered on the next visit. The bag is that place.

The bag represents not only the continuity of the minister's relation to the invalids whom he visits but the particular nature of his office. It should contain some Protestant equivalent for the Roman Catholic priest's stole, wafer, and oil. What these equivalents should be will differ with each minister. Some will want none at all because they carry in their minds all the insignia of their office. But whatever their spiritual principles, they will probably have some material representative, something to do for Protestants what the crucifix and the rosary do for Catholics.

The bag should always contain the minister's notebook. Things which need to be noted and remembered are sure to come up before, during, or after the visit. Now and then things will be said by the patient or ideas will occur to the minister which need to be set down at once, in the hall before he leaves the house, or in the corner drugstore on the way home. For these as well as for the longer and more systematic records of visits and plans the notebook should be always at hand.

For some at least of his long-time-sick people the bag will contain small gifts and surprises, something to start a new train of thought and to leave fresh after-images in the patient's mind. Most of those who send gifts to the sick get no further than books or flowers, and if many friends have had the same inspiration at the same time the patient may be rather bored with their offerings. Most friends let their attention drift off to other claims and other interests after a week or two. The minister should be able to bring a greater variety of gifts or loans than any one else, because he goes further than others along the paths of sympathetic imagination and because he devotes more time and more effort to thinking about the needs of his sick friends.

Loans are usually better than gifts, because gifts accumulate till they tire the jaded eyes. Moreover they have to be looked after. We lend Swiss-carved peasant-figures, bears or foxes, crystals beautiful in shape or color, bits of marble mosaic, a stuffed bird, a bit of moss, a fossil, an Egyptian necklace with scarabaei, a piece of Mexican colored leatherwork, Oriental metalwork, Chinese embroidery, snow crystals photographed, a sandalwood box, a fir-balsam pillow, a kaleidoscope, a victrola with records, pictures for the mantelpiece or for an empty wall. Such things can be borrowed from friends, lent to the patient for a few days, and carried away again by the minister. The patient will not want them long, but will be refreshed by them for a little while. The minister can increase his fund of loanable objects by setting some of his other parishioners the puzzle, "What could I lend for a few days to an invalid?" He can collect from many sources and so interest a good many people, sick or well, in something outside their ordinary routine.

Through these loans the patient sometimes gets interested in the lender or the lender in the patient, or one lender in another. In this way the central appeal of one sufferer can start a valuable group of personal relationships in which chance may sprout benefit that no one has planned. A doctor whom R.C.C. often used to assist took his dachshund with him on his hospital visits. The little dog's bright shifty eyes and ridiculous crooked legs seemed to do the patients almost as much good as the doctor's visit. Nearly every sufferer was amused or refreshed by him, and just because he was not brought along every day, a little holiday began whenever his clumsy pattering feet were heard trotting along the corridor.

It is a great pity that the minister cannot often bring a baby in his kit-bag. A doctor known to us did actually borrow a baby and bring him for a brief visit now and then to a patient who he knew was hungry for the sight of one. If a child can be made to settle down and play by himself in a corner of the sickroom there is no more refreshing sight for many an invalid. He can go on watching it indefinitely.

The minister's gifts may show the quality of his devotion. He will put more work than others do into finding out by inquiry among the patient's family and his friends what sort of gift suits him. The minister will keep notes of his gifts and of his remarks, so as not to repeat them. Unprepared ministers are apt to repeat the same remarks and give the same presents to many. The devoted minister will be more original about them because he puts more memory into his work. He will not be content with less than the best that he can afford and the best that the patient is ready to profit by. Realizing that spiritual gifts are the hardest of all to give, he will nevertheless be forever unsatisfied unless as he gives things, gives ideas, gives affection, he is getting nearer to his chance to give "the greatest thing in the world." That chance may never come, but he will watch and wait for it with the quality of attention that no profession but his commands.

Besides material objects, however, ideas will accumulate in the bag. The mental kit-bag packed for the visit will often, as we have said, work itself out into material objects or at least into notes for the notebook. But there will always be ideas left in the mind in their unfinished state: plans and topics for conversation, questions, prayers. These he will gather up along with his hat and stick when he starts on his round of calls. They are the basis of his regular habit of collecting his thoughts before he starts. Some of his thoughts are scattered, mislaid or shopworn. They need brushing or mending before he can use them. In particular his thoughts about the patient whom he is just going to visit need refurbishing. He needs to recall the sick man's particular history, family background, and recent misfortunes, his "growing edge," his favorite topics, and the subjects which are "dangerous" with him.[1]

Anyone who visits the sick naturally forms the habit of saving up "safe" but pointed stories, serviceable and not too ancient jokes that he can use as harmless stimulants to tired minds. Most of us trust our ability to light these little fireworks just when they are needed. Many are appalled at our suggestion to get them ready in the foreground of the mind before a visit. Well, if experience has shown you that you do not forget such odds and ends of mental furniture and that you think of them just when you need them, there is no reason to marshal them in advance. But if the type of mind which cannot do this is as common in the minister as it is in others, then only squeamishness and laziness can keep him from making preparations. He should be as methodical as any actor or public speaker in studying the ebullitions which sound so spontaneous when they finally appear. Spontaneity is splendid if you have it, whether in sermons, prayers, after-dinner speeches, or visits to the sick. But why sacrifice everything to a spontaneity which in the end you don't achieve? The habit of making no preparation for a visit is popular because it saves trouble. Original sin makes us hide our laziness behind reverence for a spontaneity which rarely comes off. We try to depend on it because we dread the labor of preparation.

"Prepare everything that you find you cannot do well without preparation," is as sound a maxim for the minister as it is for the baseball player or the pianist. Most ministers prepare their Sunday sermons. It is quite as essential to prepare for a visit to the sick. Only when experience has proved that preparation hampers or upsets us should it be discarded.

Carefully selected books are great instruments to release the spirit;

[1] See also Chapter on Note-writing.

to stir the imagination, and to give one perspective upon one's illness. We have found books in the sickroom which are poorly selected and often actually harmful.

Doctors and ministers need to be especially careful in their prescription of literature because patients have a high regard for their opinion. Miss Elizabeth Reed, librarian at the Massachusetts General Hospital, tells of a doctor who found his patient reading a Western story and said, "What, wasting your time reading a Western story? You should read ——," naming a recent sophisticated best-seller. Upon her next visit the librarian was surprised to be asked by the patient for this book, which she rightly judged would not interest him. Nevertheless she supplied it. A week later she found that the patient had not read the book; he refused, nevertheless, to follow her suggestion of another "Western," undoubtedly afraid that the doctor might see him reading that kind of book again.

The natural inclination of ministers, as well as others, is to prescribe the books they themselves like best, or have just been reading, or the book they expect to read next because they have just read a review of it. I (R.L.D.) remember going to a well-known clergyman and asking what I might read to advantage during an impending period in a hospital. That busy gentleman took my request without any consideration for the fact that I was about to play the rôle of an amateur invalid. He pulled six books from his shelves. "Take these. I know they will help you pass the time." With anticipative joy I lugged those books to the hospital with me. They were Hackett's *Life of Henry VIII, Life of Lafayette* by M. de la Bedoyère, Strachey's *Elizabeth and Essex,* Morrow's *Splendor of God,* the story of Adoniram Judson in Burma, and a large, two-volume set of Wordsworth. It was months before, with a drooping but determined enthusiasm, I was able to wade through the first four, after having read many smaller and easier books. Every one of these books, except *Elizabeth and Essex,* is too large to hold comfortably; moreover they are hard going for one intellectually listless, though all are beautifully written.

Many ministers and many doctors read detective stories for relaxation. Woodrow Wilson and A. J. Balfour are reported to have been constant readers of detective yarns. After a hard day's work, face to face with tense situations, a detective story is a relief. We should remember that often enough the sick man is in a tense situation. Prescribe for him, therefore, the kind of reading he does for fun or when he is on vacation, what he would read in the free moments of a strenuous business life. Remember that when sick one is retarded intellectually, it is only the long-time convalescent who needs intellectual stimulation.

Miss Reed is quite sure that she could never get on without mystery stories for hospital patients. She even believes that they revive the enfeebled power of concentration. Most old men, she finds, cannot read even mystery stories. They read only the newspapers. Younger men sometimes tackle ambitious schemes of reading. A stationary engineer with a second-class license was able by reading to fit himself during a long illness for a first-class license.

There are several simple principles to be kept in mind when we prescribe reading for the sick. These principles Miss Reed and her assistants have tested; having been both a patient and an observer I (R.L.D.) highly approve of them. (1) For most patients a book must be light in weight and of large print. We should like all patients to read Dr. Harvey Cushing's two-volume *Life of Sir William Osler*. But these volumes are far too heavy to be held by a patient, and bookholders are usually unsatisfactory because the patient needs to shift his position frequently while reading. (2) Reading material for the sick must be free from morbidity or vivid description of horrors. Most modern novels include at least one character, often the most outstanding one, who is either mentally ill, dying, or having a baby. A modern writer's popularity is often due to the vividness of detail with which he portrays that part of his story. An individual on his or her feet and in good health would rarely become obsessed by such a piece of writing. But the same individual ill is a prey to every form of suggestion, and often gets to brooding on physical details. Then he often identifies in himself the symptoms which writers have probably observed in themselves to make a significant bit of description. (3) Reading material for the sick must be simply written. The sick person is neither able nor interested to wade through long descriptions, nor to follow the intricate mental gymnastics which many writers enjoy. Tastes and abilities vary somewhat here. Often a combination of several kinds of reading works best. I used to prefer essays in the morning and biographies or novels for the later hours of the day when I was tired.

There are a few other general principles worth mentioning. As the patient's condition varies, one may vary the literature suggested or lent *via* the kit-bag. If a patient is awaiting a crisis or an operation he may read books which later would be out of place. I know a twenty-year-old boy who was facing an operation from which he knew he had small chance to recover. He had more than a week to wait before the operation was performed. Three days before it he told me he had built up a "philosophy about it." During this period he did not care to talk to many people, but preferred to walk about the yard by himself, or to sit by his bed reading. Ordinarily he was a friendly person, but now he welcomed those days of solitude. He read a great deal. Among other things he gave time to studying Gregg's *Exercises in Shorthand*. Another patient, somewhat older in years and maturer in his taste for literature, awaited an operation from which he knew he was not likely to recover.[2] He read the *Bible*, Macaulay's *History of England,* and Scott's *Heart of Midlothian,* which he called "the greatest fiction ever written; it takes you off the earth." In such a situation, that is just what is needed: something that will take you off the earth.

Courage is the main need of such a time. Anything that will stir the imagination yet contain an element of permanence and confidence is desirable. A life of Admiral Byrd or the story of Lindbergh's flight to Paris may strike the right note with men. Women want something less active and more romantic, but still need confidence and determination in the books they read.

[2] Chapter XXII, The Dying, p. 298.

Many patients can read but little and want something of which they can think between reading-snatches. David Grayson liked Marcus Aurelius.[3] Fosdick's little book *Manhood of the Master*, is often used by our patients. Others read and memorize the Psalms. Poetry and the memorizing of poetry is of great help with these patients. One patient who belongs in this class has memorized Milton's *Ode to His Blindness*, verses from Whitman's *Song of the Open Road* and *America Singing*, Wordsworth's *Intimations of Immortality*, *The Daffodils*, and *Westminster Bridge*, verses from *As You Like It*, Shelley's ode *To a Skylark*, and Keats' *Ode on a Grecian Urn*. By memorizing them he has them always with him.[4]

A third group includes most of the patients to whom we need to give our attention: those who are facing long convalescence or permanent handicap, from tuberculosis, heart disease, diabetes, and other chronic diseases. Unless the time of these patients can be turned to something satisfactory they become bored and difficult for those around them and their lives may be permanently warped. In this situation the minister will know each patient's needs, his likes, and his possible growth, and will prescribe accordingly. He will *not* take as his motto the words once used to describe a hospital library: "To provide occupation, recreation, and inspiration; not to instruct, inform, or reform."[5] The minister who understands a patient's needs and limitations will hope not only to occupy and inspire but to instruct and mayhap to reform. Hospital librarians tread carefully here, lest they break into sectarianism or be accused of proselytizing. The minister does not run this risk, for he knows the danger points; he will also know the patient's points of prejudice and intolerance and will deal with them understandingly. By the use of books he may be able so to broaden a narrow outlook that the patient will be forever grateful. To many illness furnishes the strongest motive that they have ever had to form the habit of read-

[3] David Grayson, *Adventures in Solitude*, (New York, Doubleday Doran & Company, 1931), p. 48.

[4] D.N., p. 345.

[5] Sarah Davis Lamb, "Five Hundred Books for a Hospital Library," *Library Journal*, 1928, vol. 53, p. 893.

ing. Some of them fall into it then and keep it up after they are well.

As a rule people are readers or nonreaders. But there remain a few who can be tempted into reading, even though when left to themselves they would never get beyond skimming the daily papers. The technique of luring people to read reduces itself to a few measures:

1. Find a special interest that they did not themselves realize that they possessed, or had forgotten about. A good many men who scorn novels, biographies, histories, and general magazines will read quite tough treatises on applied science such as electrical engineering, radio, airplanes, railroading, or manufacturing. Others will take hold of a book on biology, geology, geography, especially if well illustrated.

2. Illustrated books, especially those with photographic or colored photographic reproductions, appeal to many who will read little without them.

3. The contagion of another's interest, especially if that other is a person whose opinions the sick man respects, sometimes draws people into reading. To tell the story or a bit of it is part of the art of librarians who wish to interest children in reading. The same inviting method can be successful with adults.

The minister needs available for his kit-bag special religious literature. Doctors, nurses, librarians, ask constantly, "What books would you suggest for our patients who ask for religious reading?" May we suggest the following:

The Book of Common Prayer.
Altar Stairs (a book of prayers), Joseph Fort Newton (New York, The Macmillan Company, 1934).
The Way of Light, A Manual of Praise, Prayer, and Meditation. Compiled by Howard Chandler Robbins (New York, Edwin S. Gorham, Inc., 1933).
Prayers, Samuel McChord Crothers (Boston, Beacon Press, Inc., 1928).
A Book of Prayers, Samuel McComb (New York, Dodd, Mead & Company, 1927).
Prayers Written at Vailima, Robert Louis Stevenson.

Introduction to a Devout Life, St. Francis de Sales (New York, F. Pustet & Company).

The Manhood of the Master, Harry Emerson Fosdick (New York, Association Press, 1916).

The Meaning of Prayer, Harry Emerson Fosdick (New York, Association Press, 1916).

The Meaning of Faith, Harry Emerson Fosdick.
  (These three little books are now combined in one volume. New York, Association Press).

The Temple, A Book of Prayers, W. E. Orchard (New York, E. P. Dutton).

The Great Physician, A Manual of Devotion, A. J. Gayner Banks and W. Sinclair Bowen (New York, The Macmillan Company, 1927).

The Way, Daily Meditations on the Way of Life According to Jesus, William P. Merrill (New York, The Macmillan Company, 1933).

Centuries of Meditations, Thomas Treherne (1636-1674), (London, P. J. and A. E. Dobell).

The kit-bag should also contain suggestions for occupation or for a hobby to ride. This is different from occupational therapy which is prescribed as treatment by the doctor.[9] Occupation, as we are here using the term, is given as an adventure to break the monotony of convalescence. Perhaps the term "hobby" is more appropriate, but hobby suggests a continued interest. We are thinking of the patient with heart disease, the orthopedic patient in a cast, and the paralytic who faces months of confinement. The minister sees these patients, in the hospital or in the home; often no one else bothers to discover their growing discontent with the monotony of waiting. The minister's suggestions will vary according to the patient's tastes, his experience, his present physical condition, and the length of his illness.

We know a patient[7] who keeps a notebook of the great music that he hears over the radio. He has always been interested in music. Before his illness he attended symphony concerts and the opera at

[9] Occupational Therapy as a method of treatment for the sick developed during and immediately after the World War in hospitals for the sick. Since the war it has come to be used in many mental hospitals, tuberculosis sanitariums and reformatories. It is just beginning to be recognized in general hospitals.

[7] D.N., p. 345.

every opportunity, but his economic limitations made these opportunities rare. With the onset of his illness, a chronic disease of the central nervous system, he found that though he could still use the typewriter, he read with growing difficulty. Hence he came to depend more and more upon the radio; as this resource developed he began to keep a list of the music he heard. Last winter he listened to eighteen complete operas, parts of several others, and to one hundred and nineteen symphony programs. Neatly bound in a loose-leaf notebook he keeps a complete list of all these operas and who sang in them, of the compositions played, the orchestras, and the conductors of the symphony programs he heard. If he had missed the program announcements at the time they were given, he wrote to the broadcasting station for information. He now shows and reads this notebook with zest. It calls up the experiences of his winter. He was sick, in prison, handicapped, and yet he did not sit waiting, brooding, or crying out against his fate; he kept himself busy. He utilized an interest and forced the unavoidable curtailment of his activities to build up his mind and to nourish his spirit.

A rewarding hobby in convalescence is that of letter-writing. The minister may often stimulate this interest by suggestion, by supplying copies of letters in book form or old letters themselves. Or if he cannot see the patient often he may write to the patient and so start him writing letters in return. One of the most tragic characters in Carolyn Miller's powerful story, *Lamb in His Bosom,* is "Lias," who all his life wanted to receive a letter but no letter came until it was too late to give him any comfort. This is the situation of many patients, especially after their illness has dragged on for months. Often their friends forget. A patient we knew looked forward eagerly to a weekly letter from a priest she knew in Porto Rico. She looked forward to receiving it, and she gave eager attention to the weekly letter she wrote in response. Another patient was greatly pleased when a letter she had written appeared in a newspaper.

Another type of writing which may be encouraged with benefit is that of diary-writing or the writing of random thoughts. We who visit the sick are in need of just such material in order that we may understand the need of patients during convalescence. The writing of essays, poems, stories, may be encouraged among those who have such interests. Many people have had ambitions toward writing but have failed, largely because they had nothing to write about. Now while they are convalescing they do have something to write about.

It has been said that anyone can learn to model. Many people who have never tried it till they were ill, discover that they can find an interesting diversion and pleasant hobby in work with clay. Perhaps a more simple way to start modeling is in soap-carving.[8] For one who has the free use of his hands, whittling,[9] leatherwork,[10] paper cutting,[11] silhouettes,[12] bead work,[13] are possibilities. The study of Braille and the transcribing of books into Braille[14] is another possibility when the patient for some reason is interested in the blind.

Sewing and knitting are the most natural forms of diversion as well as of usefulness for women patients. We have known several men who also passed their convalescent hours in this way. We are not suggesting that the minister carry supplies for such work in his kit-bag, but rather the suggestions of it in his mental kit-bag. We knew a lady who decided to knit for the unemployed while she was

[8] Materials may be obtained from National Soap Sculpture Committee, 80 E. 11th St., New York, or Procter & Gamble Company, Education Department, Cincinnati, Ohio.

[9] *Art of Whittling,* W. L. Haurot, (Manual Arts Press, 1930). *Chip Carving,* H. W. Moore, (Manual Arts Press, 1922). *Wood Engraving,* R. J. Budham, (Humphries, 1929). *Wood Engraving and Wood Cuts,* C. V. H. Leighton, (Studio, 1932). *Puzzles in Wood,* E. M. Wyatt, (Bruce, 1928). *Easy to Make Toys,* C. A. Kunon, (Bruce, 1928).

[10] *Leather Craft and Beading,* H. Biggart, (Camp Fire Outfitting, 1930). *Portfolio of Designs for Leatherwork,* M. Trinick and L. E. Bristow, (Pitman, 1930). *Practical Leatherwork,* F. R. Smith, (Pitman, 1929).

[11] *Fun with Paper Folding,* W. D. Murray and F. J. Rigney, (Ravell, 1928). *How to Use Paper and Scissors in Art,* H. Swannell, (Bridgman, 1928). *Stencil Craft,* H. Cadness, (Pitman, 1921). *Paper Toys,* A. E. Pauli, (Manual Arts Press, 1930), 2 vols.

[12] *Art of the Silhouette,* D. Coke, (Sacker, London, 1913). *How to Draw Silhouettes,* C. Sprague, (Bridgman, 1929).

[13] *Beadcraft,* J. B. Littlejohns, (Pitman, 1930). *Further Suggestions for Using Wooden Beads,* E. J. Arnold, 1931.

[14] *Braille . . . and How to Learn it in Ten Lessons,* M. S. Loomis, (American Red Cross, Chicago, Ill.), 4th ed. *Braille Transcribing,* (American Red Cross Circular No. 414, 1927, rev. ed.).

incapacitated. Another patient made a quilt-top for her nurse from old neckties. Every necktie wearer who came to the ward was solicited for material.

Games are a source of amusement and satisfaction which need to be included in this list. Chess, checkers, cards, jigsaw puzzles, cross-word puzzles, all come in for their share of attention in the sick-room. Another pleasant interest which helps make life bearable to the convalescent is that of following the newspaper accounts of sports: football, hockey, occasional boxing, baseball. Every Friday while canvalescing I (R.L.D.) used to guess the outcome of the football games on the following day; colleges I had never heard of before came in for their share of attention as the season progressed. Now, years after that hospital experience, I find myself doing the same thing on a smaller scale. Life in the men's ward of the hospital takes on new interest days before a great boxing match, and during a world series practically all other subjects are taboo. The minister who does not carry current events of the sports world in his mental kit-bag is not prepared to call on the sick. But one must be cautious lest he carry nothing else.

CHAPTER XII

THE TWO MUST FACE A THIRD

In the minister's relations with the sick, the danger of their dependence on him is to be faced and if possible avoided. He must not start a schedule of visits, letters, gifts, or intimacies that he cannot keep up. He must avoid weakening the patient's powers by doing for him anything that he should do for himself. There is also a commoner and more serious hazard.

The disaster most to be feared by the minister who visits the sick is that patients, especially women, will fall in love with him. By "falling in love" I mean an attraction which calls a person away from his ordinary duties, work, and friends. Psychoanalysts accept this as a necessary part of their treatment, though they are prone to "rationalize" it by the phrase "transference," and by explaining that the lady regards the analyst as a father! In our experience with patients who have undergone psychoanalysis the lady rarely shares this delusion. She usually recognizes that she has been in love with the analyst and has had a hard time to get over it or to go on in spite of it. Physicians who do not attempt psychoanalysis view the matter more realistically and endeavor to prevent dependence of any sort. Ministers are bound to do the same if they are to avoid disasters in their parishes.

This brings us to the central difficulty: How are we to give our best service over many months to sick women without creating an emotional dependence not to be distinguished from falling in love? The answer is in part plain and obvious, in part obscure and difficult.

1. Physical distance and the avoidance of touch is the plainest answer and the one most apt to be blinked because we do not choose to face it.

172

2. The presence of a third person whenever that is possible, is our next best weapon of defense. Doctors secure the presence of a nurse or of a secretary when this does not prevent the confidentiality which is often essential.

3. *The implied presence of a third person is always practicable and always needed.* It is, however, more difficult to make clear both to the patient and on this page. To speak and to act always as if a third person were present is not so difficult, provided the patient and the minister both face the importance of it. Almost invariably the minister is a married man. The patient knows this and the fact itself tends to keep the relation to the minister where it belongs. The minister who knows the dangers facing him can contrive without awkwardness to bring his wife's name and his loyalty to her into his talks with female patients.

This awareness of a third person sounds as if it must bring forced and unnatural situations. In fact, however, it does not. The difficulty is in the will to face the facts and not to camouflage them. Given that desire, one easily learns to notice the difference between the interviews which center round "you-and-me" and those in which the presence of a third person is constantly implied. The third person is God, seen through the obligations of the two persons. The minister's obligation to be faithful to his wife, in thought as well as in deed, is a part of God's commands and of his own obedience to them. The obligation to maintain in the parish the position of one devoted always to God's work, is also part of his understanding with God. Others may frame these duties in impersonal terms. The minister, we take it, cannot do so. It will always be true, then, that he will feel the presence of a third person in every interview. To the patient this "third" may seem quite impersonal, the work which the minister urges her to take part in, the study or employment which he suggests, the home duties which he tries to help her reinterpret, the recreations which he tries to guide.

Behind these the minister feels the divine purpose which gives them worth, but the patient may not feel this and it is not essential that she should. What is essential is that the motive for work, home duties, recreation or study should be, *not* the minister's wish or command, but something more important, more permanent and more "impersonal" than he. The good of the parish, the integrity of family life, the need of education, the need of refreshment through play—these are objectives which should command patient and minister alike.

The attitude which we are describing is that toward which every human being should aim in his relations with another. Husband and wife, teacher and pupil, employer and employed, friend and friend, must choose whether they will face each other or whether both will face a third that is greater than either. Outside a movie theater we see in lurid colored posters two persons facing each other. It may be two lovers with their noses a few inches apart. It may be the hero and the villain glaring at each other in hate. In any case they see each other and nothing else. They are not furthering, admiring, fearing, or even hating anything greater than themselves. So the cheap novels depict the love affair that flares up in the last chapter. The lovers marry and live happy forever after, like an operatic hero and heroine. Each is enough for the other. They need nothing more to live on. Every one else knows that they will soon be bankrupt even of affection unless there arrives a child, a catastrophe, a summons of some sort to make them stop looking at each other and tackle some slice of the world's work that will command them with authority.

Employer and employee facing each other as bargainers or as opponents, one of whom will lose whatever money the other gains, are bound for trouble as the history of industry shows. Unless they can find common interests to work for, unless they can face a third which commands both what to do and what to avoid, they will soon fall out or persistently hover on the edge of trouble.

Teacher and pupil trying to get the better of each other are in a dangerous "two-situation" instead of a satisfactory "three-situation," and therefore face failure. Unless they can agree on something that they both need to achieve and can work for it as allies, they are in a mess from the start.

To avoid facing each other in adoration or hostility and together to face a master greater than man is our whole duty. Even inside our own souls we must not get face to face in complacency or conflict. Self-contentment and self-conflict are cured when we get an interest that will permit neither. Jealousies and squabbles in a family, in a club, in an industry or in a church, can be healed when the opponents cease to face each other and find a game, a project, or an interest to command them.

We recall these obvious facts because we believe that the minister's effort to keep sick people from depending on him is only one phase of his perpetual effort to keep his parish as clear as he can of pairs that face in toward each other and as full of teams that face forward. In dealing with women who are sick this effort has to take account of sex as well as of other tendencies in human nature which make for disaster. Sex tends to make two persons strongly aware of each other and oblivious of the rest. Rage and jealousy have the same tendency, but they are less closely linked to the best in us. They advertise themselves as enemies of society. Sex, on the other hand, is designed to develop us from a couple to a team, provided it is not allowed to balk the *other* great desires of man but is harnessed to pull them on.

In every agreeable conversation people gradually warm up to two interests—the subject of the conversation and the other person. Theme and speaker reinforce each other. When the conversation is good, when it gets results of value and develops plans and interests central in those who enjoy it, then each steadily pushes forward their common topic. Each tries to develop and to illumine not himself but that topic, and persistently soft-pedals all that dislocates attention onto himself, except momentarily. When the conversation is vapid or worse, attention is repeatedly switched off the subject and onto the persons who talk. It becomes "personal."

This decay is all the harder to avoid when the necessities of the patient's sickness demand that the patient herself shall be the subject of the conversation, for a time at least. But it is still possible to talk impersonally about a personality. This happens when it is kept clear that truth and the patient's recovery are the only objects sought by both. When each strives to exclude whatever deviates from this search the situation can be kept "triple." The minister can hold each conversation steadily to its point. He can check its tendency to drift off into irrelevancy, provided he remembers that he must steer clear of two kinds of irrelevancy, (a) that which veers from one topic to another, and (b) that which veers from all topics to the speaker.

He wants friendship with the sick person. He does not want her to fall in love with him nor does he want to fall in love himself. The distinction of love from friendship is forever difficult but never impossible, provided both parties sincerely desire it. We believe that at the right point in the development of their common enterprise, the minister should frankly put his cards on the table and state how he interprets that enterprise, what is to be accomplished and what avoided in accord with what both desire. We know from experience that this can be done without upsetting the patient and with much economy of suffering. Everything depends on clear sight and clear intention on both sides.

Praise, for example, and the expression of admiration, encouragement and reassurance, can be phrased as coming not "from me to you," but as voiced by either one toward their common goal. We (both) are thankful for what nature, time, medicine, surgery, re-education, and God through them all, have accomplished. Gratitude of patient to minister can be by him shunted off to where it truly belongs, that is, to the endeavor he represents, to the teachers he follows, and ultimately to God whom he is trying to serve. Thus to some extent the minister can hold himself aloof from the two-situation which in essentials is "the world, the flesh and the devil."

Is all this impossibly difficult? Not if the goal and the will are clear. The difficulties arise *from muddle or from wrong desire,* which is itself a form of muddle because it involves self-deceit. Many a man is really muddled about what goes on in a conversation. He does not distinguish fragments of a two-situation when they intrude themselves into an honest search for truth and cure. But he can learn and should learn to see this difference during his student days by practice with the sick and with others in trouble.

To be "upright and downright" with himself and with others is the main need and the main difficulty for every man of us in personal-impersonal relations. Exactly what is our understanding in this enterprise? What have we undertaken and where are we going? The need to ask and answer these questions is not less essential for the minister than it is for business men signing a contract or for explorers when they start on a journey.

The other great need is to recognize and repeatedly to express the fact that when we are doing anything worth while, we, the visible human beings, really do very little of it. Every doctor is aware how little healing he does, how much the physical, chemical, biological forces of "nature" make the cure. Every intelligent politician knows how little he guides the nation, how much it guides itself through forces physical and spiritual, which he controls but little.

The minister is thoughtful enough to know that the forces which make for healing, for political stability, for solid, enduring human relations in marriage and friendship, are not independent but center in the life of God. The minister therefore should find it easier than others do to keep himself where God has put him, in the background. God has made him free to be of service by voicing powers beyond him or to be a drag on the world by blocking these powers with his own personality. The success of his work in the sickroom, in the parish, and in the pulpit, will depend on avoiding "two-situations" and promoting "three-situations."

Chapter XIII

START WITH THE PATIENT

THE minister cannot swiftly create religion and morals in people who have neglected them all their lives. He cannot expect a man to be ready for prayer and meditation if he has scorned these forces up to the minute when sickness seized him. The minister has to take sick people where he finds them and work up the ladder rung by rung. In some respects they may be many rungs ahead of him. People are dull in one line and sharp in another, strong in certain muscles and paralyzed in others close beside them. So it is with their spiritual powers, that is, with their impulse to size up life as a whole and to steer for the best in sight. They are superstitious in one matter and sensible in another, perhaps one where the minister himself is weak. He will be especially keen to find points of superiority in the patient and to learn from him. Nothing heals sick minds more than serving others.

Nevertheless the minister will have to do his own share of teaching, and in that job he will grope for the patient's "growing edge" and keep his eye fixed on the Realities which he has to pass along like a football radio announcer. What is the next step for the patient from where he is? If he appreciates no music since Mozart, it is no use to feed him Brahms. If his ideals of family life are patriarchal he will not be impressed by the German "Youth Movement."

The minister can bring in his kit-bag no schedule of experiences through which the patient must grow. But there is such a series within him and it leads along a path that another's interest may help him to find. We do not pull him into our path. We help him to find his own and we urge him along it. That is spiritual growth.

To accomplish this we recommend a simple but fundamental principle: "Start with the patient where you find him." By this we mean, take in the facts of his physical illness, the present condition of his mind, his emotions, and his spirit. If he will not accept the fact of his illness, his handicap, his impending death, or if he does not know of them, then start with him there. This does not fool the patient or yourself. You study his present plight and steer your course accordingly. You are honest with him and face the miseries of his situation. You let him talk about them if he so desires. Then he recognizes you as a friend with courage.

To this the reader may say, "Yes, of course; one would naturally do all that." But lest he agree too easily, we shall point out in detail the implications of this principle, and the spiritual quality which it requires in the worker. We can start with the patient, provided we open our eyes wide to the difficulties before us before we undertake to clear them up. This is a mature outlook, neither embittered nor unreal. We see the worth of human life, yet we know how hideously it can demean itself. Above all, we recognize how pain pours itself round human existence and often balks all that is best in us.

The sickroom brings to the minister two challenges: the fact of pain and the problem of pain. If he saw no plan or purpose in the universe, if he thought life a happenstance and death a darkness, he would find no problem of pain, only the fact [1] to be remedied or checked. The doctor faces the fact of pain. His job is to conquer it. He must come to some terms with the philosophical problem also, if he is to keep his poise in face of the fact. Some never do. Some dodge it. They still are useful technicians. Nurses often dodge it; some become bitter or dull under stress of the suffering they see. Most of them pass pain by as one of life's mysteries. They hold it at arm's length and let it hurt them as little as possible. Like the doctor they concentrate their attention on relieving it.

The minister accepts a greater challenge than does the doctor or

[1] We simply mention the problem of suffering here because it relates to the present discussion. It is discussed in Chapters VII and VIII.

the nurse in the sickroom, because the minister's professional existence is at stake there. Nowhere in peacetime civilization is Christianity so challenged as in the sickroom. (We class strikes and
starvation with war, not with peacetime situations.) Christianity
proclaims Jesus's belief that God cares for his children like a loving
father and will respond to prayer. In the sickroom this belief seems
unfulfilled because prayer is often not answered, except at a great
price of suffering. The answer may come in such a way that God's
love is not recognized in it.

The minister's courage to suffer in others' suffering, to share the
Odyssey of their miseries, to feel their fears, is the strength of his
belief in God, held fast at the price of tragedy in his own life. Can
we, representatives of an ancient courage before a cross, face its
modern equivalent? The minister's message is still the "good news"
of the New Testament. Our two great national festivals, Christmas
and Easter, celebrate the good news: "I am come that ye may have
life." "Be of good cheer, I have overcome the world." When this
good news comes into conflict with the sufferings of the sick it is
one's privilege, not merely one's duty, to suffer. Suffering purges
one's love till it becomes part of the "good news." Paul's "joy that
was in Jesus" could not be silenced by the ingenious tortures of
the ancient world: scourging, imprisonment, wild beasts, execution.
None of these could silence the new message. Paul carried it beyond
Palestine with a driving force that has lasted till now.

Today the minister is still bound to carry the "good news" and to
face hostility. Paul was whipped, shipwrecked, imprisoned, in the
end, we believe, executed. No minister faces such terrors today. But,
like Paul, he knows the ugly side of things in the world as it is.
In war, in starvation, in the sickroom, the minister still faces the same
stark pain that Paul faced. When the "good news" carries the minister
into the sickroom he is tested by the conditions he finds there. He
will not be tested in argument. Discourses and ardent testimonials
will not be listened to by the sufferer. If they are expressed they
must come from the sufferer and the minister must be the listener.
In the sickroom the "good news" will be expressed first by the min-

ister's presence there. His devotion to Christ's truth will be tested by his willingness and ability to go where the patient is, to suffer with him, and to find out what he understands of life and of God. The minister will be tested when he tries to add something to such understanding of God and such control of his own life as the patient already has.

What is starting with the patient? One morning I (R.L.D.) went to see a patient who was believed to be dying but who had not been told this. She said, "I think I am going to die." I said, "You are not afraid, are you?" After considering she said, "No, I am not afraid." [2] That is starting with a patient where you find her, and moving at once toward the point which the patient needs to reach. Another patient told me of his wrath toward a minister who used to slap him on the back and say, "You're going to get well. You look a lot better today." His doctor had already told him that medical science knew no cure for his disease.

The first few seconds with a patient are significant. Many contacts, in fact we are inclined to think most of those which are failures, are spoiled or are found to be sterile at the outset. We know the chaplain of a large hospital whose only service seems to be a hearty "good morning" to every patient. To many patients it is neither "good" nor "morning." It is evening, with shadows falling fast around them, although it may be nine A.M. by standard time. The minister who uses the "good-morning approach" rather than one adjusted to meet the presenting situation handicaps himself for later helpfulness.

To start with a patient where one finds him we follow the clue of what we see and hear as we go into his room. Perhaps our coming has been announced, perhaps it could not well be. Perhaps the patient is very ill. Perhaps he is quite chipper. He may be a parishioner whose needs we know well. He may be a man we have never seen before. In any case he is a person in need. He may need to endure suffering, to be tolerant of time, to accept death, to rejoice

[2] J. L., Appendix A; p. 359.

at a handicap triumphantly overcome, to attain peace, to grow. One may find an infinite variety of needs and one cannot know much about them beforehand.

Once beside the patient how does one identify his need? By intuition? Nonsense! Intuition is a product of experience. It may be experience that works without checking in at the central office of consciousness. In work with the sick, intuition is quick observation of signs—the patient's posture, motions, and expression. Is he embarrassed, does he ignore you, does he welcome you? What of the modulation of his voice, the rate of his speech? Such signs indicate where the patient is emotionally and mentally, and what he thinks of you. One day I walked into the room of a patient I knew very well. I was greeted with the words, "Oh, Mr. D., say something spiritual." It was not what she said, but the light tone of her voice that gave me my cue. If the patient is light, jovial, bantering, one must begin with him there. One must also attempt to know the reasons for such a mood. Is it protective? Is it escape? Is it legitimate escape? Is it to be encouraged? Is it to be worked through?

One makes one's first observation before a word is said. One should get a fresh impression every time one sees a sick person. These impressions are often of great value. They may be the truest picture that we get, because our "second impressions" are influenced by what we have done ourselves. After that the patient shows us partly himself, partly a mixture of himself and us.

I (R.L.D.) was asked to see a patient by a head nurse. I have forgotten her reasons for the request. As I came to his bed the patient, a man about forty-five years old greeted me with a look of suspicion. His face was sober, his mouth slightly open, his eyes wide, there was a slight movement of his head to the side. It is months now since that day, yet these facts stand out as if I had seen them five minutes ago. I do not remember the patient's name, nor would I recognize him if I saw him again, but I do remember his look, and I know that his story bears out my interpretation of him. His life had been one of constant insecurity, economic and domestic. His attitude of suspicion toward a stranger showed his need, his limitation, his fear.

One needs to avoid getting caught in the mood of one patient and carrying it to another. To go from a patient who is happy and light-hearted to one who is in the depths of despair and not jar the second with one's carefree appearance, requires strict attention to one's mood. One must be neutral as he goes to a patient if one is to note the first full impact of his condition upon one. To glance at a twenty-bed ward is to see twenty patients all very much alike, but to know these twenty patients as people is to know twenty different stories, twenty sets of emotions, ideals, disappointments. So various must be our ways of approaching them.

One does not stand or fall, however, by the degree of accuracy of one's first impressions. We have often got off on the wrong foot with people, or failed to get off at all, and yet straightened things out later. Second or third impressions are often more important than first because one has had time in the interim to prepare the sensitive plate of one's mind for the sort of personality that is to be recorded there,[2] or merely because patient or visitor is in a better mood. One can usually get onto terms with people sooner or later if one is determined to do so. Shyness and awkwardness wear off and guiding clues multiply, especially if one can do some simple manual service. That breaks down distrust as few other methods of contact can.

One's determination to be neutral and unprejudiced at the outset of every new relation does not compel us to ignore what common sense teaches about the differences to be expected between a man, a woman and a child, between an Irishman and a German, between a banker and a hod carrier. Our expectations may be wrong; but if we hold them lightly and tentatively enough, they help us, because they sum up our experience with people thus far. We cannot ignore them unless we despair of learning more and more about our race.

Experience teaches us not only how much people differ but how much they are alike. They all like to be treated with respect though not often with solemnity, with interest but not with flattery, with a persistent effort to understand and to sympathize. These commands

[2] See Chapter XVIII, Note-writing.

are easy to write but hard to obey. Differences catch our interest, though we are often too lazy to outline them and to root them in our memory by expressing them on paper. Identities bore us. It needs more effort to act on them than to notice differences, once we have stored a good stock of types to look for.

It needs to be said again that we cannot see any more qualities in human beings than we have already learned to look for. The average schoolboy sees just two types of teachers, the cross and the likable. As he grows up he comes to own more pigeonholes into which he pops the behavior of the men, women, and children who cross his path. We cannot stop having ideas about people and all ideas are pigeonholes. The only insurance against false ideas is to have many, to hold each tentatively though not vaguely, to make new mixtures of the old ideas, and to watch for branches and buds on each type. Good novels and biographies enrich our fund of types to look for, but the fund must be in constant use or it disappears.

The minister is committed to the nurture of souls. Each needs different food. The food that the minister can most often supply is *recognition*. Sometimes he can lead people to better work, richer recreation, deeper affection, more effective worship. But such leadership is hard compared to the service of recognition. Sickness gives the minister a peculiar chance to see and so to cultivate the native qualities of souls. Even in his first contacts he must remember but rarely express the good news which it is his business sooner or later, in one form or in another, to present. He will need a long will, but if the Christian message is always afire in his own soul some heat will leak out.

The sick man is often spiritually naked, hungry, and unsheltered. He is lonely, discouraged, miserable, even when the doctor and the nurse have done all they can. Perhaps no one can help him. But the minister is bound to try. At the outset he may chat, read, play checkers, do errands, fix up the room if there is no one at hand to do it better. From that point he will go as far as he can toward meeting the patient's spiritual needs. Sometimes he will make no progress. Sometimes he will accomplish more than he deserves. But so long as the patient is glad of what the minister does and so long as there is no one else to do it as well or better, he should give such service as his other claims allow. For any interest followed home leads to religion. One never knows when the road home may open up to one's searching eyes and to the patient's half or wholly unconscious need.

We stress in this chapter the importance of fitting oneself into the patient's situation and watching his mood at the outset of our acquaintance, because we have known ministers to breeze into a sickroom and accost a perfect stranger with stock phrases: "Is your soul saved?" "Do you know your Savior Jesus Christ?" Such questions are as redolent of good intentions as they are of obtuseness. They might well draw an answer like Francis Thompson's, "What right have you to ask me that?" The questioner was a pious missionary and Thompson was a miserable outcast in the London streets when he made that startling answer; but he was well within his rights. Ardent desire to save a man's soul does not authorize us to push hard, well-meaning questions into his face regardless of his right to courtesy and to privacy. Bold assertion of Christian truth is a duty when it would be cowardly to suppress it. It was heroism in the Christian martyrs. It was noble in Stevenson's defense of Father Damien, noble though ruthless and mordant. But it may fall like a stone upon the defenseless and hungry sufferer who needs the bread of life given in compassion and in humility.

PART IV

METHODS

CHAPTER XIV

LISTENING

MOST of the minister's work with the sick is with persons who are neither very imaginative nor very fervid in religion. We find many whose growth seems to have stopped, many who are either well pleased with themselves or who have quit the struggle for spiritual growth. But to the minister who comes away from the sickroom saying, "That person has no spiritual need," we answer, "Go back! Search again. Listen again. Wait." Perfection is still the goal, perfection with all the zest of tension set up by the distance between human existence and the ideal.

The Protestant minister has seldom forgotten this command of perfection but his efforts have sometimes checkmated themselves. He has replaced the altar, symbol of worship, with the pulpit, symbol of intellect. He has set his pulpit in the center of his house of worship and turned his face not toward the altar but toward the people. His words are planned to be guideposts in the spiritual growth of his followers. Instead, his words have become weapons of attack with which he admonishes his hearers to attain the Kingdom. In replacing the altar by the pulpit he has placed preaching above prayer. His influence toward perfection becomes driving rather than leading. Then when he fails to arrive he often becomes disillusioned and his disappointment at small progress is surpassed only by that failure itself.

Great religious leaders of all time have been those who listened to the voice of God on one side and to the voice of the people on the other. In Protestant circles today listening is almost a lost art. We have developed a preaching church. We have made our people the listeners while the minister stands before them as the oracle of

God. If the Protestant Church is to renew its contact and its interest in the care of souls, its leaders must descend from their pulpits and seek out those who are in need. And they must be prepared to listen.

Where but in the sickroom does one find those who are "sick and in prison," those who are hungry for companionship, thirsty for affection, afraid, and remorseful? The Protestant minister is often accused of using only his personality in his work with the sick; in our experience he often has only words. But listening! The ability to listen, the courage to face suffering, to hear of loneliness, of boredom, of fears, to take these unto oneself through listening, is like clothes for the naked, shelter for the lost.

Listening is also the business of the doctor, the psychiatrist, the nurse, and the social worker.[1] Why then should the minister bother to do this kind of work if others can do it just as well or better? As a listener the minister stands as a representative of religion. He brings the religious perspective; a religious psychology envelops him. Religion transcends the immediate. It is not bound by today, tomorrow or next week, but by eternity. It works itself out in everyday forms of living but has its source in that which far outreaches our task of getting the job of living done. It is for this reason that religion has something to say about sickness; it has a perspective from which it can speak, and listen! The patient psychologically vests something in his minister. When I was sick ye visited me. Why visited ye me? Subconsciously the patient says: Because you are a follower, a special representative of Him who would have done likewise.

The minister's listening serves two important ends. It helps the patient to "express" and it helps the minister to understand. Much of what the patient is led by a good listener to express comes into existence while he speaks. Before that it was not full-formed but existed in a shadowy limbo, definite enough to disturb his mind but

---

[1] See Virginia Robinson's, *A Changing Psychology in Social Case Work*, (Chapel Hill Press, N. C., 1930).

not to assist his growth. We offer him a hearing. That leads him to form his thoughts and to follow their lead into consequences which he hardly suspected before. So we assist him in the process of self creation. This new birth is falsely pictured in the popular metaphor about "getting things off one's chest." The patient does not merely repeat aloud what he has already whispered over to himself. That would do him little good. It would be like telling some of his old stories before a new audience. Expression creates. Something new is born in the process. A child comes out of the patient's own life, a child he is often surprised to see yet knows as his very own. "I hardly knew myself as he made me talk and yet it was what I've been trying so long to say and brought me nearer truth than I've been before."

Besides aiding self-creation, good listening enlarges the minister's understanding of the patient's life and so fits him better to forward it, especially if he meditates on the notes that he writes after every important conversation. While he is writing these notes the ideas in them grow. They grow still more when he thinks them over and brings back to the patient at the next visit the new points which have sprouted during note-writing and reflection on the notes.

All this assumes that we never merely listen as the patient talks. *We listen through a theory, with a view to judgment and to action.* Conversation wisely directed is going somewhere. It connects with previous conversations and actions. It gathers up and projects forward a piece of the patient's life. It becomes one of his ventures. Even if the talk is only about a book that he has been reading or about the visit of another friend, his interest in the book or in the friend becomes a branch on the tree of his life. He grows or shrinks in such talks. In the struggle between new life and old laziness the minister can take a part.

He listens *to* many sentences. He also listens *with* many ideas, as clues to interpret what he hears. This constructive part of his listening is not so familiar to us as the receptive part. But in any "creative listener" who brings out the best of us and forwards our growth, most of the creativeness arises not because he has better ears or better memory than the neutral or the destructive listener, but because he listens with so much more life going on within his own mind.

At the start good listening is like playing up to a fellow actor. We "show interest." That is, we let him see that we too are rowing in the boat which his idea moves forward. Our thoughts are ready to pull with his, but not in mere repetition. His thought advances one part of our subject as a single oar pulls on one side of the boat. The good listener takes an oar on the other side of the boat. He is not against his fellow rower nor does he merely duplicate his effort. He encourages by praise what seems to him best in the talk and urges the speaker to go on with it. Knowing their common goal, he helps them toward it in his own way.

Moreover, he brings to their common adventure some experience of similar adventures. He brings to his listening as much of his relevant past as he can recall. He has rowed there before and he knows the river. Without losing a word or a look of his comrade's talk, his mind ranges backward over other talks on this subject, over books that touch it, over historical instances and contemporary variations. The more he has seen, read, and thought, the more sensitive film he has to listen *with,* the more allies spring up in his mind to support the growing life of the conversation. He carries along the patient's thought, as an actor carries on by his answers the drama which his *vis-à-vis* has started.

The good listener listens with all his leading ideas, with his whole creed. And insofar as that creed is not his whim but the best picture of reality that he can make, it may help to clarify another's ideas and to guide them toward their own goal. For their goal is reality too, a part of the same reality which the listener's creed aims to represent. We listen with our limitations and our biases, as well as with our good sense, and to this extent our listening is as much a failure as if our hearing were impaired. Then we are bored, unsympathetic, discouraging, or off the point in our replies.

What, then, is the clergyman's proper listening in sickness? He listens with his belief in God, in immortality, and in the growth that is possible for anyone not overwhelmed by acute illness or by chronic brain disease. He listens with his knowledge of human nature, gathered from the people he has known, but also from history and from that best of all psychology that is called fiction. He uses his experience of what others have suffered and overcome in sickness, his interest in the family and in the friends closest to the patient. Still more he listens with his beliefs about the patient's own life and about its "growing edge" at that very moment. His theology and his hold on Jesus Christ will be of signal service to sufferers in proportion as he manages to discover how these greatest experiences of his own life can be made somewhere to join onto the living growth of the patient before him, a growth which illness seems to check yet may be brought to stimulate.

The minister's proper listening builds in the patient more power to meet and to answer the questions which, clearly or obscurely, his illness arouses, questions about the life he has lived and about the future ahead of him. It has been our experience again and again to listen while a patient described his problems, to be stumped by them and appalled at our own failure, and prudently to keep silence and make no answer till that very silence drew the patient on to say more than he started to say. Soon he begins answering himself better than we could have answered him. Before the end of the visit we have often seen him cheered and enlightened, not by anything we have said but by what our silent interest has led him to discover for himself. And then comes the comic and pathetic farewell, when he thanks us and tells us how much better we have made him feel!

We believe that this is a good example of God's way of giving help. The patient's plea for help was a prayer, even if he vehemently disbelieves in prayer. If he presses his ignorance down into the unknown truth as hard as he can, in confidence that somewhere there is help for him, then by the desperate pull of his desire he fetches up some needed truth from the deep well. His prayer is answered. It would not have been answered unless the listener had kept still, pulling, too, on the rope that goes down to the well of truth, but not interfering between the needy man and his goal—whatever

it may be. In such a case, to interrupt, to answer, may spoil everything. But to listen with convincing concern, with evident pain in
the patient's difficulty, with complete absorption in his effort, does
help another to feel out the way to his answer.

If the patient's questions are thrown out idly or casually, as a
game or a snarl, they do not pull up truth from the Source of
Truth. It is when the hidden presence of the answer gives poignant
intensity to the questioner's search that the answer emerges. Then,
because he already knows the answer in some latent, nascent shape,
and knows the direction to push in, he gets it. The minister's listening conveys to the patient a long-practiced certainty that there is an
answer to all rational questions and that in every truth-seeking man
this answer liveth and redeemeth. How the questioner discovers
the listener's interest we cannot say, and we do not assert that it *is*
always clear or that the whole force of it is ever conveyed to another.
But we feel certain that our silent co-operation in the questioner's
effort is more apt to help him draw his answer out of God than
anything that we can say. It may encourage him to pray for the help
that he needs as in every urgently sincere question he does pray
and all the more effectively because he does not know that he is
praying. If he used the forms of prayer the substance of his desire
might be frozen to death.

Listening, at its best, is one of the ways of helping a sufferer to
pray for the particular help that he needs. Even when he does not
express his need so clearly that another can grasp and answer it, he
is heard where he needs most to be heard, and gets the answer
direct from Him, while we, the silent, listen, often marveling to see
the answer come to him through his own lips—the answer we were
not wise enough to find.

In good listening we have already distinguished two kinds of
attention: we listen to the point and we listen round it. Attention to
what the patient wishes to say divides itself again into positive and
negative. We make efforts to listen *past* the patient's terrifying
pallor, his wasted muscles, the look of suffering that makes us suffer

too. With a blind man we have to make ourselves blind to the disagreeable appearance of his blind eyes. It is hard not to look at
the twist of a paralyzed face. Such inhibitions need practice. At
first the horrors seize our attention so that we scarcely see the person
behind them. Then he sees our embarrassment and is himself
embarrassed by it.

Here the minister has a special opportunity to do well what many
others do badly. He has been trained to see past irrelevant details to
the invisible meanings of scripture, of history, of evil, and of the
material world. He ought to be better prepared than most to "greet
the unseen with a cheer" when he faces some poor paralytic or
cripple. He can welcome the sufferer's lonely soul because he has
learned by practice to disregard the surface of his body. In a hospital
the minister can learn this quickly and thoroughly. There he can
build up his power to ignore smells, sights, and sounds which
obstruct his mission to human souls. He gets used to the smell of
ether, of disinfectants, and of the unwashed. He learns to be un-
moved by the sight of blood and by the sound of stertorous breathing. He learns to be at ease with a dwarf and not to be constantly
obsessed by the shortness of his legs, to ignore the twists of a con-
torted spine and the hideous swelling of an arm or a lip.

Moreover, the minister learns like the rest of us to look past certain moral facts like crime or sexual immorality, when there is
nothing that he can do about them by direct approach. He fixes
attention on the better parts of the person's mind, which often lie
side by side with his worse traits and are curiously unaffected by
them. This strange isolation of opposite qualities within character
has been to us one of the things hardest to learn. When we find a
single, unmistakable trait like kindness or cruelty we tend to think
that it must tinge the whole of a man's personality. We learn painfully to swallow the fact that contradictory characteristics lie side by
side in many people, like the fat and the lean in a ham, and affect
each other very little. To some extent education and sociability introduce neighboring traits to each other inside a person, and weld
his character into a consistent whole. Yet we are amazed to find

even in cultivated persons contradictory qualities, not harmonized at all.

In such people the minister's work may require him to ignore for months or for years obvious moral deformities which jump in his face like the deformity of a hunchback. He cannot forget them and he watches patiently for his chance directly or indirectly to attack them. But he soon finds out that reproof and blame make things worse or block all friendly approaches. The cultivation and encouragement of the best that he can find, is like his listening for the clearly articulated words of a stammerer or the significant points in a disjointed or twisted story.

To look past a chaotic foreground to a background where he can take hold and help is, therefore, one of the minor talents needed in the art of listening.

My (R. L. D's) attention was called to a middle-aged, Protestant woman who had recently been operated on for cancer of the rectum. The cancer was removed, her large intestine opened and brought out through the side, so that her bowel movements will take place through this opening for the rest of her life. She developed a feeling of being unclean, she knew that "no one would seek her out in company," that she would be condemned as "different"; she also "knew" that "no one had ever suffered such humiliation." Her outraged ego had sunk to the point of desiring just one thing, death. Yet when, as a minister, I "sought her out," she welcomed me because in her belief I stood outside the circle of the hospital and those responsible for her condition. She never failed to express surprise and appreciation that I came. I was in an advantageous position for helpfulness over and above the position that a psychiatrist would have held, could he have been called in. Yet I did essentially what he probably would have done: I listened. She talked about her son, her husband, her home, about her church and about her husband's work in the church. Stress was released in a way that no amount of reassurance on my part would have accomplished. I am certain that as a minister I contributed something to her recovery during those dark days; my method was simply that of a listener and a bringer of quietness. With another person one might have used other methods, but with this person, aside from a little conversation always designed to stimulate her thought, the method was clear-cut: listening.

When should we listen? Always! Listen when you are in doubt, listen even when you are using other methods. Listen for your cues to be quiet, your cues for prayer, your cues to leave. The listening attitude brings the patient to the forefront of the picture. It makes him know you are interested in him, that you believe his fortunes important. Many patients will tell you about the number of hours they were on the operating table, the sensation of going to sleep under anesthetic. Some even show you a pickled appendix. Let them show it, and don't fail to look at it; an appendix in a jar is much better than in its former position. You can win the appreciation of a patient by revealing interest in whatever claims his attention.

As a method for work with the sick listening may take two forms: passive and directed listening. Passive listening means following the patient wherever he takes you. Directed listening means leading him to think and talk about a definite subject. Our conception of listening in these two ways covers a wide range of possible relationships with the patient. But in every form listening is what it implies: work, not "visiting." It carries out purpose in work with the sick, not pleasure in chatting with someone at leisure.

In passive listening the minister serves as a mirror, to reflect that which is already present. Directed listening is the creative process of which we spoke above; it stimulates the making of that which till then had not been formed, because it had not been understood either by the patient or the minister. Directed listening is teaching at its best. Passive listening needs honesty on the party of the listener, self-control, and interested disinterestedness. The patient takes one where he will and the listener must be prepared to follow. The patient selects his train of thought; he has selected it, or it has been forced upon him, before the minister enters the sickroom. The

minister does not call forth very different material than would come
to any other professional worker or friend, but the material is given
a different emphasis. Before an operation the patient will be more
apt to talk about God with a minister than with the doctor, although
his thought of God is a real part of the same thought which the
nurse or doctor hears from him. Different sides of the same feelings
are reflected: the mirror stands in a different place.

What one receives in passive listening is usually superficial. It
comes off the surface of the patient's mind and feeling. It is, nevertheless, revealing. I (R. L. D.) was asked to see a fifty-year-old
woman whose heart disease had improved but whose general condition had not; she could not walk and she did not eat. I sat down
to listen: her story came slowly and with it tears; there was little
reason why she should want to get well. She had made a failure
of her own marriage, and had nearly done the same with both her
daughters' marriages. At the time I saw her she was estranged from
one of her daughters. She was fifty, without work, without money,
and with only one friend in the world. Why should she want to
get well? I went back again. This time we talked about something
else: cats—or rather she talked about them while I listened. I knew
little about cats, but I knew enough about them to get her to tell
me what she knew. She did not know much about them either; her
interest in cats was centered in a friendly old tabby cat that she
had had some years before. But as she talked, her whole countenance changed; soon she was talking with enthusiasm about something that was dear to her, something that was friendly, that was
stable. And here was a person who listened and was interested. It
was a simple step for her to realize that my interest went behind her
conversation to herself. That was what she most needed to reinforce
her self-respect. That gave her a start in the right direction.

I stopped by the bed of a gray-haired man [2] so engrossed in reading a large book, Macaulay's *History of England,* that he was
obviously impatient for me to be on my way. Glancing at the book
I asked, "Are you English?" "Well, I'm a member of the Empire

[2] See Chapter XXII, The Dying, p. 298.

My family came from the south of Scotland," he answered. "Are you a Presbyterian?" This was a long shot; his answer came back proudly, "That I am." "I'm a Presbyterian minister," I said. "Are you? Pull up a chair."

For the next twenty minutes he talked about his church, his conception of scripture, about the operation he was facing, of his desire to live yet of his readiness to go if the time had come, of his firm belief in immortality and in the goodness of God. I was the one person in the hospital who could give him a chance to assert once more the things so dear to him. As the end of his life approached some days after the operation, we stood on the same level because we talked the same language, aside from theological differences, which I fortunately managed to keep in the background. When the crisis came they were of no significance. I had discovered the things he held most worth while and was able to keep them to the forefront. This was possible because I had listened. When the time came I was able to call them to his mind through prayer.

Directed listening may be used to get information when we suspect that the patient has something on his mind which is causing him concern. Or we may use it to get a patient to express an opinion which will turn his mind into a desired channel of thought. We all know the greater strength of an idea if an individual believes it to be original with himself. "I have often thought of that but I never expressed it before," is a common remark. Sometimes the listener ventures to express an idea, but only when he believes that the patient is thinking about it already. Listening is not just keeping one's mouth shut. It is thinking, it is anticipation, it is stimulation of thought by a question, by an opinion. But always it is waiting, and always it is concentration upon the patient and that which he is facing. When a patient says, "Am I boring you?" be sure you have been listening poorly.

As an example of directed listening in a rather special form we cite this instance. For several days I (R. L. D.) had been seeing a patient who was suspected of having cancer. Upon first coming to the hospital she had refused to co-operate with the doctors and nurses, and spent most of her time with a handkerchief over her eyes, weeping or brooding. During a period of six days she became gradually more friendly and co-operative. I came to her bed one evening to find her in the worst weeping spell since her arrival. I stood by her bed quietly.

"Some news?" I asked.

After a time, "Yes," still weeping.

I waited. "From the doctors?"

More tears. "Yes."

Again I waited. "Was it what you thought?"

"Yes, but not where I thought—it's farther up."

"In your chest?"

"In my kidney."

Pause. "A growth?"

Pause. "A tumor that may become a cancer."

"You were afraid of that?"

"Yes." Pause.

"Can they do anything about it?"

"They want to operate." Pause.

"When will they get to it?"

"He spoke as if right away."

"Next week?"

"Tomorrow, if I give my consent."

"They told you about it today?"

"About fifteen minutes ago."

I waited, then said, "Is it the operation you fear or the outcome of it?"

"Both—I suffered terribly from two other operations I had. I didn't wake up for two days." She continued, "I'm not going to give my consent right away."

"Think about it a while before you decide."

"I suppose I could have strength to go through with it."

"Strength always seems to come for these things. Think it over I'll see you in the morning."

She had stopped weeping and was fairly quiet.

In this conversation the minister said more than the patient did, yet he was essentially the listener. His early questions were so put that they could be answered in a monosyllable. By anticipating what might be in her mind, her fear was brought to the surface so that in the end not the minister but the patient said, "I can go through with this thing. I can get the strength." The minister simply added, "Strength comes—there is that which gives strength, depend on Him." She did, and is now well and working again.

In directed listening the Protestant minister makes his nearest approach to the Catholic use of the confessional. The confessional above everything else, we believe, is responsible for the strength of the Catholic Church as an institution. The confessional has given the Catholic Church contact with its people and its realistic conception of human nature; through the confessional the Catholic Church has ministered consistently and intelligently to the needs of its people. The priest in the confessional uses directed listening. Attention is centered on the penitent, not on the priest; the penitent selects the subject for his thought as does the patient in directed listening. The penitent is held to that subject by the priest; that is, he is forced to work through its implications, which are often very different from what he had imagined. Many a penitent leaves the confessional box with a new understanding of himself and his motives. When he went to confession his attention may have been taken up with a definite act. When he left he had come to realize that no single act but his accumulation of brooding, loneliness or anxiety was important for his consideration. The act was a symptom not a cause. In the confessional the priest searches for motives. His purpose is to help the penitent to see these motives himself. The priest may pronounce absolution for a given act, but unless the motive is seen and accepted by the penitent the confession is useless.[3] Through the use of absolution the priest attempts to bring to the penitent's consciousness the realization that God is interested in him and is actually enlisted in his behalf. The Protestant

---

[3] It should be understood that the confessional is set up for the use of the person who is healthy both mentally and physically—not for the abnormal.

minister attempts to do the same thing through the use of prayer.

The Catholic Church has made a sacrament of the confessional, centering around it some of its finest tradition, as well as some of its strictest laws. We conceive the Protestant minister's listening as a method rather than a sacrament. In one sense of the word listening is a sacrament just as the taking of food is. And certainly the confidences told the minister in time of need must be considered sacred. But lest listening become something formal and difficult we insist upon considering it as a tool, comparable with the other methods described here. Tools of themselves are of no special consequence, but applied to a purpose they gain value.

Consider certain limitations in the use of listening as a method in work with the sick. By a concentration upon listening in the sickroom one may make the patient work too hard. Or one may attempt to listen at times when the patient has nothing that he wishes to talk about. For this reason we have emphasized the importance of "starting with the patient where he is." But even when we do this our listening may not be fruitful, for it presupposes a certain response on the part of the listener, as we have pointed out in describing directed listening. Obviously it presupposes also a degree of intelligence on the part of the listener. Without these we may be of no use Certain patients seem difficult to listen to. In such a situation it is well to examine your own condition. Are you tired when you go to certain patients? Why? Why do certain patients bore you? Why do you find it difficult to get interested in some? Why do you dislike some patients? Perhaps you associate them with your own unfortunate experiences in the past. Perhaps they reveal in themselves limitations which are characteristic of you. Unfortunately, or perhaps fortunately, ministers have their limitations too.

Another difficulty of the listening method is that it may fail to make progress. It may take one over the same material repeatedly. It is then that we need directed listening. If one finds a patient repeating himself to no effect, if the signs of tension are not present, be certain that you have hit a dry area; push on to something more significant. But you will not always get there. It must be confessed that the patient who repeats himself, who talks for the sake of talking, sometimes makes the minister's life fatiguing.

The listening method is of limited value with three types of patients: the talkative, the unimaginative, and the very ill. With the first type, the talkative, egotistical, self-centered person, little can really be done by listening. Self-interest is a symptom of something else, and one may start a campaign to find and to combat its causes. But by the time it is full-blown in adult life one should not be optimistic about being able to accomplish anything.

One needs to be especially alert with the inarticulate person. From such a person a few seemingly irrelevant remarks, spoken out of the corner of his mouth, may be of great significance. There are some people, however, who never have risen above the mud of existence. One finds them out easily. A psychological test would verify one's first impression. They are told what to do, they do it, or they do not. They live, they are sick, they die. Some of them carry the workaday world on their shoulders. We respect them but we do not spend much time in listening to them.

With the very ill one is still to listen, but one listens more with one's eyes than with one's ears. One listens for the slight trace of a smile, for the pressure of a hand as one prays or stands quietly by. The very ill cannot say much, but what they say is of significance. In my ministry to J. L., a thirty-year-old nurse dying of inoperable cancer, my method was largely the use of prayer, but I listened also. I listened to her requests, her response, her exaltation, her outreaching.[4]

Such has been the method of the Church when it has been most effective in meeting the needs of its people. It has been like the Good Shepherd who searches the hills for those who have not found the fold. But how dependent the Good Shepherd is upon the tracks in the sand while the light lasts, and then upon the sheep's call as darkness closes in!

[4] P. 359.

Chapter XV

QUIETNESS

As I (R.L.D.) have visited individuals suffering from many types of disease and in various degrees of seriousness, I have been conscious repeatedly of an unidentified, and largely unrecognized, quality. Its presence in some instances and its absence in others forced it upon my attention. The difference between these two conditions I recognized to be the difference between triumph and tragedy, between a light that shines and a torch unlighted. This difference was not in the degree of the patient's suffering, nor in the story of his temperature chart; it was a quality seen in the patient himself. This quality which we have seen working has been called quietness;[1] but we must describe it further lest it be considered simply lack of noise.

Quietness[2] is a quality of the spirit, a state of being. In its more complete forms it may become what we imagine to be perfect union with God. Because it is an experience seldom observed in the day's doings we find it difficult to describe. To describe how quietness works, or to attempt to force it into a formula is like man's eternal effort to describe his contact with God. For quietness surely is a quality of God. It may be awakened in us as we watch the confidence of the little child asleep, or the peacefulness of the old at the end of a life well lived. One feels it through the glow of the sunset, through the penetrating odor of pine trees, in the protecting barrier of woods on a wintry day. Patients feel it through the coolness of fresh sheets after a restless night, through the nurse's objectivity,

[1] Mrs. John Finley Morgan, of New York City, was the first to call to my mind this element which I am trying to describe.

[2] *Webster's New International Dictionary* defines quietness as "freedom from disturbance, noise, or alarm; stillness; tranquillity; peace; security."

through the doctor's skill and confidence. These are glimpses of quietness. All of them are protective, for quietness is a sense of protection.

Again, quietness is patience—the terrible patience of nature, God's eternal handiwork. The slow, determined patience of nature in its healing of the broken, its knitting of the torn, its righting of the bent. I have seen its effect on a field of corn which seemed to be beaten and ruined after a storm on a Western prairie. The next morning where there had been ruin now stood strong plants waving and nodding in the breeze. That gives us quietness.

I have seen quietness in the patient who goes to sleep easily under the anesthetic cone, his confidence in "the surgeon and God"; in the young mother who smiled in response to my question, though she knew the operation was done as a forlorn hope: "Yes," she said, "it's all right. Whether I get well, or whether I die, it's all right." I have seen it in a twenty-year-old boy who knew his chances were small: only two out of a known eleven in the history of surgery had recovered from the operation he was facing. As he was going to sleep he said to me, "Tell the folks it's all right. Just another journey in life's pilgrimage."

One sees quietness hold the tireless searcher in the laboratory. Eyes glued to a microscope, tireless observations, endless speculations closely checked. Alone the searcher continues, alone he eliminates, rejects, tries again. He loves and works in the bonds of loyalty to science, goddess of man's conquest. His devotion is quietness.

Quietness stands above the world and yet is of the world. One knows it through the roar of the city, yet not in the noise of the city; not in the brutality of the city, but in the freedom of the city's streets without their loneliness. Quietness is majestic, strong because it is determined, patient; it suffereth not, neither does it stand aside.

Quietness is more than silence, for silence is waiting. Quietness is not waiting. Rather quietness is that for which one waits. Quietness is not something to be constantly sought, lest one's spirit become stagnant. It is not a free gift to mankind. It is something which the spirit earns. It is both a means and an end to attainment. By its relation to the rest of human existence it becomes a haven of renewal for the spirit. For our spirit quietness is like the sea to the traveler whose path runs hard by it. He is often within sound of it, yet is afforded only an occasional glimpse of it. Even when one comes out in the open above the sea one often finds a mist or fog lying over the water, yet, even so, one knows it is there and feels its strength.

Because quietness is a quality of the spirit, it may become a method for its own attainment. Quietness is being quiet, and even more quiet, for always there is the beyond. But quietness is not a moving into the beyond, for quietness is the beyond. Quietness needs no logic, no motion to justify itself, for it stands untouched by the heaping up of mind and matter.

In the sickroom quietness may be attained for the patient through the personality of another. Even before one actually enters the sickroom one needs to recognize the difference between quietness and activity. In the very recognition of this difference one begins the stilling of the spirit. When one puts away busyness and recognizes quietness, one is already becoming quiet. The patient will feel this quietness, will often feel the strength of a growing stillness.[3]

One of my first definite experiences with quietness in sickness was in the post-operative ward one day when I went into what I thought was the room of a patient I knew. Once in the room I found I did not know the patient, a man some sixty years old. Instead of apologizing for my mistake and making a hurried if not ungracious exit, I came close to the bed and stood by quietly. The patient nodded and smiled as I came near; I said something, quite unimportant, he answered with something similar. His features

[3] I am not unmindful of Oriental mysticism and its use of quietness, nor of that practiced by the Quakers. But in both these instances the predominating note would seem to be the individual's use of quietness to strengthen his own relation to the Divine. I use quietness for its effect on the sick.

were relaxed, his hands still, he seemed at ease. I was conscious of a definite alertness on my part; my attention was concentrated upon the patient and his need. Presently I started to leave. He nodded again and said, "Thank you." Somewhat surprised I wondered what I had done to be thanked for; I had done nothing, said nothing. Nevertheless, I was certain something happened. I am still certain.

Since then that experience has been repeated in various forms. Interestingly enough, it has not happened so many times as some might imagine that it would, and certainly not so many times as I would like to have had it happen. There have been times when I have striven for quietness with a patient only to have an embarrassed silence result. The only thing I have been conscious of later is that either the patient or I—and sometimes it is difficult to discover which—did not feel at ease; quietness needs soul searching and is often not easily attained. Again there have been times when almost unexpectedly I have come upon a period of quietness with a patient. The only rule I know for determining the use of this method in work with the sick is some such general statement as this: be prepared with all patients at all times to be quiet, but do not work too hard at it and do not be surprised when you fail in its use.

The following conditions seem most favorable to the use of quietness; whether they are essential to its use or not I do not know. Granted these conditions the method still may fail. There is some question in my mind as to which of these should be considered paramount: (1) A satisfactory rapport or working relationship with a patient; (2) a situation in which there is considerable stress or tension; (3) the right spiritual condition in the worker; (4) conscious co-operation of the patient.

(1) Just what makes a working relationship between two persons, is hard to say. Despite the efforts of modern psychology to describe what goes into a rapport or what it rests on, we still come back to such statements as: I like that person. We liked each other from the beginning. I trust you. I enjoy seeing you. We can name several

elements which go to make up a satisfactory working relationship, such as trust, mutual interest, loyalty, recognition of mutual limitations. But all these abstract elements still leave us unsatisfied in our efforts to describe what has been known from time immemorial as friendship. The element of friendship must enter into a situation before we can be of very much help in the sickroom. One of the most satisfactory doctors I know said to me, "I make friends of all my patients." He becomes genuinely concerned over what is happening to his patients, and so must the minister.

The Protestant minister is often accused of having only his personality in his work with the sick. By that, it is said, his work stands or falls. Much of the doctor's work also succeeds or fails according to his personality, for personality[4] includes far more than a "bedside manner." In the broad sense of the word, it includes knowledge, insight, skill, interest, hope, devotion.

The lawyer's work also depends upon his personality. So does the business man's, the diplomat's, and certainly the dictator's. Personality is not something on the surface, as modern psychology has shown. The surface symptoms themselves are determined by something core-deep. The manner of moving, of speaking, of dressing— yes, the very flick of an eyelash is determined by the nature beneath. These superficial characteristics often make or break an individual's work and rightly they should. Sir William Osler tells us that before he was called to the University of Pennsylvania as professor of medicine the committee invited him to dinner to see how he would eat cherry pie. Dr. Walter C. Alvarez tells of a patient who asked for another doctor because the one who came to her bed had his collar torn half an inch at the side; she said, "I thought if he were so careless in his dress he probably would be careless in other things."

Christianity has its roots in the personality of Jesus. We love the Nazarene, not only because he died for an ideal, albeit an ideal which benefits all mankind. We love him because of the nature he

---

[4] "That which constitutes a person. That which distinguishes and characterizes a person."—Funk and Wagnalls, *College Standard Dictionary*.

revealed, a nature devoted so profoundly to such an ideal. We love him because he knew the tendencies of those whom he would help, even as he knew the story of the woman taken in adultery. Yet he would not judge or condemn. We love him because he recognized the needs of his fellow men and did so much to meet these needs. We love him because in the course of his efforts he ran amuck against the civil authorities and was killed. He had no desire to die, but granted his nature, his personality, and the world he lived in, it was inevitable that he should die. Why were people attracted to him? Why has he had more influence than any other single man in the world's history? Some, it seems, did not like him, some did not believe the things he said and were not able to do the things he suggested. In those instances he failed. What he did, the devotion he calls forth, and the history of his success, his failure, and his death—all this is the fruit of his personality and not of any church or tradition through which he worked.

The establishment of a rapport, a friendship between two persons, may be instantaneous or gradual. Some people dislike ministers, not as individuals but because they are ministers. What they dislike may be a part of their own early childhood associated with a stern parent who forced them to go to church when they would have preferred to play baseball. They may associate ministers with a father who was a pillar in his church but a tyrant at home. On the other hand a minister may be called to the sickroom because of the satisfactory work done by earlier ministers whom that patient has known. But beyond the initial introduction he stands or falls not by the work of others but by himself. This is true not only of the Protestant ministry but of the Catholic as well; the Protestant has more opportunity for making mistakes, consequently they show up more seriously.

(2) A second condition which seems to call forth quietness and under which we may expect to be able to use this method in the sickroom, is a "stress situation." Quietness cannot be attained through tension. Yet in a situation of considerable stress we may

be driven to attain quietness by desperation, by the poignant need for relief. This very tension breaks down barriers and forces the acceptance of relief: (a) When a patient is very ill one may use quietness to good advantage. Some patients will desire you to be present even though they may not be able to talk. They may be semiconscious, yet they will want you near. The very presence of some people is tiring, while that of others is restful; quietness is the difference between these two. (b) When a patient is tired yet desires you to be with him, then you may become quiet, this very quietness contributing to the patient's feeling of confidence as he attempts to sleep. If he starts suddenly, as many patients do when attempting to get to sleep, because of the dull dreams or nightmares brought on by illness, he will find you alert to his need by your stillness of spirit. (c) Quietness may be used to good effect with a patient who is restless but who has recognized in you a steadying element. A misuse of one's compassion in such an instance is the repetition of "What can I do?" or "Now do try and get some sleep." Rather one might stand quietly by, at ease, relaxed within, poised without, stable in a room of unstable objects, seeing in a room of sightless objects. (d) Quietness may be used with a patient facing death, especially when he expresses hope or regret at going: for instance, "I am ready to go if my work is done." Or, "I am sorry to leave my family. It will be the first break, but it will be nice to go." (e) Finally, one may use quietness combined with listening when one meets the family of a patient who is very ill or who has died. One is apt to feel helpless on such occasions; if an element of poise can be brought into the situation, both the family and the minister may feel grateful.

(3) The worker's own spiritual condition is one of the factors which govern the use and effectiveness of quietness. Unless one can be quiet oneself, efforts to use this method are certain to fail; and that one has been able to be quiet yesterday or last week does not mean that one can today. Capacity for quiet is like fitness to participate in a hard athletic contest: one must be in condition. We are told repeatedly that injuries in football games result because the

players are not in condition. Observe with what care the professional ball players work out their pitching arms in the spring after a season's rest. This same thing is true in work with the sick. It always takes me some days to get my stride after having been away from the hospital, not because there is no work to be done but because I am out of condition. This is true as a general rule; it is true with doctors also when they have been away from their routine for a time, but it is even more true in the use of quietness as a method. One needs to have been over a course at ease to know one can go over it under stress.

The question might be asked at this point: How can the minister himself gain quietness in the sickroom; what does being quiet involve? It involves two things: First, the condition of one's spirit. One should have faced a spiritual discipline of some kind during that very day, relaxed quietly, meditated, prayed. Personally I think it unfortunate if ministers or doctors hold themselves under too stern a discipline, lest they lose contact with the world as it is. But let one save one's smoking or other indulgence—far be it from us to suggest methods of ministerial dissipation—until after the day's work, or until one has a day off.

To be able to be quiet is to call to the front of your mind that which you believe most genuinely. The times when I have felt the panic of tragedy most acutely were when I forgot the presence of God. When one goes into a foreign land but fails to take one's God it is difficult to be quiet, whether in the sickroom or out of it, whether one is a patient or a worker. Silent, unarticulated prayer is the best aid to quietness of the spirit. "He leadeth me in green pastures. My help cometh from the Lord. He is my rock and my fortress; in Him will I trust day and night. I am the water of life." These great passages give one a sense of knowing that one walks not alone into the presence of need. It is not by one's own authority that one goes to the sickroom.

Secondly, it is important to arrange certain minor details in order to obtain quietness for one's spirit in the sickroom.

(a) Allow yourself enough breath! The newcomer in the operating room sometimes forgets to breathe and forthwith faints. A speaker's voice on the public platform quivers because he does not breathe properly. Breathing, most people believe, is done unconsciously. So it is under normal conditions, but in unusual situations which call for special concentration the physical organism goes through unusual gymnastics. A few deep breaths do much to fortify one's resources.

(b) Relax! Drop your shoulders into their natural position; your arms, your hands, let them fall naturally by your side. Strange as it may seem they do not really need to be thrust deep into pockets to get them out of the way.

(c) Learn to walk without stumbling! It is no easy matter to enter a room and avoid kicking a leg of the bed, chair, or table, especially when one's attention is concentrated upon the patient and his condition. The effect is to give the impression of stumbling into the room and stumbling out. This is not a fault of ministers only. Other workers sometimes have difficulty in manipulating themselves even through a fairly empty room, when their attention is centered upon the sick patient. But what shall it profit a man if he has seemed to gain the world for his patient but kicks the bed in leaving the room!

(4) Finally, what is the patient's part in the use of quietness? Here I must confess ignorance. I do not know. Somehow the patient must consciously co-operate. That does not mean that before this method can be used it must be called to the patient's attention. In my use of quietness I have always found the condition already present in the patient, or I have consciously attempted to establish it by being quiet and the patient has responded by being quiet himself. There have been further instances when together we have seemed to come upon quietness unexpectedly. The patient though very sick has already accepted a condition of quiet; in that instance one simply steps into that which is already present.

I went to see a patient one evening who was seriously ill. She asked me to stay with her for a time. I stood quietly by for fifteen or twenty minutes. At the end of perhaps half that time she went to sleep. It is difficult to estimate the working of quietness in an experience of this kind. Perhaps it is merely that one is not noisy, but there would seem to be a further element present, which goes beyond silence, a working relationship between two persons, founded upon the mediation of God.

Another instance which comes to my mind is that of a patient who had been suffering for some days from the effects of an extensive operation on the stomach. I had seen her before the operation but not after it, until this time. Upon opening her eyes as I came to her bed she said, "Oh, I have suffered such pain! If I had known it would be like this I would never have had the operation." I said, "But you were suffering a great deal before the operation." "Yes, I know, but this goes on and on. I cannot sleep at night. The medicine gives me some relief, but then it starts up again. It seems ages since I was operated on." (It had been about six days.) She continued to talk about the difficulty of keeping up her courage and about the long nights. I stood by and said little. When I started to leave after five or six minutes she thanked me for coming to see her. Her mind had not traveled beyond her immediate condition but she was pleased and undoubtedly relieved by being able to talk about what she was going through. The element of quietness steadied her at the time; she would probably have said it was my interest in her which helped. It was that, *plus*.

In both these experiences there is the common element of the minister's strong interest in the patient and what she is passing through. The first would seem to have been more satisfactory, a satisfaction which is not easily expressed in notes or in description, not only because of the mediation of God but because we were both thinking about God at the time. That is, quietness is effective as both people center their attention upon God, not as a thinking but as a resting process. In the sickroom it is effective as the strong lends aid to the weak. The ordered mind extends ease to the chaotic mind.

One advantage of such a method as this is that if it goes wrong there is no harm done, nobody's feelings are hurt. Further, quietness itself is the ideal condition of the sickroom because, as we have said earlier, quietness is the life blood in which the torn is healed, the broken knitted.

It is natural to conclude this chapter by acknowledging the obvious need for quietness in the general warp and woof of living in our modern noisy, rushing world. With the heaping up of a mechanized existence we now face not only economic readjustment, but emotional and spiritual adjustment. That which our agrarian forbears took for granted we must struggle for. That which walked with them throughout the day—the tranquillity of nature, the spirit of quietness—we must use thought and skill to find. Quietness is not only a desirable condition for the sickroom, it is a desirable condition for any poised, healthy, happy life. If we are to work effectively in the sickroom we must understand the use of quietness. If we are to make the church an effective instrument in the modern world, we must bring quietness into its services. We must examine again the determination and the patience of a young man who stands above the world. There are wounds upon his body and sadness upon his face, but he is eternally quiet.

Chapter XVI

PRAYER

I. PRAYER: WHAT IT IS

Jesus believed that it is possible to commune with God through prayer. He did it. He did not tell his followers how or under what conditions a man can best pray. In the gospels we see that there were times when prayer and the effects of prayer seemed to be stronger than at other times. Jesus's teaching about prayer was to give his disciples a prayer. His instruction was to pray in quietness and humility; from the mystery of quietness would come a knowledge of God.

The use of prayer in the sickroom by a second person, the minister, is a method whereby the patient may be brought into touch with God. The minister plays a secondary part; he is the sufferer's representative; he fastens his mind on those whom he would bring together: patient and God. Prayer under such conditions is a learning-teaching process. The patient is the learner, the minister teacher, God and the ways of God the subject matter. The teacher often learns more than the taught. The good teacher knows both his student and his subject matter; so the minister must know both the needs of his patient and the resources of the universe which he may bring to the patient's mind.

Does God answer the prayer of the sick? Yes, but not any prayer. The contents of prayer in the sickroom should be like the contents of the patient's food tray. Steak smothered in onions and French-fried potatoes are not given a patient in his early convalescence, however much he may desire them. He is given broth, tea, soft-boiled eggs, toast, or a similar meal. So with prayer in the sickroom. The patient who prays, "God grant me strength to endure this pain," and "Patience to find through this handicap a greater under-standing of Thee," receives his answer more directly than the patient who prays, "God, take away the pain," or, "O God, I cannot endure to be injured, let me die." Pray for that which the patient most needs in the light of his condition, spiritual and physical. The answer may not come in the terms of your prayer, but time and time again one ultimately recognizes a deeper fulfillment.

II. THE TECHNIQUE OF PRAYER IN THE SICKROOM

Among the questions which ministers must consider in the use of prayer in the sickroom are: Does the patient accept prayer as a potent factor in human experience? Does he use it? Does he accept the beliefs upon which it rests? If not, is prayer the next step in his spiritual growth? Can you introduce it at this stage of your work with him? One patient we knew became greatly embarrassed at the mere mention of prayer because she associated it with the disasters of her childhood. Certain imaginings and disappointments had to be cleared away before prayer could be used.

Another patient whom we knew liked to read beautiful prayers, but did not accept the fact of a personal God and the Christian belief in immortality which he associated with such a belief in God. Religion for him was "love of one's neighbor." His love of prayers was the same as his love of poetry or music. There was in him a reaching out, a yearning, a desire for infinite good. In that sense his inarticulate desires were prayers, but one could not go to him and pray with any obvious result until he had worked through the emotional reserves which he called "agnostic beliefs."

Other points which have to do more definitely with the way we pray in the sickroom might seem trivial in the light of our object. By their very littleness they become stumblingblocks. Here are some of them. If the patient is in a room with others or in a large ward, should we pull the curtains round the bed or ask for a screen to be set up? What should one do if visitors are present? How can we use prayer with the patient in an oxygen tent? With one who is physically uncomfortable? A patient may be restless,

turning from side to side, or he may have been given a drug and
be drowsy. Suppose the nurse is present and does not offer to
leave? These are situations which the minister will face sooner or
later in the sickroom. What shall he do about them?

In a large ward we find it helpful to pull a curtain or ask to have
a screen set up about the bed. The patient prefers this and we
find it easier to accomplish a feeling of the presence of God by
closing out the bustle of the ward and the curious, if longing, eyes
of other patients. If visitors are present, do not hesitate to ask them
to wait outside for a few minutes, in case the patient does not
suggest this. A question to the nurse in regard to the patient in an
oxygen tent will usually bring a practical suggestion as to how to
overcome its difficulty. Sometimes the flap may be lifted for the
time you need without any detriment to the patient. Be certain
to let such a suggestion come from the nurse or doctor, but do not
hesitate to persist in such a situation.

Under such conditions one must be careful not to seem hurried.
With the person who is restless or uncomfortable from physical
needs, you may either wait until he is made comfortable or go ahead
if he insists. But do not fail to be alert to such signs and to inquire
if closed curtains or a closed door mean that the patient is busy.
With one who has been given a sedative and yet is not asleep, prayer
may be used to even greater effect than when the mind is active.
If the nurse does not offer to leave when you arrive, you may assume that she had better stay. She will understand your office and
her patient better if she stays.

When should we pray in the sickroom? Some ministers think
they should pray every time they see a patient. Our comment is
that they must either limit their sick calls to highly selected persons
or that they do not understand the use of prayer in the sickroom.
We do not use prayer in every instance, even with patients whose
religious lives we know well. Prayer should be varied from time to
time with other methods. It is to be used especially in times of acute
need. There will be times when we should pray even though the

patient's mood does not invite us. The old divines call it "being led to pray." The younger minister goes by the same signs and arrives at the same end—he simply calls it by another name.

With a patient who is not one's parishioner the question when to pray becomes more difficult. We believe that prayer should be used for a definite need seen in the light of our understanding of the patient's spiritual development. I (R. L. D.) found a note on my desk one evening asking me to see a certain patient unknown to me. When I arrived I spent ten or fifteen minutes talking with her quietly, or rather having her talk to me. She told me that she was to have an operation early the next morning. It was then about half-past five in the evening. This was the second operation she had had since coming to the hospital some weeks before. She was concerned about the outcome of this one, as it was to be more serious than the first. She had been a member of a Baptist church for twenty years; her own minister was sick or she would have sent for him. From that story one can draw one's conclusions. Here is a woman who has led an active religious life; she has attended church regularly; her own minister is sick; she is facing a serious operation, the outcome of which she believes to be doubtful. She sends for a minister hoping that her confidence in God may be strengthened and her spirit quieted. We know that she desires and expects prayer, and we understand what our prayer should contain. The minister may be certain that whenever he is sent for *as a minister* the patient needs and expects prayer.

The patient whom we get to know casually in hospital visitation is one we must understand before using prayer. If he is an active church member and if religion means something to him in his illness, we may be certain he will welcome prayer. If his own minister is coming to see him regularly it is somewhat presumptuous to use prayer unless he invites it.

The great number of unchurched patients who come to our hospitals have spiritual needs which are as great as those who are active church members, perhaps greater. They have not the initiative or the imagination to diagnose the source of their restlessness, their loneliness, their despair. One gets to know them easily in the hospital ward; one may get to know them in the private room if one offers one's services to the hospital superintendent and comes regularly to the hospital. To leave one's name with the superintendent or a clerk is not enough. Neither the superintendent nor the clerk is in direct touch with the patients.

With the patient who is not an active church member one must use methods which will be acceptable to him from the start. The minister may be of service in helping him through a definite crisis, but still leave him far short of becoming a person whose religious life is actively growing, and in contact with the organized machinery of religion. It is not the purpose of the minister to seek out the sick in order to enlist church membership; but the sick present needs which religion has resources to meet. It is the minister's privilege to put the sufferer in touch with these resources. He must be certain not to take advantage of that privilege by attempting to enforce upon a sufferer his own ideas, which he may mistake for the resources of religion. Start with a patient where he is, move with him in his growth. Anything short of spiritual maturity to the point of prayer, and an active working relationship with God, is insufficient.

In the use of prayer with a given individual, we have found the writing of prayers a good check upon the ground covered. Without this check we cover the same ground, include the same petitions, use the same analogies, repeat the same phrases from day to day. There is need both for repetition and for new emphasis to stimulate a breadth of religious thought. Writing notes and prayers for this purpose has the effect of holding both patient and minister to the task before them.

III. WHAT PRAYER IN THE SICKROOM SHOULD CONTAIN

Prayer in the sickroom should monopolize the attention of the minister and of the patient. Sometimes this is not so. The minister prays off the surface of his mind, especially if he uses memorized prayers. Or he is nervous, hurried, or conscious of the physical conditions under which he is working. Then satisfactory prayer is impossible. Full attention on the part of the minister is essential. By his own concentration the minister may command the patient's attention, even when he cannot do this by himself. Attention is possible in the sickroom, as elsewhere, if prayer contains the following elements: quietness, application, reach, and the language of religion.

We distinguish the use of quietness from the use of prayer, but our description of quietness shows that it contains the elements of prayer. It is unarticulated prayer. It is the raw material out of which prayer is made. We have observed that quietness is invariably present before or during the time of satisfactory prayer in the sickroom. We unconsciously attempt to establish the conditions of prayer by being quiet before it if only for an instant. Quietness is the fertile soil from which prayer, living contact with God, arises. It remains as one leaves the room.

Prayer must have *application*. It must recognize the facts in a given sickroom. It must recognize the sufferer's needs and express his thoughts about them. If he has formulated no conscious or satisfactory conception of his needs, the minister may express his own thought about them in his prayer. The patient then makes the minister's expression of his need a part of his own thought, providing that this expression is near enough to his "growing edge" and to his recognized beliefs to be acceptable. Let us be specific: a patient whom we have mentioned before held her doctors responsible for her pitiable condition. The fault, if there was any, was hers. She should have come to the hospital earlier in the course of her disease. To have prayed with her for "a spirit to forgive those who have tried to help us," would have been going beyond the patient to a point of probable rejection on her part. But to pray for "a quiet mind, that we may know Thy will and Thy spirit within us," would be more apt to prepare her mind's soil for a new plant of forgiveness—a plant which, when it blooms, will be the healthier for having been her own discovery.

By the particular applications in our prayers we may relieve certain elements of concern in the patient's mind, such as worry in regard to family or friends. One young woman said, "I hate to go, it will be the first break in our family." In my prayer I remembered "those whom we leave behind; we know they are soon to follow." In less than six months after her own death the patient's mother died also. Another patient was concerned about the financial condition of his family, but he was beyond the point of being able to help them. Our recognition of this fact helped him to accept the experience he was facing.

One should recognize not only the patient's needs but other elements which are poignant in his situation. "In the long night watches" is a term that belongs rightly in many a prayer. To recognize the weary hours of pain in the dead of night, broken only by the quiet coming and going of a nurse or the calling of a patient, is to identify oneself with the sufferer, and to speak as one with authority. Again, "the stillness of the evening," "the quiet of the morning," are references to what every patient knows.

By application in prayer we may strengthen the patient's confidence in the doctors and nurses. His confidence in the surgeon, for instance, is of vital significance. Patients usually have an attitude of reverence for the men in whose hands they are absolutely helpless, upon whose skill and knowledge their lives depend. To dedicate that reverence to God is to stamp it with even greater authority. "Surely God is in this place, in the physician, in the nurse," says the patient. A phrase we frequently use in prayer is, "We remember him who is to operate and those who are to serve as nurses. We know that we are in worthy and capable hands."

Application in prayer also implies that one should stay within reasonable limits in one's petitions. Some prayers ask for perfection, to be freed from all sin, to be washed clean. A moment's reasonableness must show us that such petition cannot be granted. If the patient is a reflective person, such extravagant demands may convince him that your understanding of God and of human nature is of the hothouse brand, lacking both experience and humility. "God, grant us patience to endure that which we cannot understand," is pointed to relieve the patient from confused brooding, and to concentrate his attention upon patience and fortitude.

Prayer in the sickroom must have *reach*. It must point beyond the immediate experience. In a following chapter we speak of the need for perspective in illness. Reach is perspective in prayer. The patient's world is falling to pieces. Former interests and values are losing their significance. This is often true even of the patient's religion. One woman said, "All my life I have been an active Christian. But now I seem to get no help from my religion. I pray but I get no satisfaction from it." Another said, "My husband and son are out of work. We have no money. I am sick and I improve very slowly. But when I turn my mind to God I am quiet and peaceful." Both these women had been active members of the church for years; the one had grown into stability of religious life, the other had not. For one God stood beyond the heat and confusion of her illness; she could transport her thought beyond the immediate. The other could not. The minister may bring perspective to a patient through his prayer. Prayers must have an application but they must go beyond the immediate so that the patient may feel the permanence of God. Presently we shall cite a prayer for sleep, which seems to have this element of reach, to bring to the patient's mind God's completeness.

The degree of emphasis upon what we call reach must be determined by the sufferer's need. Reach is not motion in prayer, it is emphasis and perspective. Reach gives leverage to prayer. To illustrate: a woman requested the minister to pray that her pain might be relieved. Here is his prayer:

Eternal God,
Thou Who dost bear us up in our travail,
And who dost comfort us in our moments of weakness,
Be Thou with this one as she suffers;
Grant her relief from this pain,

And give her patience and fortitude to endure to the end.
Wilt Thou give us peace in Thy presence,
In the quiet of the evening may we come unto Thee,
And in the still morning may we dwell in Thy presence.
As Thy glory shineth in the morning sunrise
May we reflect Thy presence by our faith,
In the name of the Father, the Son, and the Holy Spirit.
Amen.

This prayer applies to the patient's need, known through her request. Is such a prayer answered, and if not is it justified? It is not answered in the sense that some of the conditions of pain are not removed. It is answered in that the patient's concentration upon her pain is broken. The prayer contains reach at the place it points beyond the present moment: "In the quiet of the evening may we come unto Thee," and "In the still morning." By the use of the phrases "morning sunlight" and "reflect Thy presence in our faith," the patient's attention is centered upon what is known to be a stable part in her life, namely, her faith in God.

Prayer in the sickroom, like all prayer, should be cast in *the language of religion*. Our Bible contains the language of religion at its best, especially in the Gospels, in certain of the Epistles, and in the Psalms. We frequently include a scriptural verse to be certain that the strength of religious language is brought to the patient's mind. In this respect the prayer book has advantages. The language of religion at its best is poetry; it is simple, straightforward, rich in meaning, and association. It suggests dignity, patience, fortitude.

IV. WHAT PRAYER IN THE SICKROOM SHOULD ACCOMPLISH

We have suggested that prayer at its best, as used by the minister in the sickroom, contains an element of teaching from the minister's point of view and of learning from the patient's. The subject matter is God and His eternal relationship to man. Our aim as ministers in such a situation is to assist God in His Creative Process; the physician has the same aim. The physician never cures a patient; he assists nature by removing barriers or by stimulating a natural process. As ministers we attempt to place man in a more active relationship with God, that God may not only heal his body but his spirit. The physician and the minister, using different methods, work side by side toward the same ends.

Prayer is the minister's most effective way to put the patient in touch with the ongoing plans of the universe, which we call the Will of God. Such a relationship is hard to maintain; we know that well; but it is still harder to establish.

The following prayers are prepared for the sick and many of them have been used with patients. The patient himself should be encouraged to express his own prayer. While it is always the aim of the minister to make his people as independent of himself as possible, still he must not overlook the special situation of the sickroom. Some patients find difficulty in expressing their needs; others, even those who are religiously mature, are helped by the prayers of another; still others who are not able to concentrate upon formulating a prayer themselves will pray with you and receive help from a formal prayer. Always the minister must work in the light of the needs and condition of the patient.

Rest, sleep, patience, confidence, growth of the spirit, are some of the qualities most needed in illness, both for the recovery of health and for the acceptance of death. Here is a prayer for rest which contains quietness, application, reach, and the language of religion. Note the element of repetition and suggestion in it:

A Prayer for Rest

O God, I am weary with restlessness,
Make me to be still.
Make me to be at peace in my soul,
And my muscles to give over their tension;
Make me to know that as I rest upon my bed,
So I rest in Thee and in Thy support;

In Thy Peace I would abide all the days of my life,
In Thy House would I lie down unto deep slumber
As a guest rests after a weary journey;
And I would dwell in the House of the Lord forever.
Amen.

Here is a prayer for sleep which varies from the above only in point of emphasis and metaphor.

A Prayer for Sleep

Eternal and Everlasting God,
In the growing quietness of the evening and the
    deepening shadows of the night,
Grant us sleep and rest.
With the stilling of the day's doings, and the
    end of coming and going about us,
Make us to be sleepy with heavy eyes and tired limbs.
As Thy creatures are lying down in the wood,
As the bird is quiet in its nest
And the wild thing in its hole,
As the stream is still in its bed
Reflecting the great expanse of stars above,
May we in our sleep reflect our confidence in Thee,
And our assurance in Thy constant Peace.
In our sleep give us that deeper communion of our souls
With Thee which restoreth unto health.
In His name.   Amen.

One of the aims which, as above said, we consciously work to accomplish through the use of prayer is to establish or strengthen the patient's confidence in the physicians and nurses. Here is a prayer for this purpose.

A Prayer Before an Operation

Our Father, grant us thy peace,
Thou who dost wait upon us when we are restless
And who dost grant us courage when we are fearful.
Grant us quietness,
Grant us confidence,

Knowing that at this hour and in the days that are to follow
We are in worthy and capable hands.
Strengthen him who is to operate and those who are to
    serve as nurses;
We give ourselves into Thy sustaining presence;
I will lift up mine eyes unto the hills
From whence cometh my help.
My help cometh from the Lord
Maker of heaven and earth;
From the strength of the hills may we gather strength
And take unto ourselves their patience;
As the shepherd guardeth his sheep, so wilt Thou guard this one
Now and in the days that are to follow.
In the name of Jesus. Amen.

Another aim toward which we work through prayer is to maintain the patient's confidence in God. It is the task of keeping the patient from slipping back religiously.[1] We have heard many patients say, "I never doubted God until this experience." The loss of one's God in illness is far more serious that the loss of a limb or one's eyesight. Here is a prayer directed toward loneliness.

A Prayer for Companionship of the Spirit

Eternal Father,
Thou who art the companion of those who need Thee
Be our companion.
Pass with us through the valley of loneliness
And stand with us beyond its turmoil.
Stir us to find heaven in common things
And friendliness in the commonplace.
Make us to be friendly.
In the weary hours of dark nights
And the drudgery of slow turning days
We would remember Thee;
When others forget us in their business
Thou wilt not forget.
Build Thou within us a new companionship,
A companionship of the spirit.

[1] Chapter V, Spiritual Backsliding: Loneliness.

As the sea is to the ship,
As the air is to the bird
So art Thou unto us in our meditation.
So we would know Thee and Thy ways of working
For the sake of Jesus. Amen.

Here is a prayer directed against bitterness.

A Prayer for Understanding

Eternal and merciful Father;
Thou who dost wait upon us when we are distraught,
And who dost welcome us when we are discomfited,
Give us understanding.
Make us to be humble; make us to be as little children;
Still our spirit in its restlessness,
And make us to be generous with those who have misused us.
Forgive Thou our shortcomings,
For we know we are even more imperfect in Thy sight
        than we are in our own.
Make us to be understanding;
Broaden Thou our intent to forgive;
A lamp set in the midst of bitterness cannot be seen,
But a lamp of generosity gives light unto others.
We thank Thee, our Father, for understanding.
Amen. Amen.

One frequently hears a patient, usually suffering severe pain, say, "Why does God send this suffering to me," "What have I done to deserve such suffering," or, more forcibly, "Why am I punished." For a long time I accepted this question as one of those Old Testament ideas with which we are frequently confronted. I have now come to believe that such a statement is often a symptom of a sense of guilt. You will note the above questions are not followed by question-marks. They should not be, for they are not questions but statements. Most people who make them know several reasons why they might be punished. To attempt to brush away the question by saying, "That theory was exploded long ago," is to leave a thirsty spirit unwatered. If patients suffer from a sense of guilt, whether they are guilty in your eyes or not, is of no great importance. They are guilty in their own eyes and you must accept them there. Your task is to hold them up to the purifying Person of God as revealed in the New Testament, where God is forgiving. This can best be done by prayer following a form of confession which serves as a catharsis; this kind of prayer is the nearest the Protestant minister ever comes to pronouncing absolution.

A Prayer for Forgiveness

O most merciful Father,
Thou who art ever more willing to forgive than
    we are to ask,
Pardon us our transgressions.
In the lonely hours of forgetfulness
We have been unmindful of Thee
And of Thy commandments;
O God forgive us, we pray.
In our indifference we have been unfaithful to
    those we love,
And to Him who didst open our eyes to Thee,
Jesus Christ our Lord.
As a child plays and is burned,
As a child stumbles and falls,
So we are hurt by our willfulness:
Make us whole;
Give us strong limbs for walking,
And strong wills in the places we are weak.
Reward those we have hurt,
And make us strong to reward them ourselves.
We rejoice in the warmth of Thy affection
And in the peace of Thy forgiveness.
To Thee and to Jesus Christ, Thy son,
Be honor and glory, world without end.
Amen. Amen.

In almost every sickroom we find physical suffering. Patients behave toward pain in various ways. Some chafe under it, some are restless, some weep, some curse, some endure it quietly. Doctors have various methods of combating its deadly and persistent onslaught. These methods work better with some patients than with others. Probably there are few patients who suffer great pain for very long who do not pray in one way or another. Their prayer is frequently unsatisfactory because of the difficulty of gaining enough perspective for the poise which makes prayer effective. One of the needs of the sufferer is to accept his pain rather than to struggle against it. By accepting pain we mean overcoming one's fear of it, relaxing physically and mentally under it; a most difficult state to accomplish, and one which most of us can attain only after much suffering. Here is a prayer which may be used with a patient who is suffering from physical pain.

A Prayer to Accept Pain

Eternal God, whose days are without end, whose
      mercies without number,
We lift our minds to Thee in our stress:
Make us to be still before Thee,
Make us to fasten our minds upon Thy quietness;
Give us strength, O God, for the task which is ours.
Thy servant suffers from the pain.
Give him strength to endure;
Make fast his mind in Thee
And cause him to be strong in his endurance.
Thou art the water of life,
Whosoever drinketh of Thee shall not thirst;
As the tired sheep drinketh of the cool water
And rests beside the stream;
So we drink of Thy peace
And rest in the coolness of Thy presence.
In the name of that great shepherd of the sheep,
      Jesus Christ, Our Lord. Amen.

A Prayer for Patience to Overcome Handicap

O God of mercy, comfort us in our time of need;
We are bowed down in our misfortune.
We cling to Thee in our despair;
Thou who art with us when we are lonely,
Thou who dost forgive us when we are bitter,

Make us to have patience.
We bless Thee for Christ who did suffer upon the cross,
Yet was he lifted above his suffering;
Make us to know the meaning of the cross for ourselves.
Our friend doth suffer handicap
We know not why;
Make him to know that beyond the cross there is the resurrection,
Beyond the suffering of humility and imprisonment there is the
    new-won freedom of fortitude, of patience, of triumph.
Make him to turn his suffering to Thy glory
And the world will give praise for his devotion.
In the name of Jesus. Amen.

This prayer is considerably longer than the others but one feels justified in its use for the handicapped person who frequently does not suffer acute physical pain. The above prayer is an effort to put some meaning into such a condition, perhaps the only meaning possible in the light of the Christian conception of God.

Another use of prayer, perhaps the noblest of all its uses in the sickroom, is with the patient who is facing death. We believe the minister should consider it his duty and privilege to be present at, or as near as possible, the actual end of life, whether the patient dies in coma or not. The Protestant Church has been grossly neglectful of this responsibility. It should teach its people to expect such ministration. In another chapter we discuss some of the deeper problems of ministering to the dying, but we include here a group of prayers for such an occasion.[2] The following prayers were written for and used with a thirty-year-old nurse who knew that she was dying.[3] In this instance the patient had asked to see a minister before she was operated on; she lived about two weeks after the operation. The first prayer was used on Easter Day, after the patient had talked with the minister of dying. She had said she was not afraid.

A Prayer for One Dying on Easter Morning

Our Father, we are grateful for all Thou hast given us;
We thank Thee for the lessons of life,

[2] Chapter XXII. The Dying.   [3] J. L. Appendix A, p. 359.

For the friends we have known and the family we have possessed.
And above all we are thankful for Thee,
And for Thy abiding and eternal mercy unto us.
On this Easter Day we lift up our eyes unto Thee,
Thou who art near in life
And who art ever with us in death;
Unto Thee we remember our family,
Wouldst Thou abide with them and comfort them.
Unto Thee we commend our spirit,
Take us unto Thyself and comfort us
Thou who dost transcend life and death
And all things therein.
In the blessed name of Jesus. Amen.

A Prayer in the Evening

I am the resurrection and the life,
He that believeth in me shall never die
But shall have everlasting life.
Eternal Father, we lift up our eyes unto Thee in the quiet
    of the evening,
As the birds of the fields seek Thee for shelter,
As the ship sails upon the sea and comes to harbor,
So we come unto Thee and are comforted,
Knowing that underneath are Thy Everlasting Arms.
Give us rest in the night and in sleep envelop us,
And finally bring us unto eternal life.
Now may the Lord Jesus be and abide with us
In His grace, mercy and fellowship. Amen.

A Prayer in the Morning

I am the bread of life.
Whosoever drinketh of the water I shall give him shall not thirst;
But it shall become a well of living water, welling up unto eternal life.
Our Father, we have drunk deeply of the water Thou hast given us
And have felt its pull unto eternal life.
In the still of the morning give us comfort, ease us from the pain
And quiet us in the turmoil.
Thy peace be with us, the peace of the Lord Jesus and communion
    of the Holy Spirit. Amen.

A Prayer in the Afternoon

I am the resurrection and the life.
Whosoever believeth in me, though he die, yet shall he live.
I will lift up my countenance unto the Lord, yea unto Thee, Our
   Father, I would be lifted up,
That in Thy comfort I may dwell forever and in Thy peace have
   everlasting joy.
In Thee we are comforted and in Thee do we trust.
Thou who dost light the mysteries of the day,
And who dost sweep away the horrors of the night;
We commend our spirits unto Thee and unto Thy keeping. Amen.

A Prayer for Death

(Following the patient's request that I pray she might die that night.)

Eternal Father, hear this humble prayer of gratitude:
Wouldst Thou, in Thy great mercy and affection
Take this one unto Thyself,
Relieve her from the pain and the weariness.
For her great courage and endurance we are truly thankful;
In the quiet of the night may she go unto Thee,
And in her going may she not regret leaving her loved ones;
May she know they will come presently,
For we are all soon to follow.
But if it be not Thy will that she come unto Thee tonight,
Give her strength to complete the race so nobly thus far run.

The grace of the Lord Jesus be with thee,
The communion of the Holy Spirit uphold thee,
The love of God the Father possess thee,
And give thee peace. Amen.

A Prayer of Triumph

For so great a peace we are eternally thankful,
Our Father. Thou hast been good to us.
Wouldst Thou ease our weariness and give us rest eternal,
Thou who hast brought this one unto so noble an end.
May she now begin anew that which is without end,
The new life in the new day.

We commend her unto Thee;
In the name of Him who doth bear us up in the hour of
    our great need,
Jesus Christ, our Lord. Amen.

Some of the above prayers were used with members of the family present. We feel that this is desirable whenever it is possible. Much depends upon the family and on the attitude between patient and family. We believe that the minister should always acquaint the family with his ministry to a patient who is dying, for they may receive great comfort from knowing of the patient's attitude.

We have found that patients who are dying especially like the use of the benediction. A benediction, words loaded with a new richness of meaning in the face of death, seems to place a final stamp upon the past and point the patient toward the future. If the minister arrives just after a patient has died we believe that he should pronounce a benediction.

In the final analysis, adequate and effective prayer in the sickroom must grow out of adequate and effective prayer in the church. Occasionally we find a person who is ill and who has not had experience with prayer in the church; yet we not only use prayer effectively with him but teach him to pray himself. This is occasionally possible; but we believe it to be rare. Our most effective use of prayer in the sickroom is with those who already have an intelligent understanding of it, and who expect its use when they are ill. This understanding of prayer and its uses may be taught in the church school, in adult study classes, from the pulpit, and above all through prayers in the regular church services. Prayers should be said in church for those who are sick and for those who wait upon the sick, for doctors, for nurses, for the researches of science, and for the devotion of scientists to their work. Thus confidence in medical science will be maintained and practitioners of medicine will be reminded of their high task.

CHAPTER XVII

SCRIPTURE

AFTER we have established a satisfactory working relationship with an individual who is ill, after we have worked through preliminary difficulties, after we have come to understand him, his needs and his natural resources, after we have put his feet upon the path of spiritual growth, what then? Obviously we have merely started. We must do more than weed the ground, stir the soil, and sow the seed. We must not withdraw from the scene before the seed thrusts up its delicate shoot. We must continue to stimulate its growth. We must come to its aid after the wind and hail have had their go. We must: but how can we? What are our resources to assist in the spiritual growth of an individual?

We have spoken of prayer. Prayer is the minister's greatest single method in work with the sick. It is not the one he will use most often, or the one which should be most helpful to him in understanding his task. Prayer is the method which is most satisfactory in extreme crises; that which may be gained through it is most needed in the sickroom at all times; it is uniquely the minister's greatest method.

There is a resource upon which we may draw to support the attainment of prayer. There are times when a sufferer does not want to pray, times when he wants to meditate, think, brood over something beyond himself. We need a spiritual training ground, so to speak, a field for thought, where we go to discipline our spiritual lungs, to harden our spiritual muscles, to build up our spiritual determination, that we may be equal to the hard race before us. Protestants have always had the Bible as that training field.

The Bible can be used effectively with the sick, but not wholesale. A Jewish girl who knew little of religion and nothing of the Bible asked a minister for something to read which would help to maintain her courage through a difficult illness. The minister gave her a Bible saying, "Read this. Read anywhere in it. It's all good."

We have already referred to the need for "perspective" in illness,[1] and we have said that the minister has a "perspective" from which he can listen.[2] Perspective, we believe, can be gained through the use of Scripture. Perspective is seeing life steadily and seeing it whole. A philosophy of life some call it. It is the ability to accept life as it comes, and then to stretch one's imagination and one's thought beyond the immediate. We can say to a patient who is suffering great pain, "Do not think about your pain." But he cannot follow such advice without perspective. The person who faces a surgical operation must prepare himself mentally for the operation as best he can. Patients are sometimes permitted to go home for a few days or weeks between the time a diagnosis is made and the time for the operation to be performed. Others are given two or three days in the hospital before the operation. This seems to us to be wise, although apparently it is done to await the result of certain necessary tests and examinations, rather than to give a patient time to prepare himself psychologically for the operation. On several occasions I (R. L. D.) have been called at their own request to see patients who were facing surgical operations. Each time I have thought that their diagnosis of their need was correct: they needed the help of religion to gain a perspective from which they could view the experience they were facing. They needed to see life steadily. They needed to have called to their minds the stability of God. "I am thy rock and thy fortress." In such instances people do not want religion urged or lectured into them. They do not want it in the words of the minister but in terms they have always heard, terms which speak for themselves.

[1] Chapter XVI, Prayer, page 222.
[2] Chapter XIV, Listening, page 190.

If a sufferer can put his mind to the following verse, from the 90th Psalm, cling to it, repeat it, turn it over in his mind, even as he thinks of it he will be beyond his lone room with its four surrounding walls. The operation he is facing, or the pain he is suffering will dwindle toward insignificance:

> Lord thou hast been our dwelling-place
> In all generations.
> Before the mountains were brought forth,
> Or ever thou hast formed the earth and the world,
> Even from everlasting to everlasting thou art God.

On the night before one of my operations I (R. L. D.) was able to attain perspective and to get sleep by reminding myself that five years from that night I should look back upon the experience with indifference. "Five years from now," I repeatedly told myself, "how unimportant tomorrow morning will be! Even if I am dead, how unimportant this operation with its horror of enforced anesthesia will be." When we describe perspective as seeing life from the viewpoint of a future date we are reminded of those patients who are handicapped for life. I think of seven whom I know at the present time, all less than thirty-five years old. Such patients get along very well so long as they do not think of the future. The future, five or ten years hence, for them means a continuance of their present handicap; death is the next significant event, and they often become impatient for its advent. They have not gained enough perspective. They see only what they have lost, not what they can make of that loss, to their own benefit and to the benefit of the world.

A crippling wound, a coming torture takes on its proper proportions when viewed as part of a whole life. Jesus attained a perspective by going into the mountains; there he saw the road that he must follow. What did it matter to him that that road carried him to death? Death for him was not an end but an event. When Peter's world fell to pieces around him he went back to his old trade, "fishing." His Master had been killed, his own hopes had been shattered, and he himself had deserted his Master in the hour of crisis. He wanted to get away from it all, to let the wind whip about his face, to feel the pull of dragging nets upon his muscles, and so to *rest* his weary spirit. Then he would see life steadily again. Some of us gain this perspective through music, some through drama, some through reading, some through strenuous physical exercise. The feverish, restless patient cannot read, or go to the movies, or to the mountains. But he can have what Jesus found there: not the air of the hills but the mood of the hills, their patience, their eternity. That is what we would carry to the sick-room.

To suggest a perspective there are certain great truths we would recall to the sufferer's mind. These truths are best approached through Biblical passages which are the heritage of our religion and which are familiar to everyone. These passages can be quoted by the minister to those facing operation, to those suffering intense pain, to those critically ill and in a semiconscious state, and to those in convalescence who need a thought to which they can tie their minds.

Confidence in God

The Lord is my shepherd; I shall not want.
He maketh me to lie down in green pastures: He leadeth me
    beside the still waters.
He restoreth my soul: He guideth me in the paths of
    righteousness for his name's sake.
Yea, though I walk through the valley of the shadow of death,
I will fear no evil; for thou art with me:
Thy rod and thy staff, they comfort me.
Thou preparest a table before me in the presence of mine
    enemies:
Thou anointest my head with oil; my cup runneth over.
Surely goodness and mercy shall follow me all the days of my life:
And I will dwell in the house of the Lord for ever.

                                       Psalm 23.

The Eternity of God

Lord, thou hast been our dwelling place
In all generations.
Before the mountains were brought forth,
Or ever thou hadst formed the earth and the world,
Even from everlasting to everlasting, thou art God.
For a thousand years in thy sight
Are but as yesterday when it is past,
And as a watch in the night.

Psalm 90, 1-2, 4.

God as My Fortress

He that dwelleth in the secret place of the Most High
Shall abide under the shadow of the Almighty.
I will say of the Lord, He is my refuge and my fortress;
My God, in whom I trust.
For he shall deliver thee from the snare of the fowler,
And from the noisome pestilence.
He shall cover thee with his pinions,
And under his wings shalt thou take refuge:
His truth shall be thy shield and buckler.

Psalm 91:1-4.

My Strength Cometh from God

I will lift up mine eyes unto the hills:
From whence cometh my help.
My help cometh from the Lord,
Which made heaven and earth.
He will not suffer thy foot to be moved:
He that keepeth thee will not slumber.
Behold, he that keepeth Israel shall neither slumber nor sleep.
The Lord is thy keeper: The Lord is thy shade upon thy right hand.
The sun shall not smite thee by day, nor the moon by night.
The Lord shall keep thee from all evil; He shall preserve thy soul.
The Lord shall keep thy going out and thy coming in,
From this time forth and for evermore.

Psalm 121.

A Benediction

God be merciful unto us, and bless us;
And cause his face to shine upon us;
That Thy way may be known upon earth,
Thy saving health among all nations.

Psalm 67:1-2.

Freedom from Worry: Nature and Man: Working Together

And he said, So is the kingdom of God, as if a man should cast seed upon the earth; and should sleep and rise night and day, and the seed should spring up and grow, he knoweth not how. The earth beareth fruit of herself; first the blade, then the ear, then the full corn in the ear. But when the fruit is ripe, straightway he putteth forth the sickle, because the harvest is come.—Mark, 4:26-29.

Release from Worry: God's Care: Forget Today's Concern

(It is well to divide the passage.)

Therefore I say unto you, Be not anxious for your life, what ye shall eat, or what ye shall drink; nor yet for your body, what ye shall put on. Is not the life more than the food, and the body more than the raiment?

Behold the birds of the heaven, that they sow not, neither do they reap, nor gather into barns; yet your heavenly Father feedeth them. Are not ye of much more value than they?

And which of you by being anxious can add one cubit unto his stature?—Matthew 6:25-27.

And why are ye anxious concerning raiment? Consider the lilies of the field, how they grow; they toil not, neither do they spin: yet I say unto you, that even Solomon in all his glory was not arrayed like one of these. But if God doth so clothe the grass of the field, which today is, and tomorrow is cast into the oven, shall he not much more clothe you, O ye of little faith?

Be not therefore anxious, saying, What shall we eat? or, What shall we drink? or, Wherewithal shall we be clothed? For after all these things do the Gentiles seek; for your heavenly Father knoweth that ye have need of all these things. But seek ye first the Kingdom of God and his righteousness; and all these things shall be added unto you.

Be not therefore anxious for the morrow: for the morrow will be anxious for itself. Sufficient unto the day is the evil thereof.—Matthew 6:28-34.

Ask and Receive

Ask, and it shall be given you; seek, and ye shall find; knock, and it shall be opened unto you: for every one that asketh receiveth; and he that seeketh findeth; and to him that knocketh it shall be opened.—Matthew 7:7-8; Luke 11:9-10.

Unto the Weary and Contrite

Come unto me, all ye that labor and are heavy laden and I will give you rest. Take my yoke upon you, and learn of me; for I am meek and lowly in heart: and ye shall find rest unto your souls. For my yoke is easy and my burden is light.—Matthew 11:28-30.

On Faith

Then came the disciples to Jesus apart, and said, Why could not we cast it out? And he saith unto them, Because of your little faith: for verily I say unto you, If ye have faith as a grain of mustard seed, ye shall say unto this mountain, Remove hence to yonder place; and it shall remove; and nothing shall be impossible unto you.—Matthew 17:19-20.

Conditions of the Spirit

Blessed are the poor in spirit: for theirs is the kingdom of heaven.
Blessed are they that mourn: for they shall be comforted.
Blessed are the meek: for they shall inherit the earth.
                              —Matthew 5:3-5.

For Commending Courage, or Suggesting Courage

Ye are the light of the world. A city set on a hill cannot be hid. Neither do men light a lamp, and put it under the bushel, but on the stand; and it shineth unto all that are in the house. Even so let your light shine before men, that they may see your good works, and glorify your Father which is in heaven.—Matthew 5:14-16.

When we wish to quiet people who are seriously ill it is well to remember Matthew 5:21-24, lest as they seek to quiet themselves they remember they have "aught against their brother." Particularly it is well to inquire of those who send for you, when they are facing death, if there is a message you might take for them. This work of reconciliation may be of great help in releasing tension from brooding or newly awakened consciences. The shocks of illness, and the opportunity for brooding, may have reopened old wounds.

The Troubled Spirit

Ye have heard that it was said to them of old time, Thou shalt not kill; and whosoever shall kill shall be in danger of the judgement: but I say unto you, that every one who is angry with his brother shall be in danger of the judgement; and whosoever shall say to his brother, Raca, shall be in danger of the council; and whosoever shall say, Thou fool, shall be in danger of the hell of fire. If therefore thou art offering thy gift at the altar, and there rememberest that thy brother hath anything against thee, leave there thy gift before the altar, and go thy way, first be reconciled to thy brother, and then come and offer thy gift.—Matthew 5:21-24.

Peace and Quietness

Peace I leave with you; my peace I give unto you: not as the world giveth, give I unto you. Let not your heart be troubled, neither let it be fearful.—John 14:27.

These things have I spoken unto you, that in me ye may have peace. In the world ye have tribulation: but be of good cheer; I have overcome the world.—John 16:33.

A longer passage which may be used for purposes of attaining quietness and to restore or instill confidence is that beginning: "I am the true vine and my Father is the husbandman."—(John 15:1-7, 9.) Also: "Let not your heart be troubled: ye believe in God, believe also in me." (John 4:1-4.)

For Courage and Strength

But whosoever drinketh of the water that I shall give him shall never thirst; but the water that I shall give him shall become in him a well of water springing up unto eternal life.—John 4:14.

Jesus said unto them, I am the bread of life: he that cometh to me shall not hunger, and he that believeth on me shall never thirst.

—John 6:35.

I am the good shepherd: the good shepherd layeth down his life for the sheep.—John 10:11.

Eternal Life

Jesus said unto her, I am the resurrection, and the life: he that believeth on me, though he die, yet shall he live: and whosoever liveth and believeth on me shall never die.—John 11:25-26.

A second great need of the sick which we may use Scripture to meet we referred to earlier: the need for a spiritual training field, where muscles may be stretched, lungs expanded, determination set. This is a need especially for the patient who faces the remainder of his life handicapped if not totally disabled. What is there in life for the totally disabled? Why must he continue to live, a burden upon those around him, a misery to himself? To what can he give his mind and thought if he is totally disabled?

Our Catholic friends have an answer: one may give oneself to holiness. For many Protestants such a suggestion falls on deaf ears. Holiness, if it means anything to the Protestant, means something remote, something which he associates with medieval mystics, monasteries, and convents. The Catholic is more familiar with "retreats," with days and weeks spent in discipline and prayer. If the Protestant prays at all he gives only a few minutes to it in the early morning or late evening. Usually it is reserved for Sunday morning or often left entirely to some one else. The Catholic prays to the saints known and unknown; he prays for the dead and dying; he prays for the living, their past and their future; he prays because of the habit of prayer and for the sheer joy of praying. A life of holiness for the Catholic is a life of prayer and meditation: prayer whose residuum is deposited to the credit of those prayed for. The Catholic knows what to do with a life that is handicapped, total physical disability notwithstanding.

What have Protestants which is equivalent to this conception of holiness? We have, if we claim it, this same conception of holiness which we hold in common with our Catholic forbears. As a means to this we suggest the need of a spiritual training field; a body of material to which the Protestant patient may give his attention and devotion. Protestants have used the Bible for this purpose in the past, but with the advent of the modern era with its manifold distractions the Bible has become a book of the shelf, a book to own and perhaps reverence but seldom to read. The life of Jesus, standing at the center of the New Testament and Christianity, affords the best possible center of interest for study. The text is easily available. In addition there are numerous books and studies written every year on the life of Jesus which may be used to stimulate such thought. Attention to other great religious characters should follow a study of the life of Jesus: St. Paul, Jeremiah, Amos, Hosea, Job. The Bible offers us our spiritual training field; it is peopled with spiritual heroes who supply both inspiration and suggestion for a lifetime of thought. Why should one need to be active physically for such an investigation? One of the factors which seem to make religious thought so shallow in our day is that people have too many things to do. It is conceivable that the religious giants of the future, as has often been true of the past, will be those who are handicapped or physically disabled. Perhaps we shall have something to thank the automobile and its growing list of accident victims for after all.

CHAPTER XVIII

NOTE-WRITING

NOTE-WRITING is primarily a process by which the minister subjects his work with an individual to examination. This examination is the nearest approach to an objective check upon the minister's work which we have been able to discover. Note-writing is the development on paper of one's work with a given patient after that work is done. When we reproduce in writing a contact, an interview, a working relationship, we do not merely record it, we rethink it and so develop its meaning, *not while we are seeing a patient but as soon after as possible.*

Note-writing contains four values: it is a check upon one's work; it is a clarifying and developing process; it relieves emotional strain for the writer; the notes stand as a record of one's work.

I. NOTE-WRITING AS A CHECK UPON ONE'S WORK

The clerical profession has no good method by which to test its work. The physician has the autopsy table, the engineer has mathematics, the banker has auditors. But the minister has nothing except pews, full or empty, and empty pews may mean anything from a beautiful Sunday morning to the recent opening of a municipal golf course.

The proper use of note-writing enables one to check one's skill, one's understanding, and one's devotion with a given patient. The minister's skill, like that of any other worker, depends upon the understanding which directs it. A surgeon's operative technique avails nothing without a knowledge of what certain signs mean and without courage to vary that technique as occasion demands. Skill in the minister's work with the sick is the way in which he conducts himself in the sickroom. Some call this an "intuitive feeling" toward a patient. So far as we have been able to discover, "intuition," means simply the amount of skill and understanding the minister brings to a sickroom. Can he discover what a patient has in his mind? Is the patient worried, is he bored, is he lonely? Can the minister follow leads, or deliberately keep from following leads, which is often more desirable? Can he permit the patient to choose the topic of conversation and encourage him to follow through to its natural conclusions?

Skill, again, is the ability to discover a mood or an attitude and then to change it. Holding an ideal for a patient, skill is the ability to move toward that ideal with him.

A fifty-year-old divorced seamstress who refused to eat was called to our attention. After an operation for stone in the bladder she had been placed on a special diet. At the end of three weeks she found it impossible to retain the little food she attempted to eat. One of our theological students [1] went to see her. Between her attacks of nausea he told her who he was; she inquired how he came to know about her; he told her the head nurse had suggested that he see her. She was interested.

"You know about my case?"

"Only that you have been quite ill, and that your recovery depends upon your co-operation."

"I expect you're right." Then presently she said, "I used to think I would get well, but now I don't know. . . . I may be dying and don't know it." (Defiantly.) "I don't care." Again she inquired how the nurse had come to mention her.

Two days later when she was seen again she said, "I'm afraid I'm fighting a losing battle. I don't know if I will live. Maybe the doctors know but won't tell me."

"The doctors are trying their best to help you."

"I know, and I'll try."

He led her on to talk of her brothers, joking about how much fun

[1] See Appendix B.

she must have had in a large family of boys. At the end of six days, during which time he had seen her four times, she was eating better, had stopped talking about death, and was taking more interest in her surroundings. She was transferred shortly after this to a nursing home where she improved rapidly.

After the student's first visit it was obvious, once the interview was reproduced on paper, that Mrs. H. was worried about herself, and that she was impressed by the fact that she had been sought out. Her remark at the second visit in regard to the doctors, gives us further information. We then conclude: She had been on a special diet, during which time she probably received little medical attention, as the doctors were waiting for the twenty-one days to pass. But *she* had to live those three weeks. When she was given food at the end of that time she refused to eat. She thought that they had tried to starve her. Very well, starve she would; what did she care? But . . . she is interested in how she came to be sought out. She is really encouraged about her future because she finds that the doctors are reassuring when they talk to the student about her, as well as when they talk directly to her. "They wouldn't try to fool *you*."

A little time and skill turned her thoughts to her family and to her place in the family as a child.

An intelligent minister might have covered this same course with Mrs. H. without the use of notes, had he been a good listener, but he would have worked largely in the dark. Study of our notes after the first call showed us where this patient was and what her needs were. Our beliefs were verified by information received upon the second call. This showed the seriousness of her suffering, and the importance of seeing her frequently. When the doctor was sought out he said, "She is a psychiatric case. If she would eat she would get well." These notes illustrate both skill and understanding on the part of the minister. To write notes throws into relief the presence or absence of such skill and understanding. It shows whether one has let oneself and one's own prejudices, fears, apprehensions, get in the way. It reveals why one is not able to use the skill one has, and where one's skill has gone astray.

Understanding and skill are so closely interwoven that it is difficult to discuss them separately, for every move one makes in the sickroom is dependent upon one's understanding of the needs there. As notes are written one sees how much those needs have been understood. Such understanding depends upon a knowledge of people, both well and ill. It depends upon past experience, upon imagination, upon insight into the wellsprings of living water, and how those can be tapped through prayer or quietness. From this general knowledge one brings understanding to the sickroom. Notes written shortly after a visit check the extent of that understanding and reveal its limits. To find the limits of one's understanding does something to it, as we shall presently suggest.

Note-writing measures the minister's devotion to a task. Some may be startled by the suggestion that the minister, or any other professional worker, needs to estimate his devotion to a task. But such is the case in the minister's work as with other work: it is easy to forget one's purpose in seeing a patient. In fact it is easy to forget certain patients altogether. Protestant ministers are often accused of making merely social calls upon the sick; it is said that we are afraid to speak of God, to pray, or to administer the communion service. We have tried to make it clear in preceding chapters that our methods, our efforts to describe needs, and our ways of meeting them, are pointed toward overcoming this tendency to "visit." On the other hand, we are certain that any spiritual prescription taken to the sick at all times and under all conditions does not meet the needs of the sufferer. Notes, written outside the stress of the sickroom itself, reveal to the writer whether he had a clear purpose in seeing a patient, whether he discovered the needs of that patient, whether he held himself and the patient to an attempt to meet that need.

II. NOTE-WRITING AS CREATION

By what magic, it may be asked, does note-writing reach these highly desirable ends? Granted that we need to raise our standard of performance in skill, understanding and devotion, how can we do this merely by writing down what we have done? What is done *is* done. Why go back to it and duplicate it in laborious script? Our answer is that good note-writing is not merely a record of what is past and done with. It is a new creation of ideas which reveal lacks in what we have done. It is a fresh application of ideals to criticize what was done. It traces out the implications of what we have seen and heard. At one point the patient said merely, "No." What was implied in that? At another point he praised us. What can we make of that praise and how can we check the truth of our conjecture in our next interview?

Note-writing finds holes and plans to fill them up. It is self-criticism. It is self-revelation. It is preparation for self-improvement. In all these acts it ties us down to black and white and so to definiteness where thought is vague and lapsing. Lapsing, forgetting, is one of the cardinal sins of thought, next to self-deception its greatest sin. Impressions gained at the bedside begin to fade away the instant we leave it. Nascent ideas about those impressions die early unless carefully tended by note-writing. The infant mortality of newborn ideas is enormous. We reduce it by devotion to the new life. Note-writing is an essential part of this devotion.

Periodic recall is another. If we do not allow our minds to get cluttered and distracted with a multitude of sights, sounds, and smells, they will go on working fruitfully on whatever we tell them to mature. It is fashionable to call this work unconscious, but the unconscious mind is not such a fool as we try to make it. It works on what *we* are most interested in, and if we speak severely to it, it minds. Ask it for conclusions about a job given it some hours earlier and it has something worth while to say. Moreover it volunteers ideas without being asked for them, and in the middle of a journey in another direction. On a walk, at a game or at a meal we are rung up to take a message from an idea started at work by us the day before. Most of us get our best ideas when we are not thinking at all, provided we have previously set those ideas to work and told them to report at their convenience. Many of us have too little system in the household of our ideas. They are not assigned to definite jobs or told to report on them.

What has all this to do with note-writing? This: When the nascent idea has been given its task, has done it and reported, it will not go on working unless its report is recorded and developed by writing it out as far as its energy goes. Periodic assignment of problems to be worked out in one's own mind when "we" are not "thinking of them," periodic report on them and then full record of the report, is like the game of question-and-answer in which good thinking rejoices. Note-writing banks the profits.

Moreover, expression clarifies our purpose. Until we set it down in the challenging plainness of script we know only the fringes of what we intend. For any valuable purpose is like one of the rocketing spurts of water that shoot out from the descending mass of a waterfall. It is an individual yet it emerges from the greater body of one's life purpose. It has been set to work today, but if it is good for anything it reaches back at least to the yeasty fomentation-time of adolescence. It reaches forward too, for it is born in sight of the future which it will help to create. The more accurately we foresee, step by step, the results to follow if we act on our plan, the more strictly its features will be carved out by our forecast of that future. A hundred plans are born for everyone that can survive the accurate calculus of its results, its disasters or self-contradictions, its sins of omission and of commission.

The plain unvarnished truth is that when we set ourselves to work on a job such as confronts one in a sickroom we know only a fraction of what we are about. We do not mean by this that the sick person himself is a mystery to us, though that is also a fact. We mean that our own aspiration to help him is a mystery to us. Something pushes us into that room, something that started years ago in first love or first shame. But what we do and say when we get in there is terribly apt to be not the child of that aspiration but another's child—the offspring of convention, stale habit and embarrassment. Perhaps it is fortunate that we do not reveal to the patient in words the purpose with which we enter his room. It might shock him. We are not much concerned about his knowing it, but about our knowing it in all its austere beauty. For if ever we know God's holiness it is in the adventurous hopes that He puts into our minds on the threshold of a sickroom, provided we empty ourselves for His replenishment. We are often ashamed of them, scared at their command, aghast at their boldness. We shrink back into safe and sane mediocrity. But if we write out our plans beforehand and if we write them after the visit, they will not shrink so pitifully.

Many people we are inclined to believe, think best with a pen in hand. Note-writing as we are here describing it, trains our ability to recall, compels us systematically to re-experience our work in the sickroom. Some say they have no memory for recalling the material covered in an interview with a patient. Such an objection has been disproved by the large number of theological students whom we have succeeded in teaching to use this method. We have met with only one exception, a man who had an abhorrence of all writing, including examination, letter, and sermon writing.

Rethinking an experience on paper brings to one's mind certain significant underlying elements which at the time had been passed over. Often we have left a room confused in mind as to the meaning of certain things that have just happened. Upon writing our notes the confusion has cleared away. Sometimes our notes have sent us back to the patient in quest of the meaning of a reference or to investigate the patient's failure to mention a significant person or an experience that we knew should be present in the patient's story. One patient, a Protestant clergyman, repeatedly spoke of his inclination to become a Roman Catholic priest, but he also mentioned each time the defects in his intellectual make-up which prohibited his going into the priesthood. Though he was a married man he never referred to the celibacy of the Roman Catholic priesthood. He made many references to his daughter but none to his wife. We overlooked this connecting link until three contacts had been reproduced on paper. Then as we studied the notes we became aware of "a missing wife" and went in search of her.

Our most significant and frequent discovery through the writing of notes answers the question why we do or do not get on with a patient; why we are not accepted and welcomed by a patient or why we are not making progress with him. I (R.L.D.) worked for eight months with one patient, seeing him on an average of twice a week, before we ever came to discuss fundamentals. As individuals we were on the best of terms. As a sufferer and a clergyman we were far apart. I did not write notes on my work with this patient. If I had, I am sure the time would have been much briefer before we began talking of what his illness meant and what he was to do about it.

So far my (R.L.D.) most significant discovery through the use of notes had to do with R., a young mother who died as a result of a lung abscess. She never accepted my student or myself as ministers. She always held us at arm's length. In going through our notes on this patient the night before her death I found repeated references to her baby, husband, and father, and references to her married life. Later I made inquiries about this and found that I had been right in judging it to have been unhappy. While it is not probable that her unhappiness directly caused her death it is certain that it contributed to make her give up a difficult struggle too easily. The surgeon who treated her spoke to me of the necessity of keeping up her spirit. The earlier discovery of what I now consider to have been her secret, purposely guarded because of her unwillingness to face it, might have saved her life. Certainly we should be better pleased with our work with this patient could we have helped her to be more honest with herself.[2]

This type of discovery through the use of notes is the kind which one may make after many visits to a patient, when one comes to fit the pieces together. By and large those are the most significant benefits of note-writing, but it also enlarges our understanding of a given patient and his needs in the early days of an illness or of one's work with him. Usually as the summary is written (we shall presently cite an outline) one's mind sees the outline of the individual one is thinking about, or discovers that one cannot grasp it. Why not? Back we go at our next visit with a purpose. Or we may go back to the notes themselves for an answer. Thus note-writing in

[2] See p. 301.

work with the sick is an experience of growth in understanding on the part of the writer.

III. NOTE-WRITING AS A RELEASE FROM STRAIN

Much of the minister's work with the sick is done under conditions which are emotional; much of the material with which he is dealing is highly dramatic. Frequently we are asked, "How do you stand up under such work day in and day out?" Occasionally the strain does tell, but as our skill develops, as we become accustomed to the needs of the sick and the conditions of the sickroom, much of this strain is relieved. There still remains the stress of individual situations which must be taken care of. Active faith and prayer do much to relieve us, but we have found that note-writing also helps to lighten this excessive emotional load. Note-writing helps us to gain and to maintain an objectivity which is necessary if we are to work effectively in this field.

This is largely possible for three reasons: (1) Note-writing relieves one's mind from carrying the details of what has happened in work with a given person. (2) Notes show one the next step, as we pointed out above, by checking one's understanding. To know that one gives the best that one has is a relief. (3) The actual experience of note-writing, aside from helping creative thought, relieves emotion just as it does to tell some understanding listener of a problem one is facing. This is possible because of the creative experience which comes in careful rethinking. As we have said, "getting a thing off one's chest" is effective only when that thing is better understood or rethought. The penitent feels better after the confession because he has exposed his sin to the clear light of day. He sees that in the penetrating light of the New Testament there is a way past, around, or through that which blocked his path.

In note-writing one exposes problems, say the patient's nebulous needs, to the clear, calm, penetrating light of ink on paper. When those needs stand out clearly, we see that the impending death of a patient is tragic in the way that death is met, not in death itself. When a patient dies nobly and with beauty of character, where is the tragedy of his death? In the agony of those who wait near-by. We rise from our note-writing relieved of an emotional strain because we see work to be done, we go to the family and there, through companionship and faith, help them to bear their loss.

The notes of my (R.L.D.) work with J. L. (page 359) reveal a situation charged with human pathos. Yet the hope of bringing comfort to patient and family depended upon the minister's freedom from that pathos. This was accomplished partially by writing notes of J. L.'s conversation and of the prayers which I used. These notes showed me her spiritual growth. They showed the gain she was making and the spiritual stimulus, insofar as words can ever tell, which was brought her. The objectivity of note-writing regularly relieved the emotional load which I accepted each time I saw her.

On the other hand, it must be said that note-writing may cause emotional concern on the part of a conscientious worker by showing him his failures. There is a group of persons about whose condition one can do nothing. A clear recognition of this fact is usually sufficient to send one on to more profitable work. But sometimes one finds through note-writing that had one been a little more wise, a little more persistent, a little more devoted, one might have succeeded where one must recognize failure.

Our experience with R. spoken of above (page 251) is the most outstanding instance of this we have known. After her death I relieved my feeling of humiliation at our failure by writing a prayer dedicated to her and to all those who suffer as she did, and by making a summary of our work with her and of the signs we should have read, so that we may avoid repeating that mistake. One learns from one's failures; yes, provided one objectifies, studies, and preserves those failures on paper.

IV. NOTE-WRITING AS A RECORD

Notes also stand as a record. Our memory often plays us false. A glance at our notes just before we go to a patient, when many things have happened since we last saw him, refreshes our grasp of his thought and need. But although such a refreshment in itself justifies the use of this method, we emphasize note-writing more because of what it does for our understanding of a patient than for the record itself. With the growing use of written records by psychiatrists and social workers, ministers are now being urged to keep a record of their work. They are being criticized for carelessness, for not knowing why they are or are not effective. Written records would tell the story. We see legitimate objections to written records of *all* the minister's work with individuals, yet we believe the statement that the minister does not know why he does effective work is a true one. In fact we believe that until the minister develops a method of keeping records of his work with individuals he has no right to claim a place for himself among skilled workers in the field of human personality. Without records he has no objective check upon his work.

Can the minister keep a written record of his work? Of course he can! What will go into his records will be different from what goes into the medical, psychiatric or social record. We are here writing about the use of notes in work with the sick, but the same suggestions are valid for work with anyone who is in difficulty or facing a problem. For this book, however, we limit our suggestions to a use of the method in work with the sick.

Who should read the minister's notes? The minister should read them. He should write notes for the benefit he receives from them in understanding the individual with whom he is working, and how the needs found there can be fulfilled. That is why we suggest a new term. Instead of "record-writing" with the emphasis upon *record,* we speak of note-writing, with the emphasis upon the *writing.* Written notes are for the minister's own use. They are not to be passed on; they are not for purposes of research, except insofar as every minister is a searcher. The minister's notes should not even be passed on to his successor lest they be misused or misunderstood.

Many of them will be too private or too much mingled with surmise to bear the sight of another eye. But surely they could not be more private than a doctor's, and if doctors can keep written secrets why not ministers? Some doctors do not make notes of very private matters, but these are the very same doctors who write the fullest notes on the less private aspects of their patients' lives. Privacy from others is an essential part of every professional man's conscience, but beware of privacy from oneself! That's the choicest wile of the devil. Because there is much that others should not hear we put the soft pedal on our own self-accusations or the whispered hints of alarming new ideas. So we reduce ourselves to the commonplace beings whom we allow to usurp our job. We are afraid (like the monkeys, 'tis said) to speak and still more to write, because we are afraid of the work this will entail; not the work of writing but the new acts of forgiveness, of one-hundred-per-cent. veracity with ourselves. We need to be reserved with others. Yes, surely. But no reserves with God, and if we are to be frank with Him we shall hold our grip on the climbing spiral of confession by putting word after word on paper. Written words are like stairs. One foot rests firmly on the last step without danger of lapse while the other foot reaches up for the next.

V. WHAT NOTES SHOULD CONTAIN

Because our notes are written not only as a record but as a check upon our work and as a method of disciplining ourselves to recall and interpret it, we suggest the outline given on page 256. An outline should attempt to be suggestive, never exhaustive. It is a reminder, not a straitjacket. To have filled in an outline does not mean that we understand the material in it nor that we have done a good job.

Our outline is modeled on the chronological type of recording used by some social service departments. "Situations in which the client-worker relationship is the most important element may preferably be reported chronologically, since the chronological record shows more clearly than any other the way in which a contact is built up and the psychological developments in a case. Care is always necessary, however, to prevent it *from becoming diffuse and wordy.*" [3]

The minister is interested in information about the patient, his financial condition, his family, the onset of his disease, insofar as they influence his illness.[4] He is interested in the patient's present physical and mental condition, his spiritual and mental resources and how they can be brought into play to meet his need. What about the resources of the universe? The God within and the God without? The God within is the channel, the means of transportation to the God without. It is our purpose to bring these two into closer touch.

We want to know the patient's belief; his past experience with prayer; his experience with religion; his thought of God; his attitude toward his family, his friends, his physician; his attitude toward life, what he gives and what he receives from it. These and many other things we hope to learn from the patient sooner or later. The very discovery of answers to these questions should carry the patient and minister far in their working relationship. But lest someone go to a sufferer, call these questions off, and write down the answers, we strongly advise against listing them.

Chronological Outline

To remind the minister of certain important items in his work with the sick.

1. Name, age, sex, married, occupation, family, church member, physical condition (diagnosis), prognosis.
2. *Reasons for seeing the patient:* how patient came to attention of minister. *Problem* as described by whoever asked minister to see patient (member of family, patient himself, doctor, nurse, social worker, friend).
3. *First impression:* description and physical appearance. (If minister has not seen patient before, a first impression should be recorded; after that every time the patient is seen his impression should be

[3] Harriett M. Bartlett, in manuscript notes on recording in medical social work.

[4] As a leader and teacher in the community he must be interested also in the financial and sociological conditions which affect his fellow men. But in the sickroom he need not spend time searching into the causes of poverty or of any other social problem.

noted: how was minister received, explanation minister makes to patient, etc.)

4. *What happened.* (At this place should be written the main body of notes. Note whether you directed patient's thought or whether you simply listened. Show topics patient discussed, citing as many direct quotations as possible, giving worker's questions in direct quotation also.)

5. *Summary:*
   (a) Material revealed, problem as observed; needs of patient.
   (b) How can these needs be met, patient's resources, estimated intellectual capacity, attitude toward people, religious beliefs.
   (c) Brief description of patient and of this visit: Did patient seem glad to see you?

Paragraphs 1, 2, and 3 of the above outline should be used for the first interview, especially if you have not known the patient before. Paragraph 1 is only of routine importance; often it will not be filled in until after several contacts. Paragraph 4 is of major importance and should be in mind throughout one's use of this outline and method. Paragraph 5, or parts of it, should be used especially during one's early contacts, when one is trying to discover a patient's needs and to estimate his spiritual resources. Periodically the summary given in Paragraph 5 should be rewritten, lest this method become merely a recording process. A complete summary, say every five or six contacts, depending upon the nature of the illness and its significance to the sufferer, helps the worker to examine and to deepen his understanding of a patient. *After one has used the method with forty or fifty patients, one may begin to shorten it,* selecting material of special value. As experience accumulates we learn to recognize significant material especially for Paragraph 4. But at first even vague descriptions may be important. They preserve something which may otherwise be overlooked.

Following are notes made on a first contact with a patient, and showing the use of the chronological outline. They illustrate certain mistakes and are selected for that reason.

1. R. A. E.,[5] 64, woman, unmarried, shopkeeper, not an active church member, two sisters, one brother; diagnosis, cancer of the stomach.

2. *Reasons for seeing patient:* Miss D., social worker, told me about patient, saying she was to be operated on in two days, that she had been brought up a Baptist but now claims to have lost her faith, that she is resigned to death; however, Miss D. feels that she has not given up hope of living.

   When I inquired for patient the head nurse said, "She is a grand old maid." Patient was in a small room off the main ward. The head nurse took me to her room and introduced me, saying simply, "Miss E., this is Mr. D.," then excused herself.

3. *First impression:* Patient small, thin, reserved, courteous. Her face tense, her lips drawn tightly together. She was lying down in her dressing gown, having drawn a light blanket over her. She asked me to pull up a chair. I said, "Do not sit up." She said, "I guess I can be more courteous."

4. *What happened:* I said, "How are you?" "Oh, about the same, not much difference." "You haven't been operated on yet?" "No, not yet." "Do you know when you're going?" "No, they haven't told me." Then, remembering that I had been introduced as "Mister," "What is your occupation?" She almost said business, but seemed to pull the word back as being less desirable. I said, "I'm a clergyman. I'm in the hospital all the time. Miss D. told me you were here and I thought I'd come by to see you." "That's very kind of you; what denomination?" "Presbyterian." "I was brought up a Baptist, but I lived in a country where there were many Presbyterians. They ran the schools and hospitals." "Where was that?" I asked. "In China. I saw a good many of the missionaries there." "What sort were they?" (This to search out patient's attitude toward them.) "Oh, they were fine. My father did a good deal to help establish missions in foreign lands. . . .

   "I am not like you are—being a Presbyterian, you are absolute; but as the years have gone on I have dropped off a great deal. You think a great deal and come to believe many other things. I have made all the arrangements for my funeral, have written my own prayer. I want something very simple. It's hardly a funeral, it's a disposal. When the light goes out I think it's out. But I have no regrets. I have lived my life." (She came near weeping but with determination turned it into an unnatural smile.) "My prayer is simply, 'Eternal Presence, we thank Thee for the years of happiness

[5] See Appendix A, R. A. E., p. 331.

and of peace. We thank Thee for the friends we have had and acquaintances we have known. We are thankful for the bounties Thou hast given us and for the joys of life.'" There may have been another sentence, but the prayer was notable for its unity of thanksgiving as well as its address to the Eternal Presence.

Later she said, "I think of the Eternal Presence as something always here. You probably were brought up as I was to believe that God was on a throne away off somewhere. That cannot be." Then she went on to talk about her friends who were Catholics, saying she also had friends who were Buddhists. Again she said, "It is a waste of time for you to talk to me. I cannot be brought back to the formal. I should not talk that way about my religion, but I cannot believe—my prayers have not been answered. I believe in letting people be what they want to." "So do I. I'm a Presbyterian because I have to be something. I happen to be that by accident. I might well have been something else." There was a notable response to this: "Yes, I have thought ministers might like to be something else but they have to stay where they are."

There was a pause, then patient said, "I know why you came. You thought I might want a prayer, and you were going to comfort me. But I am resigned. It will be all over in a little while. I might have done something about it if I had got it earlier. But my business went to pieces in the depression and I didn't do the right thing."

After a time I got up to leave. "Well, I'll see you again," I said. "Yes, I hope so. I'll not say goodbye, I'll say, 'happy years and success, and no pain.' Thank you for coming. Come again, won't you?"

5. *Summary:* I made a bad start by attempting to center attention upon patient's physical condition and her approaching operation, but she quickly took things into her own hands. She quite misunderstood my reference to the fact that I am a Presbyterian but might well have been something else.

Here we have a sensitive, self-centered, determined woman. She has lived her own life, thought her own thoughts, and those of others as well; now that she approaches a crisis, she is determined to continue in the same way. There are few things in her life she cares to have continue, so she thinks of death as "a disposal." She thanks God for those things which she has known, "for friends we have had and acquaintances we have known"—one suspects she had more acquaintances than friends. Thus she pays her honors to

God and is done with Him, for she does not want prayers now. She says her prayers "have not been answered." She is resigned. Her next thought is that she "might have done something about it" (the disease) if she had come to the hospital sooner, but she does not really accept the responsibility for this fact. This patient's thoughts are paradoxical, one suspects that her whole life has been a duplication of these thoughts. She is facing the operation with a certain determination to die. Thus she will spite God. She is infantile, determined, inconsistent. One feels pretty hopeless in the face of such odds, especially as she rejects one as a clergyman.

One can do little but listen. This will probably be of service, for she obviously will have few people listen to her in the hospital.

The above summary was proved by later contacts and notes to be accurate. At one time the patient said that she was determined to die. When it was found that her disease was too far advanced for surgical treatment she blamed the doctors for not letting her die. She welcomed my calls and appreciated my listening to her talk about what she was facing, but I was never able to bring her the relief which she might have had could we have changed her attitude toward life and religion.

Doubtless it will be said that the minister has no time to keep notes. That sounds familiar. Lazy doctors say the same thing; but competent doctors, no matter how busy, keep notes because they know that they cannot otherwise do good work. Are ministers busier than doctors? No truthful and well-informed person will say so. Are the experiences of the minister with the sick less important than the doctor's to remember and to reflect on, less capable of being developed during the process of note-writing? No one will say so. The contrast is all the other way. Ministers need notes more than doctors, not less. Such notes will be more valuable both as a means of deepening the minister's thinking about his daily care of souls and as a help to sermon-building and to study. It is inconceivable to us that any conscientious minister can omit writing notes in some form or other.

Like meditation, good note-writing is one of the approaches or approximations to prayer. For most of us it is meditation made effective. Few can keep going ahead long in silent unwritten meditation. We tail off into vacancy or we go round in a circle. Writing enables us to hold the advances of our thought as they come. Writing favors the germination of ideas. It encourages us to throw out clear and penetrating questions aimed not at ourselves, for we do not know the answer, but at the boundless truth more of which we hope to grasp. It is no exaggeration to call this truth boundless, for we can always keep on discovering more and more of it. The truth about a patient's needs and about the best plan to meet them has no end. When we "ask ourselves" sensible questions about what the patient needs, we are asking not for what we know but for more of what God knows about him. We ask the ceiling, the doorknob, the end of our pencil, but we know that the answer is not there. It is somewhere in *"the truth."* At each step we look down a vista of the truth which we need to know. We do not often call that vista God, but there is no better name for it. Out of this truth we ask for light. That is very close to prayer. If we throw our whole weight into our questions it *is* prayer. If we merely wonder about them still we are turning in that direction.

We know well how absurd it sounds to many, this glorification of writing as a spiritual exercise. It is bound to sound foolish until we have faithfully tried it, and perhaps even then. Not every minister is fit for the ministry. This is one of the ways to test his "call." Can he accumulate spiritual resources with pen and paper or is his own pulpit voice his best reassurance?

Chapter XIX

CREATIVE ASSERTION

THE business of the minister in the sickroom is to make God more real to the patient, sometimes by prayer, listening, and quietness, sometimes by sharing his present experience of God. Human creatures hard pressed by pain rise now and then to such heroism that the minister gets a shock. He sees God in a human face or hears Him in a broken word of bedrock sincerity. Then he may seize his chance to say what he sees and to say it with all the vehemence of his vision.

I (R.L.D.) was sitting near the bed of a woman dying of cancer. She was often nauseated. One of these attacks came on while I was with her. I reached for the basin. She motioned me back and reached for it herself. Then wiping her lips with a piece of tissue paper she said, "I'm so sorry. Don't let me nauseate you. These spells come, but they don't last very long." Perhaps it was not the moment to tell her that this flash of heroism was a spark of God's life, but it was the moment to see it and to thank Him for it. Recall your own feeling when seasick. Could you be alert to another's sensations at such a time?

Later in the same visit I said, "You have attained a great peace, haven't you?" (In earlier visits I had not felt this.) She looked away wonderingly. It was perhaps a full minute or longer before she answered slowly, "I suppose I have." In that moment the peace she knew was deeper because I recognized and reinforced it. I might have added, "You are the minister now and I am the patient. In the pinch of your pain you show me God at work in you. Be glad for what you've given me and glad that God helped you to do it."

We find a clearer example of creative assertion in Shakespeare's *Henry V*. Just before the attack on Harfleur the king speaks to his soldiers. His fire kindles theirs. He sees in their faces the divine fury of courage.

> *"There's not one of you so mean and base*
> *That hath not noble lustre in your eyes.*
> *I see you stand like greyhounds in the slips*
> *Straining upon the start. The game's afoot!*
> *Follow your spirit! And upon this charge*
> *Cry: 'God for Harry, England and Saint George.'"*
>
> (ACT III, SCENE 1.)

That was creative assertion at its best. Notice the steps in its advance. A slap of sensation like the douse of a breaking wave hits Henry in the face. It is not thought or prayer but keen sense perception—"lustre in your eyes." Then comes more sharp sensation. He sees their muscles tighten and their lips seal. Like greyhounds in the leash they tug for freedom.

But these pictures on the king's retina are not mere photographs. He joins them with the fervor that is in him. He lives the ardor of his men's response. He feels it in his own muscles. Then he reinforces it with a roar of command, "Follow your spirit!" and ennobles it with the name of God.

It was in a miserable cause—the cause of battle. Yes. But the spark of God that is heroism darts up for all causes, just or unjust, so long as they stand for the best in sight. To the soldiers of Shakespeare's play the cause of England was a holy one. Henry saw their spark of nascent energy and fanned it to flame, as a good actor plays up to the daring venture of his fellow actor. So a choral conductor redoubles with hand, eye, and voice the crescent delight that shoots up to him in the voices of his chorus. So an orator hurls back with interest the response that his audience gives him.

The chance for creative assertion comes at a climax, in a moment of crisis, long prepared for by hard work. Henry had worked and suffered with these soldiers to earn this rare chance. He did not often strike the iron of their souls, and never unless it was glowing hot from blows of hard labor, hungry days, thirsty nights, fierce drills, and killing marches. Such a chance comes rarely. It must be waited and watched for. "Ye are the light of the world," said Jesus to his disciples. It needed his eyes to see it. To others doubtless they looked like other Galilean peasants. "Blessed are your eyes for they see, and your ears that ye hear. Many have desired to see the things that ye see, and saw them not."

He did not simply praise these men. He acquainted them with an awful responsibility that was also a blessing. He saw what they saw and what their light should illumine. He centered attention on a divine opportunity. He roused not conceit but aspiration.

We see God oftenest in faces lit up by wonder, determination, discovery, and most of all in the face of one who returns good for evil. Thirty years ago I (R.C.C.) saw Him in the face of a nurse, a consumptive, though we did not know it then. Rebuked by the hospital superintendent before a group of doctors and patients, publicly criticized for an act that she knew (and I knew) it had been her difficult duty to do, she said, "I'm sorry. It won't happen again." Well she knew that he was wrong and that she had been right. Yet she *was* sorry that he should be annoyed. She knew that in an emergency demanding instant action she had broken the hospital rules which it was his business to maintain. According to his lights he was right. He knew not the injustice that he did. And she could truthfully say, "It won't happen again." Such a critical need could hardly strike her twice. But her smile as she submitted to him pierced even his obtuseness and there was shame in his shoulders as he turned away. I could not say anything at the time but later when I talked it over with her I said, "Something spoke out of you that day that surprised you almost as much as it did the man it hit."

She said nothing for a while, then, "It's our job here, isn't it, now and then to build better than we know." And for the next three months, till phthisis conquered her, she set a pace and showed a quality of Christianity in her work that I have rarely seen equaled since.

The clergyman who *often* makes creative assertions will soon be like the butt of Shakespeare's Hotspur. "He can call spirits from the vasty deep." "Ay so can I and so can any man. *But will they come?*" Creative assertion is a superlative. Frequency kills it. It begins with a thrust that pierces below the range of average sight. We wish for such a glimpse so hard and so often that the wish may swap itself for reality. Then we say that we see God because we wish that we could. A false prophet and a fake seer are latent in every one of us. Laymen distrust the clergy partly because the minister seems to attain "great experiences" too easily and uses gigantic words too often. Sincerity is the test. What the minister sees with a start of wonder—the delighted admiration that the sick call forth from us again and again—*that* he may rightly try to reinforce. His enthusiasm may not help the patient. He may only stare at enthusiasm. But if the minister is one hundred per cent. sincere it can do no harm, for he only confesses what has hit him through his eyes and ears. If the patient sees it too, so much the better. If he does not he will not resent.

Are we not exaggerating? Is it really possible to see God in a patient's heroism? "No man hath seen God at any time." No, not the whole of Him but *"vestiges of his creation."* When a sick man acts with humility, courage, self-forgetfulness or forgiveness, then and there we see creation move on a step. We are eye-witnesses of the creative process which is an act of God. Dully we suppose that God is everywhere, somehow at work, but now we see it.

Creative assertion is most timely when it *accuses* a man of religion. The doubter, the deprecator, humbly sure that he has no contact with God, is the very man who speaks the divine out of his face. To catch him in the act and to show him that it is so is a delicious chance. When you convict him of religion both of you may burst out laughing at the humor and the wonder of it. You have caught him trying to escape happiness. You have trapped the crescent action just as it tried to dive out of sight. Could it be so exhilarating to catch a fox?

Humility and self-sacrifice are themselves creative, which means divine. They *must* push out the "growing edge" in order to qualify as self-sacrifice or as humility. That push is creative. Sometimes it is not the right moment to speak of it. We can only look it. That is safer though less complete. But even gratitude and delight do some work. Through our eyes then God sees His work and declares it good. Some whisper of that delight gets across to the man we admire even though we are silent.

When the minister attains the rare privilege of creative assertion he enters "the prophetic consciousness." "Thus saith the Lord," is what his eyes and ears declare. He shares the dangerous chance of the creative artist and steers his course between twin disasters. The artist creates nothing if he copies, and nothing but inanity if he "makes up" things out of whole cloth. Like the minister, he must find and follow nascent energy that is already at work. When he writes music for a poem, he feels that his music belongs to the poem because it carries the same energy further. The poet finds, loves and voices a theme that Reality gave him. Music catches the same theme and develops it further. So one poem gives birth to another, or to music or to a better social order.

But not without the creative human impulse. Art does not happen of itself, nor prophetic assertion either. Reality photographed by a machine has not moved on. Someone must risk an assertion that is, in part, the assertion of himself. "For this came I into the world."

What risks inhere in creative assertion? One vital and one trivial. Vital is the risk of insincerity. Insincere music, fake religion, meretricious literature come out of the same mean impulse. It says what will produce an effect, not what truth and labor compel one to say. The impostor plays for success even if it makes him a liar. Many a religious assertion is made for effect, out of "kindness" and indulgence. People ask for inspiration, not for truth. *That* may inspire and may humiliate. The minister feels this cheap demand and as a compassionate man is in danger of meeting it merely because he feels it.

The trivial danger in creative assertion is that it may not work.

Among certain groups in Palestine, Christ could do no wonderful work because of their unbelief, but he was no less the Christ. When a minister truthfully testifies to his wonder in a piece of heroism he may do no good to the heroic sufferer. Perhaps he has taken the wrong moment or the wrong words. But if he has done his best he learns by his mistake. When he has not done his best he learns nothing and injures the mind that is given him to use. No faithful failure injures him. He is glad of its lesson.

By many days of listening with patients, of quietness, of prayer, of careful note-writing (that is close to prayer), the minister prepares himself for the rare juncture of mood, demand, and supply when creative assertion is possible. That juncture comes without warning. It comes at inconvenient times, almost against one's wish. One obeys a command, doubtful of success but eager to take the chance. One tries to describe only what one sees, to follow every bend and blaze of truth's path, and to stop with an understatement if the itch for exaggeration is felt. Admiration, surprise, and delight are one's motives, more abundant life one's goal.

Chapter XX

RITUALS OF THE SICKROOM

When everything has been done that the best available medical advice can suggest, and when the doctor has made it clear that the patient will have to face a certain degree of permanent incapacity, say from paralysis, from rheumatism or from heart disease, then the minister should help the sick man to *build up a life under the conditions of his handicap.* Within the walls of his limitations he can make a life worth living, provided his mental or physical suffering is not overwhelming and provided that he and his family will "play the game."

With ingenuity and persistence such a life can be shaped, but it is not easy. Some invalids, when they find themselves handicapped by illness, rebel or give up. Quite naturally, but dead against their own interests, they will not try to construct a new system of occupation and amusements within the circle of their handicap. If they cannot live as they always have lived they throw up the game. They slump into torpor and bitterness, into idleness and vacancy, into peevishness and complaining. Other patients insist that they will give up nothing. They struggle desperately to play the old game. Feverishly hoping, striving, fretting for their old life, they look off over the heads of our little devices for a bearable invalid existence, and struggle in vain to live as if they were not ill. Then come physical disaster and a series of heartbreaking disappointments until they learn that they can be happy and successful only by facing the facts and learning new habits.

When the patient is convinced that he must build a new life upon a small stage, the minister can do much to assist him provided other conditions are right. The other conditions are:

(a) A good "sporting spirit" in the patient.

(b) His freedom from overwhelming pain, mental or physical.

(c) Family affection and ability to help.

Quite often all these conditions are fulfilled. Every town contains shut-ins who are not in constant or submerging pain and who are free from mental disease. Most of those who are handicapped by chronic illness have heart disease, tuberculosis, rheumatism or some sort of paralysis, diseases which produce little or no pain. Despite any of these a good life can be constructed, but it will not come of itself and many a patient cannot do it alone. He needs affectionate, patient, and devoted partners. Members of his family, with the minister's help, can give him what he needs. The family are often eager to help, longing to help, but do not know how. They lack resource and system. They see too few people, to get new ideas for their own particular invalid.

The minister's main job is to encourage, coach, and supplement the home team, that is the patient, his family, and the nurse if there is one. Now and then he takes an active part in their doings. First of all, he can pump some courage into everyone concerned by telling them in detail what others, similarly handicapped, have done. For this he must familiarize himself with the writings in which Francis Parkman,[1] Edward L. Trudeau,[2] Robert Louis Stevenson,[3] W. E. Henley,[4] Helen Keller,[5] James M. Barrie,[6] and George Thomas[7] have shown us successful life in spite of serious and crippling disease. Such facts are the best encouragements. What has once been done can be done again. Perhaps by his recitals the minister

[1] Charles Haight Farnham, *A Life of Francis Parkman* (Boston, Little, Brown & Company, 1900).

[2] Edward L. Trudeau, M.D., *An Autobiography* (Philadelphia, Lea & Febiger, 1916).

[3] Robert Louis Stevenson, "Aes Triplex" in *Virginibus Puerisque* (London, Chatto & Windus, 1916).

[4] W. E. Henley, "In Hospital," in *A Book of Verses* (New York, Scribner & Welford, 1891).

[5] Helen Keller, *The Story of My Life* (New York, Doubleday Page & Company, 1903); *The World I Live In* (New York, Century Company, 1909); *Midstream: My Later Life* (New York, Doubleday Doran & Company, 1929).

[6] James M. Barrie, *Margaret Ogilvy* (New York, Charles Scribner's Sons, 1915).

[7] George Thomas, *A Tenement in Soho*, Foreword by John Oxenham (London, J. Cape, 1931).

can rouse the sick man to read these books for himself. He will then learn another essential of good suffering, the avoidance of self-pity.

The other main task for the minister is to assist in working out what we call the "ritual of the sickroom," that is, the division of the patient's day into significant and self-rewarding parts. In most homes for chronic invalids something like this is done. The twenty-four hours of the day are plotted on a clock-face diagram, where the duties of the patient at every hour of the day are marked. This is good if the patient happens to fit the institutional ritual. But because the doctors and nurses in charge have many people to care for and little time and money with which to do it, the daily routine is seldom enough individualized. Most of the patients do very much the same thing, however widely they differ in their needs. The institution cannot afford to supply different occupations and amusements for each patient, even if the doctor knew each patient well enough to prescribe them. Moreover, such plans rarely include a progress accurately fitted to each patient's capacity.

A home-sickroom ritual can improve on this, first because there a number of people are at the service of one patient instead of one doctor and one nurse at the service of many patients; and secondly, because intelligent and affectionate devotion can supplement professional service.

The Essentials of a Successful Sickroom Ritual

1. A division of the day into manageable parts; with satisfaction in each and not merely at some remote future time.
2. A daily occupation in which the patient can make progress as long as he sticks to it.
3. An enjoyable climax or high-point for each day.
4. A family that links beauty and affection to the items of the day's ritual.
5. A chance for the patient to make himself useful.
6. A way to keep in touch with God.

Any routine saves energy because it minimizes the number of decisions. A whole week's or a whole month's is made at one stroke.

Routine also makes us form habits and these save strength. Many a healthy man has reason to bless the fact that his daily work demands his being at a certain place each day at a certain hour. It makes a rhythm which tends to go on of itself. The sick man needs it too. Sometimes the patient himself plans his own routine in essentials. Sometimes his doctor, his nurse, or his family give him the suggestions that he needs. But there remain a great many sick people whose plan of sickness will not be built wisely unless the minister helps.

Handwork is generally better for sick people than brain work, because brain work, reading especially, provides only one of the essential services of work. We learn by it but we do not easily see our gain, nor make it of use. Not many can write history as Francis Parkman did when his strength allowed him to work only a few minutes a day. Not many have their minds so stored with the fruits of past study and so trained in habits of orderly production that they can dictate book after book of archaeological research, as Professor Reisner does in the shadow of the pyramids at Gizeh, now that his eyes do not let him read or write. It needs long preparation to fit anyone to carry on his usual work when handicapped by illness.

Many a patient who cannot eat three sufficient meals a day can get in his day's food supply in six or eight small "lunches." So it is with his work. In a number of small stretches, with rest and change between them, the sick man can accomplish an astonishing amount, provided he does not lose interest in it. He is helped to hold his grip on it, if another is interested in it, suggests ways to bring variety into it, and new things to learn in doing it.

Companionship in work is a large part of most people's interest in it. Factory tasks are less monotonous than solitary work because workers can at least see one another at work and can exchange a word now and then. Sociability in work is one of the few advantages that sickness in a well-managed institution has over sickness at home. In the institution's workshop or in the ward, companionship springs up naturally. Most of us get on better with all sorts of people while we are working with them, than on ordinarily social occasions.

When the patient is sick in his own home we should try to make up to him for his lack of work-companions. Sometimes a member of the family will take up work like the patient's just for the sake of giving him companionship. Occasionally a neighbor will help in the same way. But usually the reinforcement of others' society has to be maintained for the patient by the interest of his visitors, and this interest is not always regular, vivid, or particularly intelligent.

Here, as in so many other matters the minister can do with devotion and therefore with intelligence and with skill, what others do casually and clumsily because they do not take it as their particular business. By reading up on the patient's occupation, by talking with others skilled in it, by doing a little of it himself, the minister can make his natural interest in the patient go further than otherwise it would.[8]

People do not always realize that work is essential for the sick man, but no one is likely to forget that he needs amusement. The difficulty is to find enough of it. This problem is already partly solved for him when we have helped him to find his proper work. For half the enjoyment of dropping into our amusements comes from their contrast with our work. Hence recreation is easier to plan for the invalid who does his stint of work each day. His work is pleasanter because he has something to look forward to. When his fun comes he feels that he has earned it.

The main point about amusement for the sick man is that it should be planned so as to give him *one high point or climax* which he can look forward to each day and can recall with pleasure after it has ended. He will sleep better if, when he settles himself for the night, he has something refreshing and delightful in his mind. This is usually possible if his day has contained no quarrels, no heartburnings, no disappointments. To a large extent the quality of the patient's night depends on the quality of his day. Routine helps; the sense of something accomplished and the memory of something enjoyed help more. But more still he is helped by the after-image

[8] Chapter XI. The Minister's Kit-Bag, p. 159.

of moments of affection or of a steady undertone of affection through the day.

Illness brings loss and waste. But these are partly balanced by the chance it creates for the growth of affection between the sick and those who care for them. Ordinary talk, work and play convey but little affection. But direct physical services: feeding, bathing, lifting, bed-making, lighting a fire, letting in fresh air, can be beautifully given and gratefully received. Only a poet can make love beautiful in words. But almost anyone can give simple service beautifully.

Visitors can supplement the family's devotion. The minister, beside visiting himself, can organize sick-visiting in his parish. There are people in every parish who like to visit the sick, especially if they are given a little coaching about it. Most invalids have friends who need to be reminded that a visit from them would be appreciated. The family may hesitate to suggest this but the minister can easily suggest it. In this way a patient who never had much time for friendship while he was well may become the center of a group of friends who enrich his life cumulatively as the months go on.

There is a group of young people at Trinity Church in Boston whose sole reason for existence as a club is to visit shut-ins, many of whom are confined to their beds. Each club member selects one or two persons in the parish and visits them regularly. These young people are of great help to a busy rector of a large church who must spend most of his "visiting time" answering emergency calls from people who are acutely ill or in trouble.

Of the minister's task in bringing into the sickroom the element of worship there is no need to say much here. The better he has organized work and recreation for the patient, the more he has helped to make his family and friends express in word and deed the affection which is often latent, the more natural will it be for him to sum up work, play, and love in the worship which consecrates them all.

We wish now to explain what we mean by the symbolic elements in the patient's day. The essence of symbolism is that something stands for more than itself. Money, printed words, shaking hands, a phrase of music, a goal-line on a football field, a national flag, a dinner bell, are symbols because they mean much more than the matter and motion that they contain. They rouse emotion, they start action, they wake thought, they stimulate spiritual activity. They also express it. Symbols carry out as well as initiate the impulse of the soul. Religious symbols, the cross, the bread and wine, the water of baptism, are for the religious more inclusive and more penetrating than the symbols of art or of affection. But they are like other symbols in that their material is given special value by what men have come to see in it. It takes practice to make any symbol valuable to us. No one masters all the passwords of daily life or penetrates any symbol as deeply as he might. But it is not too much to say that the richness and happiness of anyone's life depends largely on the meaning he has learned to see in fire, steel, foliage, steam, in lighted eyes and laughing voices, in darkness and in sunrise, in food and water, in sleep and waking.

Items in the Ritual of the Sick Man's Day

1. Waking and greeting those who take care of us.
2. Thanks to God for the care and the beauty around us.
3. Seeing the fire lighted, or lighting it.
4. Opening the shutters, or seeing them opened.
5. Washing and getting fixed up for the day.
6. Breakfast.
7. Bed-making.
8. Getting up (if one is not confined to bed).
9. Flowers arranged, tended.
10. Doctor's visit.
11. Getting to work.
12. Rest. Fruit.
13. Play or chat.
14. Lunch.
15. Prayer for growth of the soul. Rest.
16. Exercise or work.
17. Rest.
18. The climax of the day—a visit, music.
19. Tea.
20. Reading to oneself or being read to.

21. Rest.
22. Dinner or supper.
23. Music or reading.
24. Prayer.
25. Lights out.
26. Sleep.

Round each of these events one can learn to associate thoughts, bits of poetry, flashes of beauty, movements of affection for God or for man. Each element kindles the others, as the sticks laid together in a wood fire maintain each other's heat. Many have sat by a fire and stared into it without noticing that its flames and embers paint beautiful pictures against the blackness behind them, that the flames are like the darting points of green oak leaves, like the swift bright tongues of water in a waterfall, like spurts of ideas in lively talk. The fire is alive. So are the heat-making fires within our own bodies. Flames move, change, create, and destroy under the aegis of life, as the elements in our bodies do. We call on fire the life-giver when we speak of the fire of passion, of eloquence, of political enthusiasm, of religious fervor.

When our fire is lighted in the morning we recall the kindling of first love, we see dear eyes kindle with delight, we remember new starts in our own lives. A new household starts with a fire on its hearth, a new day begins with the fires of sunrise. There is fire in the Word of God, in Loki, and in Prometheus. The torch of learning is handed from generation to generation; the candle flame maintains its steady shape though every particle in it is born and dies again within the instant. To anyone who gathers up these memories and lights them with the match of today's hopes the lighting of a fire is surely a sacrament. No ritual at the altar could more swiftly gather past and future into a knot of nascent life.

Each item in the day's routine can be thus illumined if we will cultivate its symbolism. To wake is to take back one's conscious life out of the hands of God. Where else but in His plan for us were our conscious selves during the parenthesis of sleep? Not in the body was preserved the continuity of our souls during the night of our unconsciousness. Except for God it would be death. It is as great a mystery as birth. Where were we before birth awakened us? Not in the *genes* and juices of our parents' bodies. There is no trace of conscious life in them. We were in the plan of God for this world.

What messengers bring us back each day as we wake from the depths of His sustaining plan? Light, sound, a touch from some already wakened creature of His. We are kindled again into consciousness as the unlighted is kindled by the lighted in the first crackle of a fire. Who that has ever taught or learnt can forget how thoughts wake up at the impact of others' thoughts, wake out of the plan of creation that was somehow in us before it came to consciousness? It is recognized as true, re-known today, because the plan of it was alive in us already.

Any minister may say to any nurse:

"As you draw up a robe from the foot of your patient's sofa and tuck it about her shoulders, say to yourself: 'So the snow spreads over the grass, so bark grows over a gash in a tree, so a thousand mothers in this city will tuck their children in tonight, so naked man first wrapped skins round his shivering body against the winter cold, so protecting love wraps itself round a child. So friends have tried a hundred times to shield her from loneliness or disappointment, so God draws velvet sleep across a tired mind.'

"When she is ready to take a walk and you kneel down to tie her shoes, let your knees and your fingers remember that so you would kneel to a friend to ask forgiveness for your blunderings, that so you kneel before the emerging truth when you start to find it, that so Christ knelt to wash his disciples' feet."

We believe the minister can do much to make each recurrent phase of our sick man's day a sacramental experience and to make it clear to him that there is nothing fanciful and everything sensible in this habit of lighting up the items of our day through symbolism. It is like putting one's desk in order. The analogies acknowledge family relationships between experiences which live side by side unknown to each other. United they stand to support one another like a cluster of images in Shelley's "Skylark."

When our bodies are fed by nature and our minds by experience we compare food to knowledge because there is a common factor—God's plan—in both. The communion service mirrors this union and allies it with our hunger to incorporate Christ's life with our own. I do not see how the symbolism of the Eucharist can have meaning for us unless we carry over from it some sense of the miracle which occurs whenever we take food.[9] At that moment the creative energy of the universe, once active in animals and in plants, enters the tissues of our bodies, is transformed into their likeness, supplies strength and warmth, and supports the highest activities of our souls. This is a literal account of what happens. Our kinship with nature and our difference from nature are proved at the same instant. Every meal asserts our sonship to the Creator who feeds and preserves our lives. Food and our use of it celebrate both our dependence and our independence. The bounty of God's sustenance must be assimilated by us before it can create our strength. We put our own stamp, the human stamp, on every protein that comes to us from other animals, as the artist puts his own impress on the experiences that come to him in beauty. God cannot force our food upon us any more than He can compel us to absorb His truth. Not till we put ourselves into it can we draw His strength from it. If we are passive it cannot reach us. It runs through us and is lost.

Anyone who reflects on the simple facts of nutrition can hardly escape an impulse of wonder and gratitude every time that he takes a meal. If anything is a sacrament that is. And if we feel this and are illumined by it, we can pass on to the sick some fraction of our own feeling.

[9] R. H. Nettleship's notes on "Spirit" make this vivid. See his *Philosophical Remains*, A. C. Bradley, ed. (London, Macmillan, 1901), p. 20.

We have tried to suggest how the routine of the sick man's day can be more accurately understood as a ritual, and can be made into a series of sacramental acts in each of which some phase of God's life is transfused into the soul and body of a man. This is one of the ways in which, with the minister's help, the patient can grow during his illness into deeper realization of how the central energy of the universe creates, preserves, and renews his life. Moreover with the minister's help the routine of the sickroom can be made to increase the affection of the patient for his family. In health each of us goes his own way. In sickness the elemental acts of giving and receiving are multiplied in the day's routine. Acts of give-and-take are vectors of affection. The strongest of human affections, that between mother and child, is built up on giving and receiving. The mother gives first her own blood and vital heat, later her own milk, then countless acts of loving care. Through them flows her affection.

In sickness we come back to something more like the relation of mother and child. Strength waits on weakness. The weak may resent this. It is hard for many men and for some women to resign themselves to the passive mood. They can make little of this business of receiving. On the other hand, the members of the family may get tired of giving the plain services which illness demands. Nothing can become more disgusting than bodily services given without affection and received without gratitude. In the Spanish War of 1898 no nurses were allowed at the front. The sick had to be cared for by their disgusted fellow soldiers to whom nursing was assigned in rotation as a "fatigue duty." Other "fatigue duties" were emptying kitchen swill-pails, washing dishes and cleaning privies. Nursing added one more hateful job, detested so cordially by those who did it that their bitterness spilled over onto the patients themselves.

Women nurses of the better type seen in England and in America do their work with relish because personal service is more native to them than it is to men, and because they are more moved to compassion by the patient's helplessness and by his suffering. A good hospital nurse comes to feel that her patients are like her children or like her parents. The patients appreciate this, especially if they know by hateful experience what it feels like to be nursed by those who feel no compassion for them.

When patients are nursed at home by members of their own family the manual and "menial" services needed by the sick reinforce family affection. A person whom we care for calls out our desire to help more vividly when we see him weak and in pain. And if he responds at all, our affection is almost sure to grow. Then we grow more eager to express our love by skill, gentleness, and resourcefulness. What we feel grows from what we do, and what we do is done better because of what we feel. In this way the give-and-take of nurse and patient in the rituals of the sickroom multiplies and enlightens affection.

It is a familiar natural process when it exists at all. But like most "natural" acts it can be developed by practice, and by the suggestions of others. Keenly aware of the deepened affection and of the vivid beauty which sickroom routine can arouse, the minister can fertilize the whole process by teaching its sacramental significance. He can coach both sides—the family to express their affection with more ingenuity, variety, and skill, the patient to notice how beautifully and how tenderly he is served. Many an affectionate mother nursing a sick son has never thought of making his dinner tray attractive, dainty, and neat. She has thought much of the food and little of the way it is served. Yet to the sick the decoration is often more important than the meal. When food is prettily served he will eat it, but not otherwise. In health he was not fastidious and his mother, forgetting her own illnesses, is prone to treat him as she always has. She needs coaching.

To put affection as well as ingenuity into the way we answer a sick man's call in the night, into the way we feed him, wash him, and arrange his pillows, is an art which the minister can teach if he has imaginative sympathy and experience with the sick. The power to express gratitude for such services needs also to be cultivated in the patient. The first step in this is the habit of noticing exactly and not vaguely what is done for us. Our gratitude will be as various, and so as effective, as our awareness of what was done for us today and never before. We cannot answer exquisite attentions that we do not notice. Once having noticed them we can form the habit of tracing the motive behind them. "How she must have toiled to arrange those flowers, to get that chop here so hot, to read so much better than she used to." Most men need to be taught to express their thanks and to keep on expressing them more and more adequately.

But silence need not be all loss. Silently we can learn the sacredness of common acts, waking, eating, kindling a fire. Silence and gratitude can bring the members of a family closer. We have time in sickness to notice how much better we are treated than we deserve. We waste more time in idleness but we waste less time in heedless inattention to the essentials of human life—its sacramental values.

We make three points in this chapter:

1. That time hangs heavy on the invalid's shoulders. We can lighten this burden by planning a series of events and a climax of pleasure in each day.

2. That sickness brings us back to the elemental life of childhood, with its obvious dependence on others and on the bounty of God. By noticing our dependence on elemental gifts like food, fire sunlight, and sleep we can build up in sickness the refreshment of poetry and of sacramental beauty.

3. That sickness multiplies acts of giving and receiving. Those who find ways to give with devotion and to take with gratitude increase in every act their mutual affection.

PART V

CRITICAL OPPORTUNITIES

Chapter XXI

OPERATION

The preparation of one's mind to face a surgical operation is a task to which too little attention is given. One goes to the doctor for a discomfort which one believes is of no significance. Then the need for surgical treatment is discovered and presented at once to the sufferer or to his family. Within a few days the patient is expected to face the chances and sufferings of surgical treatment with equanimity. He is shipped to the hospital and there is kept busy, as internes collect a careful history of the onset of his disease and do numerous physical examinations. But no more attention is given to his feelings until the surgeon arrives. Perhaps not then, as he may send his assistant to announce baldly, "You are to be operated on tomorrow morning." The average man has not the remotest conception what surgical treatment involves, the reasons for pre-operative or post-operative procedure, or what he is to expect in the operating room. Everything and everybody seems to combine to increase the forbidding and mysterious threat of surgical treatment. Is it any wonder that the eagerness of those who have had operations to talk about themselves is rivaled only by those who have been psychoanalyzed?

I (R.L.D.) had my first experience with operations when, several years ago it was decreed by those who make such decisions that I ought to have my tonsils out. In the family of operations a tonsillectomy is like the village half-wit: nobody takes him seriously except his mother. Upon my arrival at the hospital early in the morning I was taken to my room, told to undress and get into a gown. This gown, the so-called "jonny," opened down the middle and was without buttons or hooks. I put it on as any normal human being would put on a shirt. How was I to know that simply because one was in a hospital one wears one's shirt backward? That was my first lesson in hospital peculiarities. A few minutes later I walked down the hall with a nurse who was as much shorter than myself as my gown was short for its assigned purpose. I suppose I had been given house shoes or socks of some kind, I do not remember, but I do remember there was nothing else from my middle thigh down, and very little, so it seemed to me, above.

Upon arriving in the operating room I was told by a formidable and none-too-pleasant woman whom I instantly disliked, to "climb up on here," here being the operating table. Someone with a much more pleasant voice, whom I liked instantly, came up behind me with an evil-smelling piece of gauze, and said, "Breathe in," while in my ear she repeated, "Are you asleep yet? Are you asleep yet? Are you asleep—" Someone with a gruff voice, whom I neither liked nor disliked, pommeled me on the chest and said, "A good stout boy." Then everybody began to talk at once. The next thing I knew the operation was over and my attention was divided between a warm fluid of which I insisted upon relieving my stomach and a very stubborn mule which insisted upon sitting on the foot of my bed. That was my first experience with operations and, except for the shortage of clothing and the walk to the operating room, it was not very bad.

My next experience was more serious. A few years later, after three years of increasing pain in my left elbow and much searching and urging on my part, a surgeon agreed to "observe my case." I was put to bed in a hospital and ordered to "stay in bed," just why I could not understand, for I felt perfectly well aside from the pain in my arm. I was anxious to have the operation done and over, for I had to be back at work by the end of the week, so I thought. Nobody bothered to explain that if I did not stay in bed while I was "under observation" my temperature would not register normally. But I was so embarrassed at hospital routine that I managed successfully to elude the watchful eye of the head nurse and slip across the hall regularly to the lavatory. When they caught me at this on the third day the nurse threatened to "tie" me in bed, but still she did not explain why.

On the third day the surgeon hurried in and said, "We are going into that elbow tomorrow to take out one joint. There are two joints in an elbow. We'll remove the one that seems to be injured and whatever else we find." I was delighted: anything to relieve the pain. The nurse told me that I could get up and do what I wanted until the next day. I asked her if I could go for a drive with a friend. "Yes, why not?" The doctor did not care and it was certain she did not. It was my own "celebration." After dinner my friend and I drove over to the next town, about thirty miles away, to see his girl. He lost track of time and I tried to; I went to sleep in the back seat. We got back to the hospital some time after midnight.

The next afternoon I was wheeled (this time I rode though I had expected to walk) to the operating room. Once inside, and as nothing much was going on, I sat up on the side of the operating table. Two nurses were doing something with a hodge-podge of needles. I said, "Mind if I look around?" They looked a little disgusted but said, "Sure, make yourself at home." A friend came in wrapped up in a sheet with a thing over his nose. He looked excited and much more ready for an operation than I was. Somebody poked her head through the doorway and said, "Dr. S. says, 'Start the anesthetic.'"

A few days later the large, dark-Negro porter who had taken me into the operating room was cleaning my room. I said, "At my operation it seemed as if all the darkness in the world fell in on me." He said, "Yuh. Ah w's holdin' yuh down." I had waked up talking about the surgeon, saying, "He didn't show his face, did he? He didn't speak to me before—he didn't show his face."

My next operation came fourteen months later. After six months of immobility in a cast my arm had not improved. Upon hearing that I was anxious to go to New York to study, my doctor encouraged me to go despite my condition. He said with a smile, "There are good doctors in New York."

When I carried my letter of introduction to Dr. M. in New York he sent me immediately to the clinic for X-rays and examination. Later Dr. M. and his assistant came to the booth where I had been waiting for three hours. It was then late afternoon, that exhaustion-period for all sufferers. He said, "We'll have to operate on that arm. It's rotten as hell. We may be able to save it but it's pretty far gone. Plan to come into the hospital in a few days, say next week. We'll operate and give you three months' rest and if that doesn't take care of it we may have to operate again. You'll have a stiff arm, but that's better than no arm at all."

He left. His young assistant, Dr. H., who was to do the operation, stayed behind. I felt as if I had been hit on the head with a mallet. What of my plans for the theological school? For four years I had planned, worked, anticipated study in New York. What about money? I had about thirty dollars; how could I afford months of convalescence and two difficult operations. And hardest of all, there was the ghastly horror of the anesthetic and its struggle with "darkness" which I had experienced before.

Necessity breeds acceptance, but necessity is often intense pain. During the next twenty-four hours I lived over that former experience with the anesthetic many times in my imagination. I tried to project myself through the next anesthetic, but never could I get further than the first sickly impact of the ether mask.

Just what happened during the next few days I do not know. I remember sitting for several hours in a park overlooking the Hudson River. There were little boats pushing around on the river. I seemed to ask myself, "What can one experience, however difficult, mean in the whole of one's life? Somehow time gets things over." The sunshine and the placidity of the river had their effect.

After being admitted to the hospital I was kept waiting several days before the operation was done. Although I grew more and more impatient I realized that time was having a good effect. My dread of the anesthetic had completely changed into a desire to have the operation over. My fatigue had given over to relaxation. To my surprise I was now able to think *beyond the operation*. I did not know, and I do not now, whether this ability to think of the future overcame my dread of the operation, or whether it was not until the dread was gone that I was able to think of the future; the two things happened almost simultaneously.

When the operation came it was as if all my apprehension had been useless, as of course it was. I had made up my mind that the way to take an anesthetic is to do nothing. Few things *seem* easier than just to do nothing. But try doing nothing during a violent thunder storm, or in a howling football crowd during a thrilling play. Multiply the emotional stress of these situations several times and you will have something like the feeling of the patient who is fully conscious as he goes to the operating room. Can one keep oneself under control, can one remember what has happened after it is over? "Yes"; one can answer to both these questions, and the second would seem to prove the first. I remember my feeling of loss when the nurse whom I had got to know pushed me into the anesthetic room, said "Good luck," and left me in the hands of someone I had never seen before. Two doctors were discussing a football game which Dartmouth had won two days before. My doctor came in; he seemed nervous. That gave me more confidence in him, for I felt that it must mean much to him if he were so concerned over my difficulty. When the anesthetic was given he was standing near-by. Then with hardly the blink of an eyelash it was over; I thought of trees, of cool air; it was warm there under the trees. It was as easy as that. There was no struggle and no darkness.

The operation which came five months later was easy to face. There was no horror of anesthesia for that had been overcome. I had discovered that in taking anesthetic one simply does nothing. One takes a mental and physical vacation. What is happening in the operating room is of no concern to you; the people there know their job, and they will not consider you any more significant if you ask questions or attempt to help them by lifting yourself from the stretcher to the table. They may say, "Make yourself at home," but at the same time they will probably consider you a fool for doing so.

We have given considerable space to reporting how one patient felt when facing an operation and the anesthetic. Some might say, But think of the glories of anesthesia! Granted, and we would add, the devotion, the courage, the skill of surgeons and surgeons' assistants, of clinicians, microscopists, radiologists, and laboratory technicians. But all this stands beyond the patient. He is a person within his own rights up to the instant he is anesthetized; beyond that he is in other hands. Beyond that instant the mystery of the unknown claims him. Should we be surprised that *facing an operation* and not the operation itself is what disturbs the patient? Let us look at the factors involved.

1. The patient commits himself, in most cases his very life, into the hands of someone of whom he knows little if anything. Is it any wonder that patients come to have such confidence in their surgeons? They *have* to have it, otherwise they could never bring themselves to submit to surgical treatment as they do. Occasionally I (R.L.D.) come across a patient who expresses the belief that the surgeon "is not working for my best interests." Immediately I get in touch with the surgeon and suggest that he "have a talk with Mr. X.; he seems to be apprehensive." I have never had a surgeon fail to express appreciation or to follow the suggestion.

2. The thought that one is to be the center of attention under such dramatic circumstances and yet is to be absent oneself, is a tough psychological burr which sticks in the patient's mind. As one patient said, "It is to be my party but I won't be there."

3. Many a patient faces death when he goes to the operating room. I suppose there are few adult patients who go to the operating room without thinking of the possibility that they will die during or soon after the operation. Certainly I have found the thought in the minds of many surgical patients. Few die on the operating table, but it is always a possibility. Some of those whom I have seen go most calmly to the operating room knew the seriousness

of the operation. Several of these instances have been cited elsewhere: J. L., page 359; Mr. M., Mrs. A., Mrs. R., Chapter on The Dying, pages 298-301; F. S., Chapter on Quietness, page 205. They all knew that they faced death when they entered the operating room. They all said in effect, "It's all right." Not a single one of them fought the anesthetic, although Mrs. A. was apprehensive lest they start the operation before she was "asleep." But so far as death itself was concerned she was not disturbed.

The experience of accepting the need for an operation and of facing it overtakes the average person as sleep overtakes him. Try observing the experience of going to sleep and you will find that you have spent a sleepless and tiring night. Pain is of great assistance in bringing the patient to accept the need for surgical treatment. Pain is nature's effort to reveal and to combat destructive forces at work within the organism. We may also recognize pain as nature's call for the resources of surgical treatment and as an agent in the psychological reconciliation of the patient to this treatment.[1]

What can the minister do in helping the patient to face this experience? First the minister must have himself so well under control that he can listen to the patient's recitation of his fears and regrets without feeling the necessity to reassure the patient immediately or of telling of "a woman I knew who had this and is as well as I am today." It may be wise to say that eventually but not the instant a sign of apprehension shows itself. By your alacrity you may increase that apprehension.

It is our belief that the patient who goes to the operating room saying, "It is all right whatever happens," is in the best psychological condition. The minister can encourage the patient to discuss this phase of the problem by saying, not when he first sees the patient but after a satisfactory working relationship has been established, "How do you feel about the operation?" The term "feel" rather than "think" seems to strike the point. Never have I had a patient do other than welcome such an inquiry. No one else in the

[1] Chapter VIII, Evil. p. 102.

hospital family is apt to propose such a question, although most patients would welcome it, especially from the surgeon himself.

Only the surgeon can tell the patient, or his parents, if he is a child, what should be known about the operation itself, its dangers, the dangers of *not* doing it, the probability of its success, the kind and degree of need for doing it now, the degree of recovery to be expected in the different powers of the body after it, its surgical after-effects, whether he will be as good as he was before or better, and if not how much he is to be handicapped and for how long. It is the surgeon's business to answer these questions so far as surgical experience gives answers to them.

Round each of his answers there is a penumbra of uncertainty. The surgeon does not always call attention to this. He cannot forever keep saying "in all probability," "in most cases," "ordinarily." He could answer in statistical terms, giving the percentage of mortality of the operation, the percentage of completely successful cases, and so on. Few people like their future put into cold, unsympathetic percentages, yet this is the only way in which he can make an exact statement, and his only alternative is the penumbra above referred to.

It should go without saying, but in fact it needs to be said, that it rests rightly with the patient, or his parents, and not with the surgeon to decide whether the operation should be done at all. He should explain the need for doing it, its risks and its uncertainties. Then obviously the decision rests with the patient. Now and then it might be the minister's business to explain the real situation here, because the doctor has taken it as a matter of course and so has not adequately explained himself. But ordinarily the minister should only relay the facts to the doctor. Some sufferers prefer that a friend or relative shall gather the evidence about the need and value of the operation from the surgeon, and make the decision. The disaster above all things to be avoided, and we have seen it now and then in great hospitals, is that of the poor confused foreigner who finds himself entangled in a net of hospital doctors and nurses and comes somehow to believe that he *must* do what they want him to do.

After the reasons for and against the operation have been clearly presented and after the patient has decided to have it done, there is still much that he ought to know about the mental side of it, in order that he may be prepared to do his best and to suffer no more than he must. All this psychology the surgeon is the best person to explain, provided he himself knows it and provided he has the time, the desire, and the ability to make it clear in terms that the patient can take in. Our experience is that many surgeons allow no time for these details because they do not themselves realize the psychical side of an operation or are unable to explain it in simple language. Then some one else must do it or it goes undone. That "someone" can be the nurse, if she has the time, the sympathy, and the knowledge. It can be the social worker or an experienced friend. But if there is no one else to see to it that the patient is prepared mentally as well as physically for his operation, then the minister may well render this service. To arm him for it is the hope of our next paragraphs.

The patient needs to know more than he is often told about the anesthetic. If he has a good anesthetist he may truthfully be assured that he will not mind the process of taking the anesthetic. Some less-irritating vapor will be used before the ether, if that is the surgeon's choice, and so the patient will be insensible before he begins to inhale the irritating ether. If "gas and oxygen" is the combination to be used the patient will feel no considerable discomfort from the anesthetic either when he begins to take it or when he is coming out of it. If the operation is to be done under ether the patient should know that he will have a more or less prolonged period of nausea and general discomfort when he is coming out of it.

If the operation is done skillfully under a local anesthetic, as is more and more often the case nowadays with weak or elderly patients, the sufferer may look forward to feeling no discomforts after the initial prick of the subcutaneous needle. He will probably talk with the surgeon from time to time during the operation, and may take food before it is over or immediately after it. The "field of operation" itself he will not be allowed to see, as his eyes will be covered.

Many patients like to have a friend with them immediately before the operation and while the anesthesia is being started, though this is less needed than it used to be because so many patients are considerably under the influence of sedative drugs by the time they are moved to the operating room. In hospitals there is sometimes a period of quite terrible suspense for the patient when the surgeon is for some reason delayed and the operation does not begin at the time scheduled for it. Then the patient may have to wait in the operating room or near it, confronted by the sights, sounds, and smells of the nurses' preparations, which are hard to bear if he is alone, apprehensive about his operation, perhaps without the reinforcement of a good night's sleep, and almost certainly without his breakfast, since most operations are done early in the morning. At such a time the patient needs a steady, sympathetic, and reassuring friend. That friend may be the minister who through prayer or quietness can do much toward helping the patient to take the anesthetic easily. To be on hand early in the morning for such an appointment is the sort of opportunity which the minister ought especially to covet.

Occasionally the patient wants a friend beside him throughout the operation. He vaguely fears that an enthusiastic surgeon may do more than he originally bargained for, may take out more organs than the sufferer has agreed to part with, or in some way may go beyond his previous agreement. This fear has no grounds in the vast majority of cases, but if the patient has it, if the surgeon has no objection to the minister's presence beside the operating table, and if the minister has previously accustomed himself to the experience, he may be of substantial use there.

When the patient comes out of the anesthetic he usually begins before long to feel pain in the wound made by the surgeon. Except in the case of abdominal operations this will be probably his sharpest suffering for the first few days. If it comes on him as a surprise it will be harder to bear than if he knows beforehand both that it will come and that it will last but for a few days. A good many people think that the operation itself will be terrible but that after all will go easily. He must be warned that the operation itself is nothing, if he has a good surgeon and a good anesthetist, but that the days immediately after may be very hard to bear.

If the surgeon's incision is a short one, if the operation has been brief and without much loss of blood, the suffering of the succeeding days may be slight. On the other hand, if the operation has been an abdominal one with much handling of the intestine, the disturbance of stomach and bowels after it, combined with pain in the incision and in the back are sometimes as bad as any suffering that we know. Operations on the brain, strangely enough, often upset the patient very little.

Convalescence is a time not so much of physical suffering as of disappointment in our distressing weakness. Friends, doctors, and nurses congratulate us on being able to sit up in bed and are enthusiastic at successive steps such as getting out of bed, walking, and putting on clothes. But we as patients feel no glory in these achievements. We manage to get through them but usually with strain and disappointment. So long as we were in bed we got along well enough. We seemed master of ourselves in a comfortable though restricted kingdom. But as soon as we try to stand, we may be in misery with dizziness, appalled at the weakness of our legs and at the difficulty in balancing ourselves.[2]

Some part of this suffering can be prevented if the minister will ascertain whether the patient has been told what to expect. In case the doctor has not done so, it is well to warn the patient, as a surgeon of my acquaintance always does, that "his legs will feel like boiled macaroni" when first he tries to stand on them. Here as in many other passages of the sick man's life, he can take unpleasant news more easily when it is seasoned with a joke. He should be prepared also to find his feet numb and prickling when first he puts

[2] More detail about this will be found in Chapter VII, Pain.

them to the floor. But above all he should know in advance that all these discomforts will diminish day by day and will pass off entirely in a few weeks or less.

If he is left to discover entirely without preparation the discomforts peculiar to convalescence he will not only be disappointed by them. He will be hard to convince that he ever can get over these disabilities in parts of his body which have no connection with his wound. Legs apparently paralyzed, back so miserably weak, head turning round and round—however can he get over such crippling ailments? But if he realizes in advance that every convalescent has just such troubles and that they will completely disappear within a short time, he can take them philosophically. He should understand, moreover, that the new motions and new positions that come with convalescence will probably bring back pain in the wound which perhaps had almost disappeared before. Especially with a long incision like that necessary in the operation for cancer of the breast some discomfort persists for a good many weeks or even months after the stitches are out.

Fits of sudden crying in convalescence are the penalty for not being adequately prepared for it or for trying to go too fast. Disappointment and weakness combined undermine self-control. Indeed it is often months before the patient's nervous system can recover fully from what we call the "shock" of a major surgical operation. In the end he does get wholly and completely balanced again, but of this he will need reiterated reassurance in which the minister may well take his share.

Not every surgeon remembers to tell his patient all that he or she ought to know about the after-effects and the handicaps inevitable with certain, though not with all, major operations.

(a) Operations that include removal of both ovaries bring on a series of annoying and sometimes temporarily incapacitating effects due to the sudden abolition of ovarian secretion to which the body has been used. This sudden and artificial "change of life" is often more trying than the gradual process that comes ordinarily about the fiftieth year. It will rarely, if ever, we assume, be the minister who should explain all this. But he may have to see to it that someone, preferably a woman who has been through the operation, or better still the surgeon himself, prepares the patient first to expect disagreeable after-effects in late convalescence, and then to realize that these too will pass.

(b) Patients who have to undergo the operation of colostomy with the establishment of a permanent opening in the colon, can be spared much fear, rebellion and disgust if someone explains to them in detail just what is involved in the technique of living with a colostomy opening. To wake up after this operation and discover then for the first time what he has to face for the rest of his life is a cruel fate. No one should be forced to undergo it. But, especially in hospitals, it happens now and then. Still oftener the surgeon tries to explain the matter before operation, but the pain and bewilderment of the sufferer or the hurry of those who try to enlighten him prevent his getting at that time the essentials of what he needs to know. The operation of colostomy is often done in an emergency on patients in a critical condition and with very little time to spare. Yet every patient has a right to know what he is in for before he consents to the operation. Realizing what it is going to mean to have his bowels move only through an opening in his abdomen he may decide to have no operation done. Life may not seem to him worth living under these conditions and he certainly has a right to choose for himself.

On the other hand, some patients get an exaggerated idea of the handicaps and discomforts which they must face after colostomy, and so decide against an operation because they have not got the facts straight. By far the most satisfactory form of enlightenment that a patient can receive is that which he can be given by another patient who has had the same operation and is now living in very tolerable comfort with a colostomy opening. With pains and foresight such an "experience meeting" can usually be arranged, unless the operation has had to be done in an emergency. Even then some thing can be done by one who has practiced to condense the essentials of a clear explanation into a few words so that the patient is neither terrified by false apprehension nor lulled into false security.

Someone ought to do this. That someone will not always be the doctor or the nurse or the social worker as it might well be. Then it may well be the minister.

(c) Patients who have to suffer the amputation of a leg ought to be warned of the tedious though ultimately successful maneuvers which will be associated with fitting an artificial leg and getting used to it.

(d) Those who are persuaded to have an operation for the deformity of the great toe known as "bunion" should be warned that although in the end the results will in all probability be excellent, it may be many months before they can walk without pain and a limp. The operation seems in itself so slight a one that patients often fail to realize how slow their complete recovery will be.

(e) Patients who submit to a gasteroenterostomy for peptic ulcer of the stomach or duodenum are not always warned that the operation will not make them proof against errors in diet, or enable them to live as hard and as recklessly as they could do with impunity before the ulcer started. Despite the great and often permanent relief which the operation gives, most patients are still handicapped. They still have to take extra care of themselves and they ought to know this beforehand. Else they may be disappointed, may reproach the medical profession unfairly.

Our chance to serve patients forced to undergo a surgical operation arises from the fact that doctors and nurses are so busy and so practical in their mental habits that they rarely take time to prepare the patient's mind. If he knows what he has to expect, what groundless fears he may expunge, when his hardest test will come and when it will be over, he will take the operation more as the doctor and nurse take it—a series of things to be done with some suffering involved, but less than the groping imagination fears when it has no solid facts to guide it. The minister has often a Samaritan's opportunity here. If he knows what to say and when to say it he will deserve the thanks of patients, doctors, and friends. Perhaps the best fruit of all from going through the whole experience of an operation with a patient is this: We are friends for life with many of those who share with us a grinding test. Foundations of confidence are laid for valuable work later on.

Chapter XXII

THE DYING

When I (R.L.D.) first came to work in a general hospital as a minister I went around the wards looking for patients who were discouraged, lonely, apprehensive. I saw such people and they were responsive. I became more bold. I felt, "If I can just find somebody whose illness is very serious, and if I can help turn the tide for that person, then the power of religion will be demonstrated."

So gradually I began seeing people who were not expected to get well, and who did not get well: cancer patients whose tumors were inoperable, patients with heart disease, and others. I saw them first in the capacity of an observer. In a paper I had written a year before to clarify my mind on the subject of "Religion's Contribution to the Recovery of Health," I had included a short sentence on death: "And those patients who are not to get well—whose task is it but religion's to aid them to die nobly?" Now I was facing that task and I found the short thought which had gone into my former paper quite inadequate. People were facing death and I, a minister of religion, "whose task it is to minister to people dying, that they may die nobly," must minister to them. Yes, I must minister to them. And so I did, the best I could.

One day I stopped by the bed of a Scotsman, a proud, old-school religionist. Although we never discussed it openly I soon discovered that our brands of religion were different. Mine was flexible, tolerant, academic, tinged with humor; his was vivid, Biblical, other-worldly and somewhat tense. I was fascinated by his strong confidence in the face of death. He seemed to enjoy my coming to see him, and I did so regularly. After he was operated on I went to see him as usual; I prayed with him, prayers that I knew were balm to his chaotic memory. I included phrases which reasserted his ever-active faith, and he responded to them with gratitude. For a time he got better, but his physical reserve was inadequate and after ten days he became weaker and died. Then I realized what had happened; I the minister had gone to him and he had ministered to me out of his abundance. We did not talk the same religious language but his religion was real and he died "nobly." "I am ready to go if my work is done," he said.

I stood by the stretcher of a thirty-year-old woman in the operating room. Two days before the surgeon had told me, "I probably shall have to operate on Mrs. A. It is the only thing left; but if I do she may die on the operating table." Now she was being given a blood transfusion before taking the anesthetic. There was a feeling of tension in the surgical amphitheater. Everyone, even the patient, knew that this was a desperate effort to save her life. She looked up at me and smiled nervously. A few minutes before she had said, "I shan't wake up while they are working, shall I?" We had reassured her. After a little time I said quietly, "It is all right, isn't it?" She looked at me questioningly for a moment and then said, "Yes, it is all right; whether I get well or whether I die it is all right." She did not die but it was weeks before the implications of my statement and of her response to it began to be formulated in my mind.

As my hospital experiences multiplied I slowly came to the conviction that the ideal which we want for patients who are face to face with death is summed up in those words: "It is all right; whether I get well or whether I die it is all right." And we want patients to come to that conclusion themselves. Death is an incident, it neither proves nor disproves, it neither destroys nor overthrows. Hope was high on the day this idea broke through to full realization. But then before my very eyes I saw that death did destroy, that it did overthrow, and again I saw that it created. I saw that under the stimulus of approaching death something new was attained, something was laid hold of which the individual had not known before. And again I saw death come to people who were still living as they had always lived, rebellious, fearful, dull, and stupid.

There are two ways to die, with infinite variations between them. One is desirable, satisfactory, noble; the other is tragic, sad, disheartening. One I think may rightly be called religious, the other not. One relieves the tragedy. The noblest deaths are those that end a period of enhanced intimacy with those nearest and dearest, of special nearness to God and of expressed gratitude for love, for beauty, and for the everlasting arms. Fear and regret are banished by confidence that the great adventure is in the keeping of infinite Wisdom. Some attain this, many almost attain it,—"almost," perhaps the saddest word in the English vocabulary.

By this time my interest in the hospital had somewhat changed. I still looked for the discouraged, the apprehensive, the lonely patients in the wards. I still encouraged the staff workers to tell me about patients who seemed out of the ordinary. I was still interested in religion's contribution to the recovery of health, but my interest did not stop there. Mrs. A. had expressed it well that day in the operating room: "If I get well it is all right, if I die it is all right." It seems to me that this is religion expressed in its purest form. To attain it is the final triumph of religion.

A thirty-year-old patient, J. L.,[1] facing a serious chest operation sent for me. She was apprehensive and worried. I tried to discover why, but could not. She knew that patients came through operations, she said, but she also knew the surgeon could do only so much; the patient must do the rest. She was afraid she would not be able to do her part. I saw her three times, one of them on the morning before her operation. She was quiet and courageous that morning. At the operation the surgeon found a large, rapidly growing tumor which could not be removed. After eight days she began to lose strength rapidly. On Easter morning, nine days after the operation, I saw her. She said, "I think I am going to die." I

[1] Appendix A, p. 359.

said, "You are not afraid, are you?" She considered this, then said, "No, I am not afraid." I said, "It is Easter, you know. It will be an especial Easter for you." I saw her again that day and four times the next, each time to pray, and each time to hear her express appreciation for my having come to see her and for what I brought. On the following evening she said, "I think I am better, and I am sorry. It would be nice to go." I saw her twice the following day, and three times the next. She died the following morning. On two occasions she asked me to pray that she might die that night. The surgeon, two special nurses and her sister remarked on the peace that she had attained and how easy this made it for all concerned. The patient herself constantly expressed appreciation for the help she had received. Facing death she had attained that which she had never attained in life. Some might say it was the exhaustion that comes to all who are dying, or that it was due to the medicine she took. Her special nurses did not think so, the patient did not think so, and the surgeon spoke of the change in her attitude. I think she had won the victory over death.

On the other hand, there was R., whom religion did not touch. R. was a young mother who had developed a stubborn abscess of the lung. For months her condition failed to improve. Her husband came to see her regularly, but there were little signs that made one feel they had not been happy together. Several times she told me that her baby was well taken care of. She talked little about her husband, and when her father, to whom she was deeply attached, remarried, she said, "Well, that is a load off my shoulders." These things did not piece together until after she was gone, so that while she lived we had little indication of what we now believe to have been an unhappy home situation. R. and I were on good terms, and I went frequently to see her, but I always knew that she did not want me to pray with her. This was true even when she became very ill. I do not know why I now feel badly about her death, for certainly she died nobly, although she attained no special peace. I saw her a few hours before she went; there seemed to be a certain desperation in her dying. She was essentially courageous, patient, determined, beautiful. There seemed to be something of the fundamental elements of religion in her make-up, but in the final test they were not sufficient.

Again one finds oneself checked by the very truth one is trying to express: that to the religious person health, disease, and death are incidental features of a continuous growth. There is D., a thirty-three-year-old engineer facing an early death with multiple sclerosis. He and his wife discuss death with calmness and maturity. They do not actively disbelieve in a personal God or in the Christian belief in immortality, but they find it difficult to believe anything positively. D. once said to me, "My mind is open on the subject of immortality. I do not believe it, neither do I disbelieve it. But I do not feel I have done all I can for humanity." Certainly one can say D. is religious. Does it make any difference whether he lives six months or sixteen years? Is it that one wants his attitude to change, that one wants him to say, "I believe. Help Thou my unbelief"? I was not happy at R.'s going because her unhappy life seemed to be accentuated in her death. A desperate sort of death it seemed. To see J. die was a trumpet-call of triumph. In her going there was no tragedy except for her family. Her change was effected in four days, yes, in two days. D. has many of the qualities of a religious person and in his last hour he will not want for courage, but as for getting present help from his religion as J. did, as my Scottish friend did, I doubt it.

We are forced to this conclusion: religion may transcend death; some religion does. In the light of some religious experience the transition from life to death makes little difference. Is it the people that make the difference, is it the type of religion they have, or is it our relation with those people? In the light of the New Testament and in the person of Jesus, health or illness, life or death, cannot be imagined to make any difference. To him the universe was essentially spiritual. For him, to aid in the recovery of health for certain individuals was desirable and he gave much attention to it; but death was surely no defeat and nothing unnatural. Neither does it seem to us unnatural as we watch a soul pass through it with faith strong and confidence complete. One is forced to admit, however, that this is an ideal which many do not attain.

Occasionally the Protestant minister is sent for by a patient who is dying,[2] or by a member of the patient's family. Often this is a person who has long intended to join the church and "do a better job of living," as one patient expressed it. Or it is a person who has something on his mind which he feels guilty about; or we get a call from a member of the family who desires "to have the word of God said" with the patient before he dies. In these instances the minister may size up the situation, estimate the sufferer's needs, and attempt to fulfill those needs by bringing him into touch with God. But in many cases we have found that the patient is his own best physician. His own unforced repentance is sufficient for his forgiveness in the eyes of man and, one may be certain, in the eyes of God. His evident compunction for much of his past is really a form of confession, and the minister may seal it with a prayer of gratitude and assurance of God's mercy. For some patients the solemnity and peace of the occasion may be deepened by a baptismal or by a communion service. If a patient is really making a final confession, such a service is of help in removing his mind from the restlessness of the world and by stamping upon his consciousness the presence of God.

We cannot expect, we cannot even desire to change the outlook of sick people radically within a few days or weeks. Each of us builds up the tissues of his life as he meets its routines and its surprises into an effectively tough fabric. It has to be so. No one could work with himself and no one else could know what to expect of him unless his character had been molded into something almost as fixed as the shape of his hands and the expression of his face.

We cannot change him easily or swiftly and we should not want to even if we were sure that we could improve him. For if our hands could remold him, others' could remold him again and again until he would have left no character of his own. A life so

[2] See Appendix A, In the Afternoon.

limp and malleable as to be capable of one rapid conversion after another would soon be shapeless from the impacts of rival converters. But there is one exception to this. If a man is already ripe for change, if he is like an unlighted candle which needs only a match to set him burning steadily, or like a prisoner waiting only the turn of a key to set him free—if all his energies are set and tense for effort in one direction, so that a fulfilling touch can liberate them, then the act of liberation *can* be done in an instant and its effects may be profound and lasting. But it will be a liberation not a conversion, not a reversal of energies long and purposefully accumulated in him.

In the moment of first love something like this seems to happen. In the call to war Rupert Brooke heard such a summoning and transforming voice, God's voice, he believed:

> *"Now God be thanked who hath matched us with our hour*
> *And caught our youth and wakened us from sleeping."*

Even in the hour of death such a call might come to a man through a parish minister or a hospital chaplain. But we ought to recognize that so profound a change can come only to those who are prepared and sensitized to it, tense with conscious or half-conscious longing for it; so Christian writers have pictured to themselves the state of souls ripe for conversion. Such souls are rare among the sick whom the minister should visit in his parish rounds or in a hospital. For most of them no sudden change can be made for good or for evil. They are not balanced on the edge of conversion and ready to be pushed into it by a few words or prayers. If their souls are to be saved they must first come to believe in souls and in salvation.

But that is no reason why the minister should make no effort to befriend and to encourage the unchurched as he encounters them fighting death in a hospital or in his own parish. Unless they are already friends of his he will have to be content with small returns, perhaps with no tangible returns. But in the challenging moments of perilous illness, of bereavement, of disgrace or humiliation he may do much. Anything is possible then.

It is usually with the members of his own church that the minister does his most effective and satisfactory work in ministry to the dying. With the exception of those to whom death comes quickly and unexpectedly, the minister will have been seeing the sufferer regularly before the crisis arrives. Then the minister's work with his dying friend is a continuance of his regular work except that it is more intense and concentrated. He needs to be more alert to the patient's condition: to his expressed needs and his unexpressed thoughts. It is the minister's rare privilege to think with him beyond the physical existence. It has been our experience that the patient is again his own best physician in this respect. We can think with him through any regrets he may have at going, reassure him in regard to his family, bring the presence of Christ to him through the communion service, minister to him through our own poise and faith in God in the presence of death. All or any of these are the needs of the individual facing death, and the better one knows the patient the more effectual such a ministry will be.

Ordinarily, we believe, little can be accomplished for the Protestant patient through the communion service that cannot be accomplished through prayer; and there is always the danger that an unfamiliar instrument may get in his way. But if the communion service is a welcome and not an unfamiliar instrument, then by all means use it.

One should see the dying patient frequently; this usually is possible from the minister's point of view for his time with such a patient should be brief. I (R.L.D.) saw one patient four times in one day; this was possible because I was in the hospital and made it a point to go past her room as often as that. She said, "Come in every time you are in this part of the building. I don't care if it's ten times a day." Obviously such a ministry could not be carried on over many days. It would not be effective except during a crisis in the patient's condition.

With a person like the one just described, a person who is not afraid and who has no regrets at dying except concern for her family's sorrow and her own natural affection for life, one should do much passive listening. That is, one should listen to her requests or to anything she may wish to tell; then one should use quietness and prayer. Scriptural passages may be used in the prayers, utilizing the best we know of the language of religion. The very symbol of death is quietness and peace; anything else seems out of order.[3]

With a patient who has regrets at going or who is fearful of going, one may use directed listening and quietness. A desire for any direct ministrations about death should come from the patient. That does not mean that the patient must ask for a minister before he will come; but it does mean that the minister must wait for some indication on the part of the patient *that he knows he is dying* and for some sign of how he feels about it. If there is fear or regret in the patient's mind the minister may direct the patient in his thinking by the use of questions. When patients know that they are facing death and when they are not suffering from a sense of guilt or regret, most will become reconciled to it if given a chance to think it through. Some prefer to talk to their doctor rather than their minister. The doctor and minister should work shoulder to shoulder with the dying, regardless of which the patient depends upon most.

The first problem the minister faces in work with a person who is dying or who is soon to face death is: what does the patient know of his condition? This problem involves the physician, the nurse, and the family as well as the minister. Some physicians object strongly to telling a patient that he may not recover, even when the physician is fairly certain what the course of the illness will be. Some doctors say that patients never really want to know what they are facing, even when they ask. Others believe the patient should be told only when he asks. Still others believe that every sick person has a right to know the nature of

[3] "Then I Sleep," Allen Hoben, *Christian Century*, January 11, 1935.

his illness. Many instances could be cited to support or to weaken all of these positions. Usually the physician does whatever his experience, his temperament, and his own religious faith dictate; often he wisely shifts the responsibility for such a decision to some member of the patient's family.

We believe that the question how and what to tell a patient about the danger that faces him is the doctor's problem only when the patient is not a member of a church. When the sufferer is a church member and trusts his minister, it is the minister's problem, unless the patient has indicated by action and comment that he prefers the doctor as his spiritual as well as his medical adviser.

In answer to my (R.L.D.) request that a patient be told the nature of his disease, after the patient had told me that he had asked the doctor and had not been given a satisfactory answer, the doctor said to me, "But you have the minister's point of view." This is not an adequate answer. If the medical profession and the clergy have different points of view in such a crisis, then one of them is wrong. The correct answer is not what one or the other holds professionally, but what is the most desirable from the patient's point of view. In the final analysis it would seem to us that there is no single answer to the question, no decision that is best in every case. The question must be decided on the basis of the individual patient's needs and by those who know him best. In the average situation that would be the family doctor and the minister; together they might decide whether it is desirable that a patient know the seriousness of his disease. Together they will minister to him and to his family during the experience of death. Together they can do much to relieve such an experience of its tragedy.

It should be remembered by the minister that it is ordinarily the task of the physician to tell the patient whatever he is to be told after the decision is made. Some patients nevertheless will question the minister rather than the doctor about it. This is either an indication that they do not want to know or that the physician has not given them a satisfactory answer. When asked by a patient about his diagnosis or about his probable future we should always refer him first to the physician by asking, "Have you asked the doctor?" or, "What have the doctors told you?"

The goal toward which I (R.L.D.) try to work with every patient is: "Suppose you are to die, as we all shall sooner or later, what difference does it make?" One would not put it so baldly with a very ill patient; rather one may begin by some such question as, "How do you feel about it?" or, "You are not afraid?"

The minister's contact and working relationship with a patient who is dying should be established before a crisis is reached. This is impossible if the minister is first sent for after the patient has reached a critical stage in his illness. The difficulty which may then arise is illustrated by the following experience. A head nurse told me of a woman who had had a serious operation and who was not expected to recover; she was discouraged and emotional. It was because of her emotional rather than her physical condition that she was called to my attention. But as soon as I told her I was a minister she asked, "Am I dying?" I assured her it was not for that reason I had come to see her. In this case I am sure that my coming to see her *did not* implant such an idea in her mind; it merely led her to express what she had been thinking already. But with nonchurch members one needs to be alert to the fact that the calling of a minister or of a priest is often associated with death, because they do not see the clergy at any other time. Such a shock is to be avoided. It can be avoided, by both the priest and the minister, in case we can see the patient before he becomes critically ill.

We must remember that the dying are often lonely, even when they are so sick that they show but little signs of consciousness. "Don't be away too long. I get lonely without you," said a dying wife to her husband. Yet for hours before that she had shown almost no sign of consciousness. Merely to have someone sitting beside one, quiet but ready, may be a boon in our last consciou hours. For suddenly the world changes its color for the dying. What had been accepted becomes now merely terrible; what had

been familiar becomes strange. Time starts over again years back.
Of a sudden the slate of experience is wiped clean and we are
back in childhood's fear of the dark with all childhood's need of
simple reassurance. Or we are lost somewhere and need a familiar
voice or a firm hand to bring us back. The watcher must be
alert and imaginative if he is to meet such changes. He cannot
let his thoughts wander nor can he safely interpret the sick
friend's words in the light of those spoken ten minutes ago. In
that interval he may have moved fifty years; he may have flitted
back again in an instant from his own far-off, helpless childhood
to his clearest, maturest self, with no remembrance of the former
state.

We must remember that the dying are often entirely conscious
even though motionless and incapable of showing any response
to what they hear around them. We are accustomed to judge the
degree of consciousness by the patient's signs of response—words,
smiles or other movements. But this habit misleads us with the
very ill. They may be all there save for the power to show it.
"I'm all right but I can't talk very well," said one patient sufferer
only a few hours from the end of her earthly life. Another whom
we had supposed to be entirely unconscious showed after some
hours of immobility a slight twitching of his lips. With my ear
close to them I just made out the word "Water," uttered in the
faintest audible whisper. We gave it; soon after he opened his
eyes, smiled and talked. "I knew everything and heard everything," he said, "but I couldn't move or talk. You gave me up
too soon."

Those words have burned into me (R.C.C.) for life two absolute imperatives for watchers by the dying:

First, never give up hope or the attempt to be helpful until
the sufferer's heart and breathing have been silent for more than
a minute. Long after you think all is over you still may be
needed.

Second, In the presence of the apparently unconscious person never say anything that you do not want him to hear. You never can tell that he is unconscious and you never can be sure how much he hears. He may be cruelly hurt when you speak or even whisper words that he is not intended to hear. This has happened several times in my experience. Two watchers, each tending the one dearest of all to him, said what they would rather have died than have overheard, found out later that it was overheard, and carried for all their remaining years the scars of that moment's agonized self-reproach.

Say nothing, therefore, in or near the dying man's room except what you will be glad to have him hear and to remember later that he did hear. There is, we repeat, no proof that he cannot hear until heart and breathing have been long silent. Only the physician can be sure of this. Awaiting his decision all others should "carry on" as if the sufferer were fully conscious.

It is not enough to avoid terrible blunders in the presence of the dying. Since they may at any time be conscious and may need the very words of love and courage which we think it too late to speak, we should speak them and keep on speaking them, by faith and without any response. Whatever we should ourselves most want to hear if we were aware of approaching death but unable to make any sign of response, that we should say from time to time, not loudly but with all the meaning that we can put into our voices.

One great difficulty is to avoid showing signs of grief. To avoid this, and especially to help the patient's family to avoid it, is one of the minister's most important duties. Many affectionate families are very stupid about it. Overwhelmed by their own sorrows they easily forget the patient. They approach the bedside with red eyes, with mournful expressions, and even with tears and sobs. Conceivably this may not always depress the sufferer but so far as our experience goes it has always done harm. Those who cannot better control themselves should keep out of the sickroom until they can. To do otherwise is to be inexcusably selfish at a moment when every thought should be for another. This is so obvious that most people with any power of self-mastery can be made to see it and to act on it if the minister does his part rightly.

Spontaneity is never more out of place. When most spontaneous in our grief we are thinking most of ourselves. We picture *what we are soon to lose,* not what suffering we may save another, what comfort we may give him. It is amazing how few people remember this even when their last chance to help is at hand. They have to be taught (and they can be taught) to prepare their faces and their words before they enter the sickroom, to imagine vividly what they themselves would want around them at the last—all that asserts immortality by assuming it, all that takes it for granted and so carries on present life at its best, through our delight in one another, in the beauty of God's world and in Him.

Naturally enough, few of those nearest and dearest to the now-retiring soul can keep at their best for long in the sickroom. They must take turns there and must fill in their intervening hours with whatever will best restore them to full awareness of the life that death cannot conquer. Fatigue and confinement often dull this. They must do whatever most refreshes them and restores full command over themselves. Sometimes all the watchers are worn out. It is then that the minister has one of his golden opportunities to take his place among them and to be at hand, perhaps in the night hours, *as one of them* and not as an outsider, to give whatever he can of physical or of spiritual service. When he can be at the bedside as one of those who care and who show by their presence that they care, his professional powers will have their best chance for service to the patient and to the family. Doctors often do this, not because they think their medical skill is needed but because they know that the members of the family are worn out. They need some rest if they are to give the sufferer what they alone can give—when at their best. Night watching is equally the minister's business. Incidentally such night watching in a pinch does more to cement his good relationship with the doctor than anything else we can do. The doctor will remember that minister with gratitude and will be glad of his aid in other cases of illness.

"But how," someone may ask, "can the minister bear the physical strain of such night work when he has all his other regular duties to attend to?" He can bear it as the doctor does, because he has to bear it and because he is methodical and ingenious enough to find times when he can snatch his moments of necessary rest in between the items of his ordinary routine. His next Sunday's sermon is apt to be the better and not the worse for such experiences with his sick parishioners. Watching as well as study helps the sermon.

We have made no reference to *salvation* in this chapter or in the former pages. Some will ask: "Is it not the purpose of the clergy to work for the patient's salvation especially at the time of death?" The conception of the ministry as a life of "saving souls" by pulling them back from the brink before they plunge to their doom, involves beliefs which we do not hold. At what point in a person's spiritual growth salvation begins or at what point it is accomplished is beyond our power to estimate. Some will object to our conception of spiritual growth, perhaps will believe that we have fallen in with an easy, nineteenth-century optimism. But such is not the case. Our conception of growth, which encompasses our conception of salvation, leads us to place the individual as an individual at the center of the picture. It is the minister's task, we hold, to go to the sufferer and to minister to the sufferer's needs as he finds them and not as he assumes them to be.

Often that is exactly what happens. When the representative of religion goes to the sickroom and attempts to have the sufferer conform to his own theological concepts he is ministering to his own supposed needs rather than to the patient's. The minister must have views of his own and be certain of them. In fact we are certain that unless he does he will not go day after day to the sickroom nor will he stir from his comfortable bed in the middle of the night to go to the dying. It is the faiths and certainties of his own spirit that become significant once the minister is there. Hence our emphasis upon a listening method, upon the importance of starting with the patient, upon quietness and upon individual application to his present state of mind in our prayer. All are formulated in an effort to meet the patient's religious needs rather than the minister's.

But if this is our attitude the question may be asked: In the face of death what does the minister bring? What justifies his ministrations being sought, and his being admitted to the room of the dying? First and foremost, we should say, his own religious confidence, his faith in the fact that God is a loving and merciful Father, as revealed by Jesus. Moreover he brings the Christian belief that one may be so strengthened by faith in God that one passes through the experience of death and into continued life, lifted above the ordinary routine of the sickroom. How is such a faith, such a rising beyond the commonplace accomplished for the sufferer? Never by lecturing, but by listening, by being quiet, by prayer, by revealing in one's own make-up, and sometimes by reassurances, a faith that is not bowled over.

We would go to the person who is dying whether he accepts any of these beliefs or not. We would go whether he knew he was dying or not; and we would not bring undue pressure either on the physician or on the patient to have him know the seriousness of his condition. We would go for two reasons: first, because of the need one knows to be present in almost any person who is dying—tne need to have despair stamped from his mind, to have his loneliness assuaged, and his deepest desires expressed. Secondly, because it is the least the minister can do in the light of the New Testament, in the light of the personality of Christ and his devotion to all sufferers. "Inasmuch as ye have done it unto the least of these my brethren, ye have done it unto me."

People should grow accustomed to expect the ministrations of the church through its clergy in illness and also in death. They may be taught to expect this as they are taught to pray, in the church school, in adult study groups, from the pulpit, and by actual ministration to the dying. Parishioners may be taught not only to expect such ministration, but what to expect as a matter of course. The form of it will vary somewhat among different Protestant groups. By and large such teaching will be fairly simple. The ministry to the dying need not be more complicated than ministry in ordinary illness; the difference is largely a difference of emotional content. An occasional sermon or talk by the minister in the church school will do much toward smoothing the way for future tasks in the sickroom.

For good or for ill the hell-fire-and-damnation conception of death has pretty much gone by the board in the Protestant Church today and we are among those who wish to pronounce a hearty "Amen" to its going. There is, however, a need for constant teaching within the Church on the subject of the Christian conception of death. We talk and teach freely of many other subjects. Why should we not of death? We must repeatedly emphasize the fact that that which we love in a person does not die at death. The Christian religion, the Christian conception of God implies the fact of immortality. Cannot immortality and death be as easily preached and taught as the concept of God or the life of Jesus? Mystery, tears, and tragedy need not make up the whole of our associations with death. Let us get people used to the truth that death is a release, a fulfillment, an experience to be passed through with the calmness with which one passes through any meaningful event. The tragedy or the victory of death is in the way one dies, not the fact of death itself.

Chapter XXIII

THE BEREAVED

UNLESS one has been much with the family during the latter days of the illness one does not realize how tired they are, how much on edge their nerves are, and how much they need rest. Relief from the strain of seeing a loved person suffer is often their dominant feeling. Loss of sleep and the strain of mingled hope and fear leave many so exhausted that they are almost numb emotionally and reproach themselves because the sense of relief overshadows grief. They need to be assured that this is normal and right, that they have nothing to reproach themselves for. By intense emotion they have exhausted their present capacity to feel. In order to do their best later on they need the rest which nature is now forcing upon them.

Some have been shocked by the repulsive aspect of a dead or dying body. They need time to forget this and to get back the remembrance of their loved one at his best. Unfortunately the conventions of mourning lead many to tire themselves still further by shopping and by worry about funeral arrangements, at the very time when they should be resting. It is the minister's privilege to run errands and save people fatigue so far as he can during the earliest days of their bereavement. More especially his business are suggestions about the funeral, in case people have given no thought to this beforehand.

If the funeral service is at all what it should be, those who have suffered are relieved for the time of their most crushing burden. The days which follow are more trying. It is then that we often hear the bereaved wrongly urged to get busy, put their sorrow behind them and face the future. For some people this is the right course, but for the majority just the opposite is needed. They need to pause and to dwell upon the whole life of him who is gone. There has never before been a time when his life could be seen as a whole, understood and appreciated at its full value. To focus on his life, to recall it year by year, to gather and reread the letters or diaries that remain, to talk and to write about him, is the proper way to fill the earliest days of bereavement. In this period it is especially those who knew and appreciated the loved one that we want about us. To talk with them about him, to add their remembrances to ours, is our chief desire. But now and then the minister has a more flexible sympathy and a larger vocabulary than those who are more intimate with the sufferer. Together with his religious faith these qualities may fit him to serve in this period of tender recollection and synthesis.

Above all things to be avoided are the false "consolations" offered to Hamlet by his uncle. Shakespeare makes him say nearly everything that should not be said:

> "... Your father lost a father;
> That father lost, lost his; ... 'tis as common
> As any the most vulgar thing to sense ...
> Why take it to heart ...
> To reason most absurd ... who still hath cried,
> From the first corse till he that died today,
> 'This must be!' ... To persevere
> In obstinate condolement ...
> Shows a will most incorrect to Heaven;
> A heart unfortified, or mind impatient;
> 'Tis unmanly grief."
>
> (HAMLET, Act I, Scene 2.)

That death is common. That it must be. That grief is rebellion against God's will. That grief is unmanly—this is what one would say if one planned deliberately to increase a mourner's suffering It is true that when one mourns, rejoices, discovers or creates, one does what thousands of others have done. There is a common element in all these acts. But the significant fact is the uniqueness in the common. To pass over this as Hamlet's comforters do is deliberate falsehood.

That this evil had to come at this time and in this way is what no science and no philosophy can truly assert. Better morals, better medicine, might have prevented it. That physical death has thus far come to every man makes it highly improbable but not impossible, that physical death will some day be conquered. Nothing but the self-contradictory is impossible. But even if it were true the necessity of death is no comfort in grief, rather an aggravation.

To suffer is not to rebel. Suffering is a fact, not a plan or an argument. It is a part of the fact of love. If you rejoice in the presence of him you love, you are cut by his absence. Else you are as fickle and as mindless as an insect. Condemn sorrow and you condemn love at a moment when it most needs reinforcement.

To many a male, grief, or at least any emotional expression of grief, seems unmanly and is humiliating. He hates to add the suffering of shame to the suffering of heartache. To tell him that whatever he does show is unmanly is to say what he knows is not true.

Another stupid insult to a man already burdened with misfortune is to say, "Six months hence you will be feeling very differently." Yes, possibly. That is the most terrible part of it, for if sorrow goes, a good part of love will go too. Only indifference can obliterate the pain. Forgetting is all too easy. Engrossment by other interests is highly probable but it is just what we fight and ought to fight in the bitterest time of our bereavement. A love forgotten is a love dead, and while it lives there will be suffering in it as well as joy.

To be told that all the world gets over its grief and that we are probably like others is the most discouraging word that can be said to us. It is like telling us that we never can get over a fault or be faithful to a friend. It may be true but no one can be sure of it, and no one has the right to burden our efforts with the weight of his disheartening guess. No one wants to take comfort for his sorrow in the reflection that the part of him that loved is soon to wither. That is an insult to the dead. If one can only keep his love by continuing to suffer, one wants to suffer. The price of ease would be disloyalty.

Beware, then, of trying to "cheer people up" at a time when that means faithlessness to the dead. They should be encouraged to cultivate the recollections and meditations which inevitably bring grief as well as thankfulness, reverence, and deepened love. Love can be entrenched once for all in one's life by this invaluable period of integration. Those who can share in this experience can help to revive memories of the departed or to add new outlines to the portrait then being stamped once for all on the souls of the bereaved. They will find their own affections strengthened too. Such friends will come to form a unique band of intimates joined by the possession of memories that are precious.

Don't say, "Nothing is lost. You have your deathless friend forever." That is not Christ's doctrine of the Comforter. He said that our souls must be broken and ploughed up by the trial of absence before they could win new growth from the Comforter's presence. Nevertheless, absence is as great a fact as presence. The dead are not with you as they were before death. Present still are the harvests of memory. Much of the past is glorious and invigorating. But the present and the future life of your beloved is not here but elsewhere. You do not want it otherwise. It would be horrible if, after their bodies' death, souls had no fresh work ahead of them. If they are vividly alive in that new work elsewhere they cannot be here about our earthly life at the same time.

Except in memory and in dream we do not want them present. That would enslave their new life. They are not, as Shelley said of Keats, "a portion of the loveliness that once he made more lovely —bursting from trees and beasts and men." They are individuals not natural forces, and no individual can be in two places at one time. We hope they know our lives, but their present life is not and cannot be here with us. To mistake our thoughts for their words is to belittle the privilege of individuality. To confuse our ideas with the present creative acts of our beloved dead is to make them one of our dreams.

When a friend is in Europe and does not write, there is still a sense in which he is at home with us. His ideas, his plans, we can carry forward in imagination because our memories of him are a part of our being. But our pictures of him are built on intimacy with his life up to the time he left us. It is precious. We may carry on by the strength of it for years. We are forever grateful for it. But his present and his future actions, thoughts, feelings, experiences, are hidden from us. It is no different when he dies. We are certain that he still lives and that is much, but it is not and ought not to be an experience of his present life. We can grow by reason of what we are deprived of, but we *are* deprived.

We venture to say that no man who has taken delight in the voice, the motions, the eyes, the smile, the new ideas, the firm rejections, the amazing furtherance to his world that one loved friend has shown, can say that *this* life is still present. The most vital thing about a person comes to us in the surprises he gives us, in what we could not foresee until he did it because it was beyond us to conceive it. When all that goes, we have still our long accumulated lessons from him and our stored memories of what he did. But it is blasphemy to chart his creative future out of his past. He is more than that. His present life is different by as much as he has grown since he left us.

I (R.C.C.) once heard it said, after someone's death, "You have not lost but gained her." That is a false alternative. You both lose and gain. When a poet or a musician dies, we lose his yearly output which may be of immense value. With every live person there is something corresponding to the artist's output. This is lost to us when death comes.

On the other hand, the mere fact that we no longer enter the stream of new gifts from a person's presence, makes us able and eager to see his past more completely than we did in life. Pushing further into the interior essence of the vanished life one may talk with it as children do with an "invisible comrade." As we see more and more in a great writer's work when time ripens it, so we may understand a person better after his death than before, and so living ideas that were his grow more powerful in us.

The call to work in a time of sorrow need not be a call to distraction and forgetfulness. If our work is for ends dear to him we have lost, it can help us to keep his memory green. What we have known of his standards, his hopes, his beliefs, is a part of his life. His cause is an essential part of him. He would want it forwarded by our efforts. Sometimes this can be made true only by an improvement in our standards of work. When we are urged to go back to our work, not as a soporific like wine, but as the fulfillment of an unspoken pledge to the soul that has left us, we can take comfort in our work.

Men go back to their work sooner than women after a death. Men find less relief in talk and more in action. Emotion tears them more and enlightens them less. Many are violently awakened to fear of their own death by the death of another, and so want to get away as soon as they can from all thought that threatens them. That is inevitable so long as annihilation and not immortality is what they see at the end. The minister has little or nothing to give to such people when they are bereaved. They can do no better than drug themselves with work and attempt to forget their fears. But death itself often argues for life beyond the grave. A belief in immortality that has been hitherto rather feeble is often strengthened when we stand at the grave and try to conceive it as engulfing the soul that we have loved. So much vitality, so much creative power and energy would never have been built up in a reasonable world, we feel, if it were suddenly to be wiped out. We feel this most after the death of one still in the prime of life. The more unnatural the death the surer one is that the life goes on out of our sight.

Can the minister still further strengthen this confidence? He must try, and he will often succeed provided his influence has not begun with the illness just concluded. What is said at such a time does matter. Witness the indubitable and sometimes lasting effect of a funeral service in which the great assertions of scripture are marshaled to feed our hunger. It makes a great difference who says these things. A minister who long before this illness and this death has come to be trusted, can carry over into the crisis of acute need the authority built up earlier. He cannot create a belief in immortality; especially he cannot create it by argument. The chief value of argument is to show up fallacies, not to create confidence. The minister who strengthens people's belief in the soul's permanence does so by the contagion of his own certainty, and especially by the evidence of this that he gives unconsciously in the way he behaves, in the things he takes for granted, in what he treats as important and what as trivial.

Aside from study and talk about reasons for belief in immortality, which in our experience are rarely if ever a help to the bereaved, there is the accumulated wisdom of scripture and poetry which like living friends can help us by contagion. St. Paul, St. John, Tennyson (*In Memoriam*), Emerson (*Threnody*), Shelley (*Adonais*) do not argue but assert conviction in impressive ways. What they see we can glimpse when we are stricken. In this the minister can help, especially if he knows bereavement by personal experience.

PREPARATION FOR BEREAVEMENT

Part of "adult education" ought to focus on preparation to meet misfortune, illness, and death. We expect sound business firms to build up reserves far in advance of the need to draw on them. In good times, when we are vigorous in health and not distracted or hurried, we ought to build up a reserve of spiritual life on which we can draw when the blow comes. Philosophic study of the grounds for belief in immortality, the reading of great scripture and poetry, and above all these, the attempt to face and conquer similar trials on a smaller scale, are what we need to build our reserve fund.

By "similar trials" we mean the death of one not very intimate but still near enough to hurt us. We mean minor illnesses and minor deprivations. Though the experience of meeting illness is very different from that of meeting death, it has elements in common. Fear of annihilation has seized people who had nothing worse than the measles. The loneliness of bereavement can be felt in the death of an uncle or a cousin not of our most intimate circle, if we do not push the experience aside or let it be crowded aside by the routine of daily living. In such ways anyone who wants a disciplined and steady life, seaworthy in storms, partially immune to the invasions of spiritual suffering, will make his preparations. Many do so half-consciously and half-heartedly. It might become the custom to do so methodically as we do now in far less serious matters of money, health, and fire-risk.

A clergyman who has won leadership in his parish can stimulate and systematize the stray gropings of his people in this direction. Doubtless many ministers do something like this now in Bible classes, in preparing children for confirmation, and in week-day classes as well as in sermons. We believe that training in sound spiritual investment, in the accumulation of spiritual reserve funds, in spiritual hygiene and spiritual immunity, would be more effective if we borrowed the terms of business and of medicine more boldly.

Spiritual needs are not merely analogous to financial and medical needs. They are partly identical. Imaginative foresight, whatever calls it out, is the same quality. To live beyond the needs of the moment in money and in hygiene trains the same muscles that will be called on in spiritual disaster. The same common prudence is in order for the one emergency as for the others. Common sense is not enough to make us prepare for financial or for physical disaster. There must be imagination and detachment too. Aspiration alone will not draw many to build up spiritual reserves. There must be sagacity as well. The minister should appeal to both motives and emulate the methodical yearly accumulations of a wise board of directors, as well as the spiritual enthusiasm of St. Paul.

Though we have not much experience to prove it, we are inclined to believe that an effective way to attack the problem of *Spiritual Reserves* is to include it in a study-course on *Success and Failure,* itself part of the adult-education course which every parish ought to contain. In such a course success and failure will be found, without profound investigation, to be what Kipling called them: "twin impostors." They are similar fakes because they both invite us to feed on husks. Success is not permanent, reliable, a flaming credit to the victor. Failure has its elements of gain. It is not so accidental or so sudden as it seems. Both twins point us ahead, though both seem to pin us to one spot. When studied more attentively, success and failure are seen to be twins in another sense. We must learn to be always prepared for either if we are to be solidly prepared. *Utroque paratus* means a position so fortified that whatever happens you win. In military, financial and medical affairs there is, we take it, no such position. It is in scientific work and in religion that one meets often the men who win whatever comes. This may sound Utopian, but it can easily be verified in the following illustration.

From 1910 to 1933 I (R.C.C.) was in charge of a course at the Harvard Medical School, in each exercise of which I read aloud the written "histories" of three patients who had died at one of the Boston hospitals and on whose bodies an autopsy had been performed. These histories had been multigraphed so that each student had had one to study a week in advance. The history contained all the known medical facts about the patient up to the time of his death. The results of questioning him and his relatives, the data of physical, chemical, bacteriological, microscopic, and X-ray examinations were included. The temperature chart, the nurse's reports, the notes of progress in the disease and of the treatment directed against it— these facts were set down. Before I began to read the record aloud each student handed me on a card the diagnosis which, in view of the record which he had studied, *ought,* he thought, to have been made. None of us knew what diagnosis the attending physicians *had* made during the patient's life nor what had been found at autopsy.

Reasoning aloud from the facts of the record as I read it, I arrived at the diagnosis which seemed to me demanded by the known facts. This committed me fully and ended my part of the exercise. The pathologist who had done the autopsy then told us what had in very truth been found. Then all of us, students and teacher, faced the truth and compared it with our beliefs.

This experience of early tension and final release was a poignant and a deeply human one. Step by step we built up a prediction with the certainty that within a few minutes it would be shown right or wrong, illogical or well-reasoned. It typified the three steps in spiritual growth: problem, hypothesis, and verification: challenge, venture, result.

Still more enlarging to my outlook was the discovery that if the question was well put, if the case was fairly stated, we were sure to win whatever happened. If our reasoning was correct and our diagnosis right, then our success was obvious. Our methods were proved trustworthy, our confidence for future attempts increased. But if the pathologist proved us wrong, the adventure was still gain for us. For, despite the chagrin of a teacher proved wrong before his students, I learned something each time. I learned what I especially needed to learn, namely, the gap in my armor of attack on the problems of medical diagnosis. Some future attempt could now be successful, some future patient could be helped, because I had not only blundered but learned how to avert that blunder in the next attempt.

For twenty-three years the "growing edge" of my medical knowledge stretched itself out each week to receive its food. Thus far and no farther went my diagnostic fitness. But it was sure of its chance to grow. Groping, stumbling, I was each week a little less of a groper and stumbler. Sure, clear gain. More gain when I failed, and so located a dangerous weakness, than when I succeeded. For success, though it increases the confidence which we all need for our next job, does not stimulate growth so much, and growth, I take it, is the only absolute need of a human soul.

In this illustration of the secure position attainable by the lover of truth during a considerable part of his working life, I have already suggested that there is a joker in the pack. You inevitably gain whenever you are shown right or wrong. But when the problem is wrongly put you neither succeed nor fail. Then your time and others' is wasted. If the facts given you to study are not facts, then your correct reasoning and your faulty reasoning are alike fruitless. The question must be rightly put or no answer is sensible. To the question, "Have you left off beating your wife?" the answer "Yes," is as absurd as the answer "No." In perhaps a fifth of the approximately ten thousand autopsied cases which I have studied I gained nothing, because the problem was not put in the form of a *crucial experiment*. When we ask our scientific questions in the right form nature is bound to answer us Yes or No. But the art of questioning is not easy. Much labor must be expended in getting that step of our study right or we cannot take the next. It would take too much space to explain the ways in which the question can be wrongly put in medical diagnosis. The important point is that it can very often be *rightly* put merely by conscientious labor and without extraordinary talent.

Carry over now these ideas to the experience of the person training himself for *success-and-failure*. He must know something about his growing edge, that is, he must have learned where his powers end. This is hard. We cannot know *all* our limitations. The challenges of experience bring out now and again some new ones which we do not see even when we look for them with tenacity and system. But most of the coastline of our growing edge we can map accurately. We know how we behave when people are rude to us, when we have lost the last train home, when a friend proves false, when the pipes freeze and break in winter. We can be sure whether we do or do not yet know how well we could bear being refused in marriage, whether or not we have faced bankruptcy, famine, flood, severe pain, public disgrace, imprisonment, a "vamp," a skillful flatterer, speaking before a group, the test of holding public office. Somewhere along the line of these alternatives any of us can locate his growing edge. What next? He would be a fool or a lunatic to go in search of such trials as "experience." Many pretend search for experience when self-indulgence is all they are after. They are not crazy or idiotic. They merely deceive themselves a little more than the average. No; one does not look for trouble if he wants to grow by experience. He finds it and before that he imagines and prepares for it, steering his course by the troubles that he has already met.

In the study of spiritual insurance one tries to imagine disasters which one has not yet met and to fit one's powers for the test. The bridge builder tests his materials for the strains they will have to bear. He allows a wide margin of safety. He also sees to it that these materials get a fair chance to show their strength. If the ends of a bridge are not properly supported its materials will never get a chance to answer "Yes" when asked if they can support the weights apt to pass over them. The bridge will go down even though its materials are perfectly adequate.

During his interneship the medical student tests his diagnostic powers and his capacity to keep his head in emergencies. He is not thrown into medical practice to sink or swim. He does not have to settle the diagnosis on which a critical illness will be treated. He works out what he would do if he were really up against it. He suggests this to his superior in the medical hierarchy, usually the visiting physician. He then watches the actual decision and corrects himself against it.

This is what happens when he trusts his superior. If he does not trust him he learns nothing. His powers are not tested; no proper answer Yes or No is obtained to test them, but ordinarily he gets his answer.

Further back in his training he tested himself on tasks still further from the front trenches of reality, on simple cases, printed cases, hypothetical cases. In the stages of his progress he learns both how to succeed and how to fail. He learns how to peg down successful acts into habits and how to straighten crooked reasoning, faulty memory, clumsy motions, so that in the next attempt they will work better. Part of his training time is wasted because he hits neither failure nor success in his morning's work. Then he goes along in a fog of lazy note-taking and torpid reading or merely stares at operations. He puts no clean-cut question and so he gets no answer.

Training to meet misfortune, including death, might follow the medical interne's plan. It might start from printed "cases"—novels, biographies. The success of such a course would create a habit of welcoming all fortune, good and bad, that can further spiritual growth. Some people need far more good fortune, some more bad fortune, for their growth. The habits trained in the minister's course should be as good for meeting the seductions of good fortune as for facing disaster.

In the chapter on note-writing we show how our knowledge of practical theology can grow by failure as well as by success. The "autopsy" which proves us right or wrong is not so decisive as we could wish. But if we write down our spiritual diagnosis and treatment, if we commit ourselves definitely on what we believe the patient needs and what we plan to do about it, the lapse of time will usually show whether we were right or wrong. Then if we have a fair amount of humility we are sure to win as much by our failures as by our successes.

Training to make success out of failure can go on all one's life. It prepares us to meet the great enemy death, because it gives practice in meeting loneliness and fear. When we fail in athletics, in examinations, in public speaking, in business, in friendship, in love, loneliness and fear pounce down on us unless we keep them off by two maneuvers: first, by nonresistance to the accusations of failure, and then by hustling to strengthen the weak points that caused our failure. In our early failures we protest that we did not fail. We try to deny the damaging facts and bolster up our self-respect. We blame others. We curse fate.

Gradually we learn to talk less and listen more to the lessons that the failure can teach. It or something like it may happen again. We do not want to be caught twice in such a position. If we are to prevent this we must find out where and why we blundered. The failure itself will usually tell us if we will keep quiet and listen.

The letters of St. Paul glow with light from a soul prepared for either fate. "For to live is Christ and to die is gain." "I know how to abound and I know how to be abased." If he lived he would spread the "good news" and rejoice. If he died it was in a good cause and his death would advance that cause.

So we believe that Jesus faced life as well as death in the Garden of Gethsemane. "If it be possible let this cup pass from me. Nevertheless thy will, not mine, be done." At that instant he was not sure that he must die. He longed for life. He saw rich chances for work still ahead of him. He did not welcome death as the only way to advance his cause. But he was ready for either path and sure of victory by either. It is easy to rejoice in life. It is not always difficult to acquiesce in death. Indifference may settle like a mist on us in times of trial. The Christian is not indifferent in the choice between life and death. He has no eagerness for martyrdom. He hotly prefers life. He is certain of God and so whatever comes to him after he has done his best, must be good. He will win even when he loses.

APPENDICES

STORIES OF WORK WITH THE SICK

THESE histories are used with the permission of either the patient or the family.

1. R. A. E. BITTERNESS

July 15. Miss R. A. E., a sixty-year-old, unmarried woman, was called to my attention by Miss D., social worker, who said patient had just been admitted to the hospital suffering from a growth in the stomach. She will probably be operated on day after tomorrow. Miss D. described patient as being "reticent, apprehensive, fearful." Miss E. had said, "They want me to come into the hospital but I don't want to come. What is the use? It is the end anyway."

I went to the ward to see Miss E. late in the evening. The head nurse took me to her room, a small room off the main ward. The nurse introduced me, saying simply, "Miss E., this is Mr. Dicks," then left.

Miss E. was lying down with a robe on, with a light blanket over her. She asked me to pull up a chair.

I said, "Do not sit up."

She said, smiling, "I guess I can be more courteous."

(a) I said, "How are you?"

"Oh, about the same, not much difference."

"You haven't been in yet?"

"No, not yet."

"Do you know when you're going?"

"No, they haven't told me." (a-1.) Then, as if remembering that I had been introduced as "Mister," "What is your occupation?" She had almost said "business" but seemed to pull the word back as being less desirable.

(b) I said, "I'm a clergyman. I'm in the hospital all the time. Miss D. told me you were here and I thought I'd come by to see you."

(c) "That's very kind of you; what denomination?"

"Presbyterian."

(d) "I was brought up a Baptist but I lived in a country where there were many Presbyterians. They ran the schools and hospitals."

"Where was that?" I asked.

"In China. I saw a good many of the missionaries there."

(e) "What sort were they?"

(f) "Oh, they were fine. My father did a good deal to help establish missions in foreign lands. (g) I am not like you are. Being a Presbyterian you are absolute; but as the years have gone on I have dropped off a great deal. You think a great deal and come to believe many other things. I have made all the arrangements for my funeral, have written my own prayer. I want something very simple. It's hardly a funeral, it's a disposal. When the light goes out, I think it's out. But I have no regrets. I have lived my life." (Here she came near weeping but with determination turned it into an unnatural smile.)

"My prayer is simply, 'Eternal Presence, we thank Thee for the years of happiness and of peace. We thank Thee for the friends we have had and acquaintances we have known. We are thankful for the bounties Thou hast given us and for all the joys of life.'"

I think this is a general rendition. There may have been another sentence but the prayer was notable for its unity of thanksgiving. Later she said, "I think of the Eternal Presence as something always here. You probably were brought up as I was that God was on a throne away off somewhere." (h) Again she said, "It is a waste of time for you to talk to me, I cannot be brought back to the formal. I should not talk that way about my religion, but I cannot believe—my prayers have not been answered. I believe in letting people be what they want to."

(i) "So do I. I'm a Presbyterian because I have to be something. I happen to be that by accident; I might well have been something else."

(j) There was a notable response to this: "Yes, I have thought ministers might like to be something else but they have to stay where they are." (k) There was a pause, then patient said, "I know why you came. You thought I might want a prayer, and you were going to comfort me. But I am resigned. It will all be over in a little while. I might have done something about it [the disease] if I had got it earlier. But my business went to pieces in the depression and I didn't do the right thing."

After a time I got up to leave. "Well, I'll see you again," I said.

"Yes, I hope so. I'll not say goodbye, I'll say, 'happy years and success, and no pain.' Thank you for coming. Come again, won't you?"

Summary: This was a bad start. The minister immediately takes charge and centers attention upon the patient in a rapid-fire order. While it is desirable to center attention upon a patient rather than upon oneself it is not desirable to focus that attention upon the patient's illness. As a minister you desire to let the patient know you are interested in him (or her) not because he is sick but because he is a person, who happens to be sick.

At (a-1) the patient takes things into her own hands in an effort to find out what really is going on. She almost says, "What business is it of yours anyway? You are not a doctor. By what right are you so interested in what has happened to me?'"

(b) This explanation should have been made at (a). Thus the above bad beginning would have been avoided, yet the patient's interests would have been paramount. An introduction in the sickroom, whether it be made by a second person or by oneself, should be natural, clear, *brief*. One may or may not, according to the situation, explain how one comes to know of the patient.

The casualness of the above explanation at (b) might be questioned; but here we have a patient who, we know by our above observation as well as by the information given us by the social worker, is "touchy," suspicious; she challenges our right to see her. Therefore, we must not assume even to be vitally interested to say nothing of coming to see her particularly.

(c) The subject is shifted back to the worker.

(d) One does not know whether this is an effort to establish a bond of common interest or to shift the subject away from herself, but either way the minister must follow her thought.

(e) is an effort to find out something of patient's attitude toward people as well as toward religion, for the missionaries would be closely assiciated with their religion in her mind.

(f) tells something about patient's family but little about her attitude toward people. At (g) she finally takes things into her own hands and comes to that which is uppermost in her mind; she tells the minister what he thinks and sets her own thought against his. She reveals what has been in her mind for weeks, perhaps months—her thought of death. She has made her own arrangements for her funeral; what does that mean? Perhaps there is a trace of Oriental influence here. No! she tells the minister what she thinks of death: when the light goes out, it's out.

(h) is another effort to be done with this meddlesome parson who by his very presence makes her think of that which is a closed book. But she does not feel comfortable in talking that way—Her prayers have not been answered.—"I believe in letting people be what they want to"—or—"Why don't you leave me alone? I have made up my mind."

(i) is an effort on the part of the minister to establish an understanding of tolerance which the patient had denied him earlier when she reads into his mind her own dogmatism. (j) Patient quite misunderstands this effort. She has often thought ministers may not like their jobs any better than she likes her own thought at the present time.

(k) One waits for the patient's next move, having failed so completely at (i). Under the pressure of silence—perhaps painful—she reveals the real crux of her thought, "I am resigned. It will all be over soon. I might have done something about it earlier but now it is too late." What is it? And what are the prayers which have not been answered?

Conclusions: A sixty-year-old, unmarried, Protestant woman who was brought up in a religious family. She is courteous, independent, determined. God has not answered her prayers that she be cured of the disease she has. God has deserted her; she will, therefore, be through with Him. She has written her prayer for her funeral. She asks nothing more of God, and she heaps coals of fire upon Him by thanking Him for that which she has had in life. She has not accepted her illness; she has resigned herself to it and desires nothing but death.

Despite a bad start the minister leads the patient to reveal her need and her mental suffering. She does not accept him as a minister and she is annoyed with him for his interest and kindness, for has not God already deserted her? She has made up her mind to that and does not care to have the subject reopened.

On the face of it this problem is helpless. The patient has been thinking these thoughts for a long time. Her mind seems set. On the
other hand, she passed her childhood in a religious home; she addresses
her prayer to the Eternal Presence; she dislikes God so much she has
gone to the trouble of arranging for her own funeral—a mere disposal; but it is not a closed question with her for she reveals her whole
thought the first time she sees a minister. There is the coming experience of an operation which may shake her conviction.

July 16. I went to the ward later than I had planned. The patients
were having supper. Miss E. was in a corner bed; she seemed to take
no notice of me. I went over to her saying, "Well, I see you've been
moved up; I didn't expect to see you out here."

She spoke quickly yet in a friendly tone: "Good evening, Mr. Dicks.
Yes, they moved some men in the room today. I don't like to be in
the large ward with so many people. I don't like many people around.
But it's only for a couple of days." Said she had had a terrible night;
had suffered more than she had for twenty years. "The doctors very
kindly let me have a hypo and since then I've quieted right down.
(a) They have been very kind. You know, they go so cautiously they
almost convince you they can get you better over your own [pause]
poor best judgment."

When she paused I expected her to say "desires"; she obviously
searched for another word. She said she had mentioned me to one of
her brothers today. She thanked me for coming to see her.

(b) Again she said the doctor had told her they would "cement her
up" and "They almost make you feel they will, but if they do they will
have the power of gods."

(c) I said, "They do some marvelous things here."

She responded, "Yes, I know they do! They're very cautious and do
all sorts of tests."

As I was leaving I said, "I hope you have a good night tonight."
She smiled appreciatively.

(a) and (b) bear out our belief as pointed out in the first contact
summary. She has not made up her mind to die; there is a lingering
hope. The doctors almost convince her she is wrong by their going
calmly ahead as if her "poor best judgment" did not exist. (c) was an

opportunity missed for directing the patient to talk more about what she was thinking.

Summary: This contact revealed little. Patient accepted the minister in a natural and friendly way. She spoke freely of what she was thinking and of the impression which the doctors made upon her by their "caution," *i.e.,* their care as to detail. Something more might have happened if her statement at (b) had been followed instead of the minister being so anxious to reassure the patient.

July 17. Patient operated on. The cancer was found to be inoperable.

July 18. A nurse was arranging the bed; she told me to come in. Miss E. wet her lips from a glass of water near by, "so I can talk." When I spoke to her she looked at me as if she did not know me, then said, "You must not stay now. (a) Come back later and you can say a prayer for me. I'm sorry I'm so inhospitable, and thank you for coming to see me (b), but you might make me scream even with a pat of the hand."

I said, "All right, but I wouldn't mind your screaming."

The nurse followed me to the door saying patient was disoriented and that I was not to mind what she said.

(a) This was not a request for a prayer but an effort to dismiss minister.

(b) Apparently some one (perhaps a nurse) had been patting her hand to her dissatisfaction.

Summary: Contact reveals a weak rapport which could not stand up during post-operative experience. Should give patient time to quiet down before seeing her again.

July 27. Miss E. was in a semi-private room. The curtains were partially drawn and she was moving about in bed, the head being elevated. She had slid down in the bed with her blankets and cover twisted by much pulling and turning; her pillow was crumpled up under her. I knocked lightly on the chair-back at the foot of the bed. She gave a start, looked up quickly, then said in a resigned manner, "You always come when I can't talk to you."

I said, "Would you like me to come back later?"

"No, it would be the same later. I've been having a terrible time. You have not been by since you came when I was feeling so badly. It's awfully nice of you to come when I talk so terribly."

I said, "You were in the other ward and I lost track of you in the shuffle."

She said, "Yes, I know, and it's awfully good of you to come. I was just moved into this little room last night, for which I'm glad. I've had such a terrible time—" Tears came to her eyes. "I feel sometimes that God has deserted me."

I said, "Do you think God ever does desert us really, even though it seems that way?"

"No, I don't, but it's so terrible. You don't know what it is if you haven't been through it, the shame, the disgrace, the ugliness. I do love the beautiful. I have always had everything you could want, and this is so terrible."

She was becoming more hysterical; with a determined effort she bit her lip, shaking her head as if fighting off an inclination to weep. Then with great calm she said, "This is a great hospital, a wonderful system, but they are so busy they can't do the little things that are needed, to fix your pillow, to straighten your sheets. They bring me trays of food; I see them beside me but I can't eat—" She told of being lifted up into a chair without notice, of needing "medications" and of no one being able to give them to her, just why I could not gather. She went on to say, "I know how difficult I am to take care of and that I am a pig to want attention, but if I could only get my strength back a little so I could take care of myself. It does look like I am going to have to leave the hospital alive, and I did not want to." Again tears came to her eyes. "You will say a prayer for me, won't you? Only the Eternal can help me."

Another patient was sitting near. I was standing at the foot of the bed and could see the other patient as well, while Miss E. could not for the partially closed curtains. This patient said, "The will of God," nodding toward Miss E., "the will of God is that she is like this, suffering." Miss E. did not pay much attention to the other patient. I said, "These things are very difficult to understand as the will of God."

Miss E. went on talking, thanking me for being "so patient and listening to all these terrible things."

I came nearer. "You must not hesitate to say anything you want to when I see you."

She lightened up, trying to smile. "It is nice of you to come—and you will remember me with a prayer?"

I held out my hand after assuring her I would. She drew back. "No, no. You mustn't shake hands with me, I'm not clean enough to be touched." I smiled and said, "I will remember you and I do hope you get along nicely."

July 29. As I walked in Miss E. said cheerfully, "Oh, I was just thinking of you this very minute and wishing you would come. Sit down. You've always come when I was feeling so terribly. Now I'm feeling better and clean and you have come. I was wanting you to come. I wanted to tell you—I thought you probably wanted to ask me but I have felt so terribly you never have—but I wanted to tell you,—perhaps you think I'd have a better chance if I'd been baptized. I have. I was baptized as a child and then again later, but I have to confess it was to please my parents. But I was devoted to the Baptist Church for years. Then I got traveling about and never got affiliated again. I think I should have, perhaps I wouldn't be so friendless now. I'll tell you how it was. We were playing baseball in the road, no automobiles to bother then, and the minister, a kind man but not diplomatic, came along and interrupted our baseball game to ask if we were going to join the church. We told our mother and father, and father said, "Aren't you?" And I said (I was always the spokesman), 'No.' Father said they, my mother and father, would not either then. Father always got his way. My mother" (stopped to close eyes to keep tears back), "was the most perfect woman: never an unkind word." Strongly, "Father was good too, but strong-minded. Well, we joined to please mother, but it never made any difference in our lives. I never felt any difference."

She continued: "I want to tell you about a miracle. My bell doesn't ring, so they can't hear me when I want anything. I called, 'Nurse, nurse, please, please.' I was in awful pain in the night, three nights ago. Well, I pulled myself up and put a pillow tightly against my stomach, and looked out that window at the moonlight and prayed, 'O God, why have you deserted me?' And I thought, 'God hasn't deserted me. He has simply made me do something. Tomorrow I will walk.' They had tried to get me up and I was too weak. Well, then I knew, God comes and spurs us on to something else. In an hour my pain was gone. The next day I got out of bed with the nurse's help." (She had made two tries on days before but was too weak to succeed in walking.) "I walked—shuffled across the room and back, sliding my shoes on the floor." (These shoes she had borrowed from under another bed, thinking if she could only have the aid of putting feet in shoes she could walk.) Today she walked to the laboratory across the ward. "Don't you think that was a miracle? You remember I asked you to pray for me? I think that has helped."

I said, "Absolutely."

She continued, "I lay here thinking, 'Take up thy bed and walk.' " (Amused.) "When I was a little child I used to think that meant a man picked up a big four-poster and carried it on his head, and that that was a feat. But it meant a mat. When I was in the Orient I saw them, little mats on which they slept. So I lay here and thought that out. I'd never thought of it before.

"There's another thing I'm thinking of,—I want to know if I have cancer. My chart is there in the corner. It would be written in their language, which I couldn't understand. It makes a difference, you know. If you have cancer you won't have long and you want to plan your life. So I have that on my mind and I want you to remember that in your prayer. I'm not anxious because I shall find out, but I'm just thinking about it."

I was ready to go. She said, "Now is there anything you'd like to say—go ahead." But she gave me no chance. The remark seemed meaningless. She asked me to turn on a light. I did, then standing by the bed I said, "Would you like a prayer now?"

She moved restlessly as if she felt uncomfortable. "If you like."

I took her hand. "I will lift up mine eyes unto the hills, from whence cometh my help. My help cometh from the Lord, Maker of heaven and earth. Our Father, we are thankful for Thy healing strength, the strength of the hills. Give us patience and confidence unto health. In the name of Jesus. Amen."

There were tears in her eyes. "I always dislike such things. They are so beautiful they hurt me. Those words are very appropriate. I need strength, the strength of the hills. I will remember those beautiful words. Thank you. Good night, come again."

August 1. Since my last visit Miss E. had asked if she has cancer and has been told that she has. Miss D. suggested I see patient and tell her she is to go to a convalescent home tomorrow.

When I walked into the room Miss E. was sitting on the side of the bed writing. I have never felt or seen a look of such hatred as was turned upon me. Immediately I became quiet. "How are you?"

She looked down, the corners of her mouth twitching. "Not so good. I've learned the truth. But I can't tell you. It's all over. I won't get better. They didn't do anything for me. My pain is just as bad. I figured it all out in the night. They couldn't do anything for me. This is a great efficient mill, they do wonderful things here, but they don't have much time. If I could have had the doctor I wanted he could have saved me but it would have taken a long time and I didn't have the money. Only a miracle can save me now. I wake up in the morning and I say, 'This is God's perfect day,' and I say, 'Now, God, take away the pain,' but it does not go—God cannot take it away. God is nature, circulation, He cannot take away the pain. You see, I deserted God. I would stay up and work until twelve o'clock because I needed the money. For two years I have fought this pain instead of having it taken care of. It went too far; then nothing could be done. I hate to leave my brothers." (Several times, as tears would come to her eyes she would strike them away, determined not to give in to them.) "I will not cry. Why should I? There's nothing to cry about." (Calmly.) "Your prayer made me weep, like beautiful music that you love. I tried to repeat it to my brother but I couldn't remember the words. Like old hymns that I hear. I love them because my mother liked to sing them, but they hurt me."

After consideration I said, "I once had an operation that was very painful."

"You have suffered?"

"Yes, the pain would not let up and I, too, prayed as you have."

"But you are well, you had good care—they took time."

"Mine was not a question of life, it was a bone infection. But God would not take the pain away, because, as you feel, He could not. But He suffered too."

"No, God's above pain. He does not suffer. But I hope you never suffer again. Are you married? You must get married, not hurriedly, because there is so much incompatibility, but you must marry. Those are the things that count. I am expecting a visitor. I may be going home soon."

"Yes, I just heard you are going tomorrow."

"Oh, I'm glad of that because there are some things I need to have done. I need to get some of these bandages off before I go so I can put on decent clothes again. But it's like dressing up a corpse— Thank you for coming to see me all these times."

"I may see you again."

"Yes, maybe."

September 27. In the nursing home, where Miss D. had seen Miss E. twice and found her in "good general condition."

The patient was sitting on the side of the bed when the nurse took me into the room. Miss E. smiled, saying, "It's Mr. Dicks. How nice of you to come to see me all through the rain." She held out her hand, a very unusual thing for her to do. "My hand will freeze you," I said. I was ushered outside while patient was put to bed. Then I sat near the foot of the bed while she talked. I stayed about thirty-five minutes. Patient was very much thinner than when I saw her a few weeks ago. She was cheerful, talked easily without emotion or concern, although the whole time she was touching this and that with her hands, taking a swallow of milk, moving something on the desk beside her, and pulling at the blankets.

She talked about herself, saying she suffered great pain, that she was under medicine most of the time, that noise made her nervous. (Some one was talking in a loud voice; Miss E. stopped and with difficulty kept from screaming, then went on talking quietly.) She said, "It does seem like science could do something to relieve such suffering. If I were them I don't know what I would do, I suppose go round and visit people, like you do."

"That's pitifully little."

"That's a great deal and helps a lot. Did I tell you I had forgiven the doctors for what they did?"

"You spoke about it."

"But I hadn't completely, had I? Well I have now. They did what they thought was right, but it is a shame."

She spoke appreciatively about Miss D. and her calls, and about her work at the hospital. Then she insisted on knowing something about what I was doing. There were several times when the conversation came to a standstill. In these instances I was quiet, waiting for her to take up the conversation again. During these periods she seemed quiet, sometimes preoccupied, yet they were not embarrassing. *This* was something I was never able to attain with her at the hospital. There she had always been nervous, agitated, anxious to talk; now she was not. I believe this to be a test of her attainment of spiritual reconciliation; on the other hand this may have been the effect of medicine, but she did not seem drowsy or heavy-minded as patients under morphia usually do.

As I was leaving she said, without any show of emotion, "I expect I'll not see you again. I once asked you to pray that I will be taken quickly. It seems like I should be. Why do I have to go on when I'm not really here, just a frame? I ask you again to do the same, and I wish you good luck in whatever you do. It's awfully nice of you to come."

I said, "And I hope you will——"

Before I could finish she added, "Be comfortable. That's all you can say."

October 19, in Nursing Home. Nurse said Miss E. had been upset; did I want to see her in that condition? I replied I did not want to disturb her, but that her being upset made no difference. The nurse went upstairs to see patient. After some time she called me to come up.

Miss E. was lying very straight in bed, with blankets well up around her chin, something quite unusual for her. She did not seem to have changed much from the time I had seen her some weeks ago. She wore the same knitted hair-net which I had come to associate with her. I stood by the bed quietly.

She spoke, in what I at first took to be a weak voice but discovered it rather to be constrained. "Hello, Mr. Dicks, it's nice of you to come to see me. I've just had a scolding."

"You have?"

"Won't you sit down?" nodding toward a chair.

I went around the bed and sat down; nearby was a small table loaded with many objects; I noticed especially four glasses, a basin, a box of letters, and a pile of tissue paper.

She said, "Yes, about this time every day my hypo wears off and I have great pain. I wanted them to open the door to let in some air. There were several people in the hall, so I rang the bell. The nurse came from downstairs and gave me a scolding. I know she's terribly busy but I was suffocating, and it was such a small thing to ask. She gave me a scolding."

"Did she open the door?"

"Yes, it's open now, see."

Here she became nauseated. I reached for the basin, she motioned me back, reaching for it herself; then wiping her mouth with a piece of tissue-paper, she said, "I'm so sorry, don't let me nauseate you. I can't keep anything on my stomach. These spells come, they don't last very long. I can help myself. I have to force liquids down." Taking a drink from one of the glasses she explained, "Soda bicarbonate," then a sip of milk from another glass, followed by a sip of water from a third. This was a sort of ritual: each glass had its cover, two of them being paper napkins; a small pencil served as a weight for one. After each sip each cover was carefully replaced. She explained, "I'm so fussy about everything. I like to have covers on all the glasses, but of course they can't give me covers enough so I use these papers." She said, "I suffer so much. They give me three hypos a day, one at six, at one, and at seven. They come in and wake me up so as to have some regularity. But it's so long, just waiting to go. I hate these deliriums. They tell me I wake up screaming. They are always about going out, or some one helping me to go, in one way or another." After a time she looked at me steadily. "Your prayers aren't very strong"—(pause)—"or I would go."

I said, "It's very difficult—"

She picked my word up quickly. "Difficult telling the Divine what to do, yes, I know. But don't you think it's terrible of the doctors not to have helped me? It would have been so easy. I would not have screamed the least little bit. It would have been so humane."

There were more sips from the various glasses, and explanations about "forcing milk down to keep up my strength." Then, "Tell me about your work. I think it's wonderful, the thing you are doing."

I said, "We are busy."

She changed the subject. "My brother has a baby that's sick. His wife is in bed with a cold. It's like a curse over us. Just a touch of the hand or a word of sympathy helps so much."

I said, "You have attained a great peace, haven't you?"

She looked away wonderingly. It was perhaps a full minute or longer before she answered slowly, "I suppose I have. I used to think I must do something about it and then I knew I couldn't. I would just have to wait. How do other people get through things like this? I suppose some live by their faith, that they are going out into something more. My mother did. But I lie here and wait for the end. How could there be anything else? Who am I? One among millions. A mere nobody."

I said, "There is a nice sentence in St. Matthew's Gospel, 'I believe, help thou my unbelief.'"

She said, "I still remember your prayer, 'I will lift up my eyes unto the hills,'" this haltingly.

I said with her, "'From whence cometh my help.'"

I stopped. She continued, "'My help cometh from the Everlasting God.' Is that it?"

I continued, "'Maker of heaven and earth.'"

She said, "A friend of mine writes me she still has hopes I will get well. She doesn't know the half of it. I'm just waiting here for the end."

I asked, "Are you glad they told you?"

"Oh, yes, I'd have been frantic if they hadn't. I'd have been worrying about everything. Do they know what it was? Did they want to know?"

"What was it they told you at the last?"

"They didn't tell me much of anything, they wouldn't."

"Did they say it was a tumor?"

"No, a cancer, they said. Do you know the men that operated on me?"

"What were their names?"

"Dr. B. and Dr. K. Dr. B. did it but he didn't come in before the operation. I wish he had. He kept in the background. He had examined me, giving me a couple of jabs and thumps. He was jovial and genial but wouldn't say much." After a time she said, "I suppose to some one else who believed differently from me you would have something more to say?" (Waiting for creative assertion.)

I said, "I hold the same hope for you that I hold for myself."

"Hope? What hope have I? I just lie here and suffer, waiting for the end."

I said, "The hope of the spiritual, beyond the physical. The physical drops away. This happens to all of us one way or another but the spiritual gains strength. I don't know why such suffering comes, I suppose we shall never know—"

She said, "Why! There is no why. There can be no why."

I continued, "But I am convinced that That which creates and sustains the world as we know it, complex and minute, is able to know and claim every one of us, regardless of who we are."

"It is too terrible, too terrible, terrible.—How is Miss D.?"

"Fine."

"She is so nice."

"She wanted to be remembered to you."

"Remember me to her, rather what I was, to her, not what I am." After a time she asked, "Have you been out of town?"

"No, I'm going on Monday."

"Where?"

"To New York."

"It's nice you can go. I hear people talking about the newspapers but it seems like another world. But what's the use of talking about that. It's so nice of you to come to see me and listen so patiently."

I rose to go. "I will remember you."

"Do, and speak to Miss D. and Miss —— the nurse on the ward. She won't remember me, and if she does she shouldn't."

"Miss B. I'm sure she will remember you. Miss D. will probably come out to see you."

"It's terrible to have to come to see any one like me, but she's brave, I guess she can stand it. Good fortune to you and goodbye."

Miss E. died the following week.

2. D. N.   LONELINESS

March 28, 1934. A thirty-three-year-old engineer, of medium height, fair complexion, quiet disposition, friendly, intelligent, with a good sense of humor. He is a member of the Unitarian Church. He has multiple sclerosis of two years' duration. This is a slow, hopeless paralysis.

Miss E., one of our social workers, heard of D. N. through his wife, who brought their little boy to the Out-Patient Department. At present few people come to see D. N., and those who do are not interested in the things he is interested in. When the minister, to whose church D. N. would go if he were well, comes to call he always says that D. N. will soon be better again. Both D. N. and Mrs. N. know this is not possible and both resent the minister's attitude. Miss E. had suggested that I go by to see the patient; Mrs. N. had thought this a good idea.

Miss E. and I went to the home together. When we came in N. was listening to a symphony orchestra radio program. He told me about the programs he has heard this winter; in one day he has listened to as many as three. He is keeping a list of the symphonies he has heard, together with the orchestras and directors. He has heard about 125 symphonies already this season. From this we went on to discuss current events. N. said there has been so much war talk over the radio that he turns it off.

He explained how he had been converted to pacifism. It was while attending a young people's meeting that he first became interested in the anti-war movement. At that time he held a commission as a reserve officer. A speaker had said he felt the decision for or against war should be left to the politicians. This opinion had made Mr. N. very angry and he rose and answered the speaker. The next day he found himself on a committee to prepare a course of study on the causes and cure of war. This led him to the complete pacifistic position, causing him to resign his reserve officer's commission.

He spoke of his work in the church, how he and his wife had been responsible for a program of "progressive" speakers. This program they had encouraged for a period of three years, in an effort to interest the public in a dying church, but it was of no avail. The church had had to close its doors. He said, "You are of what denomination?" I explained I was Presbyterian, but that I was working in an interdenominational movement having no connection with any local church; that I spent all my time in a hospital. He said, "Well, if you are interdenominaional, you won't mind my being a Unitarian. I think our church is rapidly dying. The Unitarians in New England are conservative. The young men going into the church are of not too high caliber. They seem to look on it as an easy way to make a living. If they come out very strong on reform of social conditions in their preaching the members start looking for a new man. There was a Rev. S., of whom my wife and I were very fond. We enjoyed four years with him as our pastor."

"Was he primarily a preacher or did he do pastoral work too?"

"He did a great deal of pastoral work. The board members seemed to think if he could turn in a definite number of calls he was doing good work."

Miss E. and Mrs. N. came upstairs as it was time for us to go. N. said, "Now I have talked all the time, and you haven't said a thing about your work."

"That would take a whole hour, so we had better save that for another time. Would you like me to come back next week?" N. said that he would.

Summary: One gets the feeling of a courageous, intelligent man, who has touched life vitally at many points and is facing a difficult situation with genuine courage. One suspects that he has lived rather a lonely life and is now most lonely of all. There is a feeling of (real) affection and devotion between the patient and his wife.

April 6, 1934. D. N. was lying on the bed; he asked me to bring a chair from the other room. He got up and sat in an arm-chair. I inquired how he was; he said he was feeling pretty depressed, guessed it was the day, maybe it was because he was hot.

Turning to me he said, "You told me you were a minister, but that you did not have any connection with a definite church, I believe. Just what are you doing?" I explained. He seemed interested. "To my knowledge that's a new thing. I haven't heard of it anyway."

I explained that it was new, that formerly ministers had gone directly from seminaries to work with people, understanding very little about their needs or how to minister to them. Yes, he agreed with that and thought "some of our men would be better off if they had some of that work." He asked what it was we stressed. I explained.

He went on with his life story begun last week. "When I finished college I didn't think I was qualified to do the job I had been trained for. At that time the ministry held a great appeal for me. Judging from some of the men who have gone into our church I don't think I would have done so badly. And it might have been my salvation, saving me from the condition I'm in now because it would have altered my life. But my family held out against my taking up the ministry."

"What was it you did take up?"

"Architecture. I was an architect. That was all I ever mastered."

"Did religion have a strong appeal to you?"

"Yes. I had got interested in pacifism and had made a number of talks and written some papers. Several of our men wanted me to go into the ministry on that account." He continued, "Yes, not many of our men would do much good in seeing a sick person, or help him much. I don't know of a preacher in S—— who could do other than preach about 'the will of God and the strength that comes from affliction,' and there's not much comfort in that. I can look back now and see certain causes which I might have avoided if I had lived a different life. Last summer when I got so depressed, largely because I was lonely, I blamed it on God. I had to have some one to blame, and a person isn't very anxious to take the blame himself. I saw very few people last summer. People aren't anxious to come to see a person with an affliction like mine. Well, the minister who would be my minister if I was up and could go out, sometimes comes to see me. One day he said he was coming to talk to me about 'the mystery of Jesus.' He has been here several times since and never has mentioned it." He smiled amusedly.

I said, "Whatever that is."

"Yes, whatever that is."

"What do you think religion can do to help the person who is sick?"

"I know very little about the Bible. I can't quote you many passages. I do like the prophets. The Book of Amos is the one I use most."

"Do you ever use Jeremiah?"

"No. I know the story but I never read it. A friend of mine wanted me to read the Gospel of John. I had been fond of the fourth chapter; the story of Jesus at the well was one that used to move me very profoundly. I got about half-way through and couldn't go any farther. I like the Book of Mark best. It being, as I understand, the oldest, and therefore most likely to be true. I have always liked the Sermon on the Mount, Amos, Hosea, and parts of Genesis. But I never could see the truth of the Beatitudes. I consider the Bible to have underlying truths in it and I also consider it to have lies in it. My philosophy spins

itself out in a rather complicated way. I'll tell you about it some time."
He seemed weary as he thought of it.

There followed a discussion of his use of the radio and his interest
in symphonies and operas. I inquired if he had thought his experience
along these lines had been equivalent to religious experience. He replied
by telling me of "the emotional kick" he had received from them. He
went on to say how a friend had suggested that he memorize passages
from Wordsworth and other of the romantic poets, to keep his mind
occupied. So he had memorized passages from Wordsworth, Keats,
Shelley, Emily Dickinson, Milton, especially Milton's "Sonnet on his
Blindness." He repeated this poem to me, saying that when he found it
"it became the Scripture of my life."

I attempted to discover how N. had developed his taste for music
as well as for good poetry. He showed me a loose-leaf notebook in
which he has kept a careful list of all the symphonies he has heard
this winter, as well as the operas, with the names of the singers. This
book is carefully and neatly arranged. He had expressed the desire to
have a system of religious ideas about which he could think, "and in
that way keep my mind occupied." Yet he went on talking about something else.

April 14. In discussing the recognition of Russia N. said, "I have
long felt that if the American people understood the spiritual program
—I mean social program—of Russia they would feel differently."

N. thinks he may get better, yet he knows his medical diagnosis.
He expressed strong dislike for the house in which he is living, which
belongs to the heirs of his father's estate. He said that he had few
friends who come to see him, and that when they came to see him
it was out of pity or kindness for him and not because they had any
affection for him. "They have no spiritual kinship like you and I
would feel, and no interest in coming to see a person like you would
have."

Later D. N., Mrs. N. and I were talking. Mrs. N. said, "Mr. D,
what do you think of death?" N. explained he did not have his mind
made up about after-life, his mind was open, he did not believe it
definitely, yet neither did he disbelieve it. "Two weeks ago," I said, "I
went to see a thirty-year-old patient who was dying. I saw her as
many as four times in one day for a period of four days before she

went. The whole thing was so real during that time I could have stepped over without any regrets. Her going was not a tragedy. She did not think so and neither did I. I mentioned her one day when I came to see you."

"Yes, I remember your speaking of her."

"Two weeks before, when I first saw her, she was a most apprehensive person."

"Well, I had never had to think very much about death until this came. My father's death meant little to me. The day of his death T. [Mrs. N.] and I went down town to buy a new lamp-shade. And when my mother died I knew I could do nothing about it." (Patient had been in bed sick at the time. His doctor thought the news would make him worse, but instead he began to improve.) He continued, "Last summer when I got to brooding about my condition I came to the conclusion that God had handed me a back-handed slap by giving me something I didn't deserve. But that was mainly because I was so lonely. I have told T. that when I did go all I wanted was some great piece of music played and no spoken words. But of course other people would say, 'How strange!'"

April 26. N. said, "I hope our discussion last week didn't leave you—[I do not recall the word]. I know you expressed several opinions which I do not hold and T. does not either. I have my mind practically made up, perhaps too much I should say, to views that are somewhat contrary to those you hold, and I hope you didn't think me irreligious."

"I found out you were religious long ago."

"I didn't know whether you felt if one didn't believe as you do you had nothing in common or not."

"The thing I am interested in is whether a person's religion works or not."

"That's it. I'm not sure that mine does. I think I'm a religious person but I'm not sure I have anything to which I can cling and which will bear me up."

"What about prayer? We have never discussed it."

"Prayer is the thing that always stumps me."

"What has been your experience with prayer? Have you experimented any with it?"

"No. I haven't. Not directly. I have perhaps unconsciously. T. and

I have read books of prayers and been greatly inspired by them. My difficulty is that I don't believe in a personal God so I find difficulty in praying because I don't know what to pray to, due to my early training."

Just then Mrs. N. who had been working in the adjoining room came into the room where we were and sat down on the bed. She spoke of a minister who had preached at King's Chapel, reading a prayer Stevenson had written, which contained the sentence, "God, Maker of the quieter hour, quiet my heart in Thee."

There was some doubt as to the exactness of these words. The minister had promised to send them to Mrs. N. but had not. The prayer had contained all that either N. or Mrs. N. thought a prayer should. The two exchanged glances and smiled. Mrs. N., "Shall I tell him?" N., "Yes, do. I think he'll appreciate it." Mrs. N. then told the following story. She had been coming from the store when two of the neighbors' little girls had run out of the house saying, "Oh, Mrs. N., we're so happy. We looked for some candy and didn't find any so we went in the other room and said the Hail Mary and when we looked for the candy next time we found three pieces, so we thanked Jesus for it." Mrs. N. had been amused, and had told N. about it. She had told it quietly; although the radio was going and C. (aged four) was busy in the other room he had still apparently overheard her for he immediately started downstairs. She asked him where he was going and he replied, "I'm going to get some of that Jesus-candy." Mrs. N. explained, "That's sort of the way we feel about prayer. It's the use it's put to." She continued, "However, Dr. ———'s prayer at the King's Chapel was different. There was everything that one could want."

I said, "It did contain a reaching out, and there did seem to be a response of something to that reaching out?" She agreed.

May 3. Mrs. N. came in to tell me about Dr. B.'s visit this week to see N. It had been some months since he had seen N. Dr. B. had said, "If you can get out from under the load of emotionalism you are carrying we may see some improvement." Mrs. N. said he was to get no more sympathy. He took it all good-naturedly. Later when we were alone he said Dr. B.'s visit had helped a lot, had greatly reassured him, and that now he was going to try to forget some of the "things which I believe are responsible for my condition. I'm going to try to get over some of my emotionalism. I realize I have to do it myself. The doctor can't help me."

"Well, I'll check up next week to see how much progress you have made. I'll take your emotional temperature every week." We both laughed.

June 2, 1934. N. inquired if I was familiar with Wordsworth's "Intimations of Immortality," saying it expressed something he had long felt and yet had not found written anywhere. Last summer, upon rereading the poem, N. had decided to memorize the whole, although it is long. He said it expressed a view that immortality was similar to the trustful acceptance of a child. He felt that as one becomes sophisticated one blocks himself away from his fellow men and hinders his usefulness to humanity, but that the faith expressed in Wordsworth's great poem and the simplicity of it appealed to him.

"I have told you several times that while I could not believe actively in a personal God and a personal immortality, neither do I disbelieve it. This poem somehow expresses my feeling very satisfactorily. I can understand the continuation of a certain element in one's existence. Both Mrs. N. and I have felt for a long time that childhood is the happiest time of one's life. Certain people's ideas of immortality are rather repulsive to me. A cousin of mine lost her mother shortly after my father died. She said, 'Won't Uncle S. be surprised when he sees Mother walk in!' " N. said,

"To any one who holds such views and gets comfort from them I have nothing to say, but they are not sufficient for me."

"I suppose you find difficulty in imagining what would go to make up immortality?"

"Yes."

"Have you ever thought much about what makes up creation, and how creation is carried on? That the borderline between physical, mental and spiritual is dim? There seems to be constant interplay between them, one affecting the other. Is it not conceivable that creation may be aided by the use of the mental and spiritual even though the physical is dropped away?" N. said this expressed something he had long felt but never had got into words.

N. has memorized the following poetry: Verses from Whitman's *Song of the Open Road* and *America Singing*, Milton's *Sonnet on His*

Blindness, Henley's *Invictus,* Tennyson's *Little Flower in the Crannied Wall,* "short in length but volumes in content," he explained; certain sonnets of Shakespeare and several verses from *As You Like It,* Shelley's *To a Skylark,* Keats' *Ode on a Grecian Urn,* Wordsworth's *The Daffodils, Westminster Bridge,* and *Intimations.* I asked if he had learned any of the Psalms. He replied that he had not, so many people had tried to convince him that if he only believed strongly enough "a miracle would be performed" that he had turned against the Scriptures.

He explained that Mrs. N. and he had come to the conclusion that organized religion as they had seen it held little for either of them; that a year ago he had felt he must have something to steady him; he had lost the use of his eyes, his hands and his legs. What more was there to live for? A Unitarian minister had called, who upon leaving had said to Mrs. N., "I don't know what we have in our religion for any one at a time like this." N. had repeated this remark to another Unitarian minister, who agreed that the ministers themselves had no idea "what they had to give in a time of crisis, if anything." In desperation N. had turned to Christian Science. An aunt who is an ardent Christian Scientist had made him so mad about "what she called science but what I call piffle"—he laughed—that he had not wanted to have anything more to do with it. "But I am in better shape now than I was a year ago."

"Do you feel religion has contributed anything to this gain?"

"You asked me that once before and I said, some people would say no, but I call it religion."

The N.s have moved to the country and it has not been possible for me to see them regularly. *From a letter written to N. August 12, 1934:*

"N., you remember that you and I once talked about prayer and its possibilities. At that time you expressed appreciation for certain written prayers you had come across at various times. I feel that prayer is that time when the inner self stretches beyond one's common experience to mingle with the noble spirits of the ages. A wise man once called it 'the communion of the saints.' The cue to satisfactory prayer is quietness. Prayer must contain poetry, imagination, appreciation, reach—thus taking one beyond oneself. With these thoughts in mind, I am enclosing a prayer which I wrote a few months ago, adapted to the needs of some of the patients at the hospital. I thought you might like to see it."

A Prayer for Sleep

Eternal and everlasting God,
In the growing quietness of the evening and the deepening
    shadows of the night,
Grant us sleep and rest.
With the stilling of the day's doings and the end of
    coming and going about us,
Make us to be sleepy with heavy eyes and tired limbs.
As Thy creatures are lying down in the wood to rest,
As the bird is quiet in its nest
And the wild thing in its hole,
As the stream is still in its bed
Reflecting the great expanse of stars above,
May we in our sleep reflect our confidence in Thee,
And our assurance in Thy constant peace.
In our sleep give us that deeper communion of our souls
    with Thee which restoreth unto health.
In the name of Jesus. Amen.

September 11. In the new home.

N. said, "You said in your letter that you hoped I had continued my good fortune in music. Well, I have. I've heard twenty-six symphonies this summer by radio. In your letter you spoke of prayer. I think we had some discussion on that subject before and I indicated that due to my agnostic up-bringing I had not had much experience in it. I think my feeling is about the same now, although I think the prayer you sent, which you had written, was very beautiful. You know T. and I have always agreed on every other subject. We have always shared completely as a matter of course, finding we felt the same way about everything. This is the only thing we've ever had a rift about." There was an exchange of laughs between N. and Mrs. N.

She explained, "Well, I've thought about it a lot and I found I had a definite feeling that way. I just had to have a time each day for taking stock if I was to keep my equilibrium. It was more a period of stock-taking than anything else. I would call it prayer." She turned to N. "Tell them about your birthday present."

"I had expressed the desire for a group of prayers by Stevenson some two years ago."

Mrs. N. said, "We had heard one of them used at King's Chapel. One expression D. had remembered and quoted, but I guess it made more impression on me than on D. It was, 'Give us courage, joviality and the quiet mind.' I found Stevenson's prayers were collected in a little book, so I got them for D.'s birthday recently."

"I had expressed hope to own a copy of them some day."

"But as I read them to him I felt the lack of any response in D. There was a definite disappointment."

"I think I've gotten farther away than ever. I've accepted what has happened to me, and that I could do nothing about it. So I feel probably farther away from it than at any time."

Presently N. and I were left alone. I said, "D., have you ever thought much about quietness?"

"No. I don't have that and I need it. You have asked me about the great music I listen to and I have felt I got a definite kick out of that. I have been a little surprised at not feeling a resentment against myself for feeling that way."

"I've written something recently on quietness. I'd like to send it to you and see what you think of it."

"I'd like to see it very much. Do send it, but don't be disappointed at my reaction to it."

November 15. D. N. was admitted to the hospital this afternoon in what seemed to be a serious condition. I saw him this evening about 7:15; he talked with great difficulty, seemed exhausted and utterly discouraged, but he did not express anxiety about his condition. Asked about the radio, said he hoped he would be able to hear the Philadelphia Symphony tomorrow afternoon.

November 16. I went by to see D. N. at eleven o'clock. The radio was being connected. He talked with difficulty but looked stronger. I went by again at five. He had not felt like listening to the orchestra. I stayed about forty-five minutes. He said that his legs are paralyzed, that he hopes he may wake up and find he can move them. He talked about Mrs. N.'s teaching Sunday School, and taking C. to the kindergarten.

November 17. I went by to see D. just before visiting hours, as he was expecting Mrs. N. He was facing the door with an eager look on his face, revealing his hope that she would come. He said he didn't know whether she would be able to get in or not. "They put me through a new course of tortures this morning. A constant string of doctors and nurses have been coming in. I feel like a museum piece." He did not seem to mind, made some humorous remark about their coming, and told me in a matter-of-fact way of being able to move his legs today. "I thought I was done for when I came in here. Wednesday night I thought sure I was dying, but I guess it isn't that easy." Laughed. "I told T. to be good to C. and all the things she was to do for him. I guess I made it pretty hard for her. But it didn't turn out that way. Now I've got to do it all over again." We both laughed. "I didn't care whether Mr. —— who brought me here hit a Mack truck on the way or not."

Mrs. N. came in. She said she had called the hospital yesterday. The nurse had said D. was quite cheerful: "That doesn't mean anything because he's always cheerful regardless of how he's feeling."

November 20. Mrs. N. told me again how D. came to know about the disease he has. A year ago last summer, while they were at the Cape, a woman who lived next door and whose husband had multiple sclerosis, came to see D. while Mrs. N. was away. She said to him that it was a shame nothing could be done about "this disease." When Mrs. N. returned the woman said, "Well, I hope I haven't let the cat out of the bag." Mrs. N. then told D. what the doctors had told her about multiple sclerosis.

She feels D. is a "bigger person" because of his illness. She says she has told him that but does not think he agrees.

Later in the afternoon I went to see D. He was sitting up and in a jovial mood. Said he understands there is some real hope for him, that he had come to the place where he had pretty much given up the struggle and had not "cared whether school kept or not." T. had urged him "not to struggle against it, but accept it." He now feels this may have been the wrong attitude. I asked him if he did not think he had been a good deal happier by taking that attitude, however. "Oh, yes, undoubtedly."

He said, "I have felt this fall that T. was turning more definitely to religion while my own feeling has remained the same. If I were to get well I would take an active part in Church affairs again, but my feeling is the same as before."

"Have you resented Mrs. N.'s turning to religion more?"

"No, I can't say I've resented it. I just couldn't see it, was all." We went on to talk of other things.

During the next three weeks I saw D. N. regularly. Dr. Cabot went to see him one day with me. N. enjoyed this call very much; they spent the time discussing Greek art. D. said later he had had a "terrible case of blues coming on that day," but that this call did much to drive them away.

I took a description of "Quietness" to D. N., reminding him that I had promised to send it to him some months ago. He expressed appreciation for it and asked to have a copy to keep. (See Chapter XV, p. 204.)

December 17. D. N. inquired if I knew Masefield's poem "Dauber"; he said he thought it one of the greatest poems he has ever read. He quoted Masefield's poem "Sea Fever," and spoke also of a poem by Emily Dickinson in which she tells of thinking she was dying on two different occasions. "I know what she was talking about. I have thought I was dying two different times; the first time was at home when I had this spell before I came to the hospital, and once since I've been here. I didn't think I'd ever wake up. But I guess it isn't that easy." He continued in much the same calm manner. "Dr. T. had a good talk with me yesterday. He told me something I have tried for two years to get Dr. B. to tell me. He told me about this darn disease. He was very considerate. He guarded my feelings and told me just what I'm to expect. He told me he could not make any definite predictions, that he had known people to get better even when they were as bad as I am and worse. The disease could be arrested, not cured."

I asked, "How did you feel after Dr. T. told you?"

He said, "I was relieved. He didn't tell me anything I had not surmised, and nothing T. had not told me, but it was backed up with medical authority. I've lain awake many nights wondering about this. I had wanted T. to write Dr. B. and ask him about the nature of this disease but she wouldn't do it. I told Dr. T. I was extremely grateful and I am. Now I'm anxious to get home by Christmas."

December 18. I said, "You told me once you thought your present condition is due to the kind of life you had lived. What did you mean?"

"To my early family life. I wasn't conscious of it until T. pointed it out, but then I recognized it. I was always the under dog and while I didn't recognize it I must have resented it."

"When we were living in P. my brother wrote me a letter asking me what did I think I was doing, paying out money for rent when my mother was living alone. He said it was my duty to go and live with her. At the time I couldn't write. I intended to answer the letter as soon as I was able to, but then after a few weeks I decided to ignore it. From the time I received that letter I went down rapidly. But that is all a closed book now. A year ago I couldn't have talked about it this way without becoming emotional. You're the first person to call it to my mind for months."

"Are you sorry I did?"

"No, it is a closed book now."

December 19. A group of singers came to the ward. By request they came to his room and sang several numbers. He enjoyed their singing but it had tired him very much.

He asked me to find Masefield's "Cargoes" in a book on his desk and check his memory on several words. I did. He quoted Whitman's "The Open Road," saying how much he liked it. He quoted Emily Dickinson's poem which he had spoken of before.

> *"My life closed twice before its close;*
> *It yet remains to see*
> *If immortality unveil*
> *A third event to me,*
> *So huge, so hopeless to conceive,*
> *As those that twice befell.*
> *Parting is all we know of heaven,*
> *And all we need of hell."* [1]

"That's given me something to think about. You know twice during the past month I thought I was dying. At the time I was quite reconciled and ready." He smiled, then continued, "Those last two lines, 'Parting is all we know of heaven, and all we need of hell.' I've often wondered just what she means by them. It would seem to be that it is not possible to really prove heaven but that at parting from earthly things and loved ones we know they have made up heaven for us here so must later also, and that parting is all the hell we need. Emily

[1] *The Complete Poems of Emily Dickinson* (Boston, Little Brown & Co., 1924), XCVI, p. 52.

Dickinson is such a mystic it's hard to know what she means sometimes."

He quoted another short poem of Emily Dickinson. We discussed "The Vision of Sir Launfal." He spoke of the desire to learn "The One Horse Shay," because his father had liked it so much. He spoke of "Hiawatha," saying he had never liked Longfellow but thinks that C. is about ready for the story of Hiawatha now. He said a year and a half ago he had known very little about poetry and cared little for it, that now he thinks of poetry constantly. "I have said Wordsworth's 'Intimations of Immortality' almost every day since I've been in here."

Presently he turned to talk of music, speaking of one of the student nurses who is fond of music. He spoke of Brahms' First Symphony. "I have analyzed it to be an attempt to prove immortality. At one place a cornet solo expresses nature's reaching out for heaven. Then there is the arching over in the first movement. In the second movement the arch rises higher." He hummed a part of the fourth movement saying, "There the arch seems to be complete, joining heaven and earth. A horn quartet comes in to express the great culmination of all forces. That's a poor imitation of the music but you get the idea."

"It expresses a great peace, doesn't it?"

He spoke eagerly. "Yes, it does." He went on to speak of Beethoven's Fourth Symphony and César Franck's Symphony.

D. N. went home on December 20th. Since that time I have seen him several times, but nothing of significance has happened beyond the continued deepening of our friendship.

3. J. L. DEATH TRIUMPHANT

J. L., a thirty-year-old, single, Protestant nurse, came to the Hospital for an operation on cancer of the chest. She knew she had cancer and that it would be a difficult operation; she had been sick about six months. Her sister came to Boston with her. Two days before the operation Miss L. expressed the desire to see a minister. Miss B., the social worker who had been told by a mutual friend of Miss L.'s arrival at the hospital, offered to call me. Miss L. said she had wanted to see her own minister before leaving for Boston but had not called him; she said, "When he came in before he always gossiped about all the news in the church. When leaving he would always say, 'Keep up your courage.'"

Miss B. introduced me to the patient. She is a nice-looking, friendly woman of thirty but appears younger. In the ordinary events of the day's job one would judge her to be a genial, good-natured, responsible person who probably does not bother about ultimates.

She is worried about the operation on Friday. She said she knew a surgeon could do only so much and then the patient must do the rest. "And I'm afraid I won't be able to do my part. . . . I am only thinking up until Friday." We talked of several other things, but I was not able to discover why she felt she might not be able to do her part. I left saying I would see her tomorrow.

Summary: A thirty-year-old nurse who is apprehensive as she faces an operation she knows will be serious. Today I failed because I tried to strengthen the patient's courage by reassuring her (although my notes do not show it) before I knew her definite need. There is considerable question as to whether I know it now or not. I tried: (1) To strengthen her confidence in the surgeon, as a result of patient's saying, "You have seen Dr. C. operate, I understand." (Miss B. had told her that.) (2) To get her to look beyond Friday, by calling attention to the fact that she knows other patients get through operations. (3) To relieve her stress by having her talk.

March 22. Miss L. is to be operated on tomorrow at nine o'clock.

She had just been prepared for operation when I went to see her. She seemed quieter. She said, "I just knew I would get up and go home when they came in to prepare me." "You really didn't think that, did you?" "Yes, I did," (hesitatingly.)

Today I tried listening and quietness. Both were somewhat effective. She said, "The Catholics have a convenient religion for a crisis. The confessional helps you to get it all out and then strengthens your faith." I said, "How do you think the confessional helps?" There was no significant response to this. After a short time she became a little restless. I rose. "You are coming in in the morning before I go to the operating room, aren't you?" "Yes, wouldn't you like me to?" "Yes, I really would."

Summary: I used the method of listening and quietness today to learn something more about the patient, and to quiet her. I also wanted to save prayer for tomorrow morning, thinking it would have more effect. On the other hand, there was the opportunity and the moment for prayer, both of which I was conscious of but did not grasp. Had I used it today it might have given her more confidence, and established me better with her. *Note:* Patient had sent for me yesterday. In such an instance I feel one should use prayer, not at once but before leaving the patient. I am inclined to think a reversal of my methods in this instance would have been better. As it was, she was expecting one thing and I did another. If I had first done what she expected my other efforts would have gone better. The point on which this decision rests is that the minister was sent for. This makes it different from the cases in which the minister goes to a patient of his own accord. In the latter he may well use other methods than prayer first.

March 23. I went to Miss L.'s room at eight o'clock. Her sister and her sister's husband were with her. After introducing me to them the patient indicated that they were to leave. I stood by the bed. "How do you feel?" She said, "Oh, much better." There was no evidence of nervousness, neither was she very quiet. She was more like a person going on a trip, and busy with last-minute preparations.

"Did you sleep last night?"

"Yes, I really did. . . . In an hour it won't hurt."

"Would you like me to say a prayer?"

"Yes, I would."

I took her hand, praying. At first it was confused for I was trying to remember the prayer I wrote last night; then I became quiet and it went better:

> Our Father, grant us thy peace,
> Thou who dost wait upon us when we are restless
> And who dost grant us courage when we are fearful.
> Grant us quietness,
> Grant us confidence,
> Knowing that at this hour and in the days that are to follow
>   we are in worthy and capable hands.
> Strengthen him who is to operate and those who are to serve
>   as nurses.
> We give ourselves into Thy sustaining presence;
> I will lift up mine eyes unto the hills
> From whence cometh my help?
> My help cometh from the Lord
> Maker of heaven and earth;

From the strength of the hills may we gather strength
  and take unto ourselves their patience;
As the shepherd guardeth his sheep so wilt Thou guard
  this one now and in the days that are to follow.
In the name of Jesus. Amen.[2]

The patient's eyes were moist when I had finished. She thanked me.
"You will come in and see me, won't you, and say hello so I will
hear you?" "Yes, tomorrow especially."

At the operation the surgeons found a large non-removable cancer.
During the next few days I saw Miss L. only once, and then with little
satisfaction as she was in an oxygen tent. Both Miss B. (the social
worker) and I saw her sister every day, however.

March 31. The oxygen tent has been removed. It is not believed the
patient will be able to leave the hospital as was originally hoped. The
family has been told this. Miss L. looked feverish and restless when
I went in. I stood by the bed, prayed:

The Lord is my shepherd, I shall not want.
He leadeth me beside the still waters
He maketh me to lie down in green pastures:
In my Father's house are many mansions
If it were not so I would have told you.

We lift up our eyes unto Thee, Eternal Father,
In our restlessness we cling to Thee,
In our pain we seek Thy comfort,
In our seeking we find it.
For Thou art always near,
In the long night watches
And in the quiet of the still morning;
Lend Thou thy peace unto us
And bear us up in our weariness.
Be Thou a constant comfort to this one,
Rest her when she is tired
And quiet her with Thy consuming peace.
In the name of Jesus. Amen.

When I had finished she said, "Come in every day. I need your
words."

---

[2] This prayer and others that follow here have been used in Chapter XVI,
on Prayer. The prayers used here were all used originally with this patient. They
were either prepared before going to see her, or were written down shortly after they
were used. Sometimes I simply had a verse of Scripture in mind when I went to her
room.

April 1. Easter morning. 12:30. Miss L. was very ill and talked with difficulty. She said, "I think I am going to die."

"It will be all right, don't you think?"

"Yes, I would rather die—"

"You are not afraid, are you?"

"No—I am not afraid."

"It is Easter today. For you it will be a special Easter.—There will be others there, you know." She nodded, smiled. I prayed:

> Our Father, we are grateful for all Thou hast given us;
> We thank Thee for the lessons of life,
> For the friends we have known and the family we have
>   possessed.
> And above all we are thankful for Thee,
> And for Thy abiding and eternal mercy unto us.
> On this Easter Day we lift up our eyes unto Thee,
> Thou who art near in life
> And Who art ever with us in death;
> Unto Thee we remember our family,
> Wouldst Thou abide with them and comfort them.
> Unto Thee we commend our spirit,
> Take us unto Thyself and comfort us
> Thou who dost transcend life and death
> And all things therein.
> In the blessed name of Jesus. Amen.

She said, "Say the benediction."

> May the grace of the Lord Jesus,
> The communion of the Holy Spirit,
> The fellowship of God the Father Almighty,
> Be and abide with you now and forever. Amen.

"Amen."

"Would you like me to come by this evening?"

"Come as often as you can. I need you."

April 1, 7 P.M. Miss L. was in better condition than when I saw her earlier today. She introduced me to her night special nurse; then she said, "Mr. D. is going to say a few words for me."

> I am the resurrection and the life,
> He that believeth in me shall never die
> But shall have everlasting life.

Eternal Father, we lift up our eyes unto Thee in
the quiet of the evening,
As the birds of the fields seek Thee for shelter,
As the ship sails upon the sea and comes to harbor,
So we come unto Thee and are comforted
Knowing that underneath are the everlasting arms.
Give us rest in the night and in sleep envelop us,
And finally bring us unto eternal life.
Now may the Lord Jesus be and abide with you
In His grace, mercy and fellowship. Amen.

She smiled her appreciation. "Did you have a nice Easter?"

"Yes. Now I am going to hear the English boys' choir."

The corners of her mouth twitched. "I want to— I want to——"

I said, "You will send for me if you want me, won't you? I'll come
at any time."

She was pleased. "Do they know where to call you?"

"Yes. Good night."

April 2. 9:30 A.M. Patient was very tired. I prayed:

I am the bread of life.
Whosoever drinketh of the water I shall give him shall never
thirst; but it shall become a well of living water, welling up
unto eternal life.
Our Father, we have drunk deeply of the water Thou hast
given us and have felt its pull unto eternal life.
In the still of the morning give us comfort, ease us from the
pain and quiet us in the turmoil.
Thy peace be with us, the peace of the Lord Jesus and communion of the Holy Spirit. Amen.

When I had finished she smiled, said, "Thank you for coming to
see me."

April 2, 1:30 P.M. Miss L.'s sister was present. Miss L. had sent for
me. As I came in she smiled, and asked her sister to stay. She had just
come through a difficult attack when it was thought she was going.

I am the resurrection and the life.
Whosoever believeth in me, though he die, yet shall he live.
I will lift up my countenance unto the Lord, yea unto Thee,
Our Father, I would be lifted up.
That in Thy comfort I might dwell forever and in Thy peace
have everlasting joy.
In Thee are we comforted and in Thee do we trust.
Thou who dost clear the mysteries of the day,

And who dost sweep away the horrors of the night;
We commend our spirits unto Thee and unto Thy keeping.
   Amen.

When I had finished she said, "Stop in every time you are by. I don't care if it is ten times a day."

April 2, 5:15 P.M. The patient had just had a stimulant and had revived a little. When I came in she smiled. I took her hand. She said, "You know, I'm feeling better."

"You are?"

"I'm really sorry. It's so nice to go. I'm really anxious to go. But I hate leaving my sister. She feels badly about it."

"She feels much better now. She's pleased you feel this way about it."

"You have made it this way."

"I'm glad I have helped a little."

"You have helped a lot. You have made it possible. I was so afraid two weeks ago. Now I'm not. And I have known what you said too. It has been so comforting." She smiled.

I prayed; this was truly a prayer of thanksgiving:

Our Father, we are thankful Thou hast brought us through the
   darkness into light.
We are grateful Thou hast given us eyes to see Thy presence;
For the faith and confidence of this one we give Thee praise;
Enfold her in Thy constant peace
And take her unto Thyself, unto Thy comfort, and rest and
   joy,
Unto Him who has given us confidence and courage,
To Him who by His noble revelation of Thee has given us
   this vision,
We give Thee praise.
And unto Him we commend this one dear to us;
In His name, and for the grace, communion and fellowship
   of God, the Father Almighty,
We give Thee most humble thanks. Amen.

April 2, 8:15 P.M. She said, "You are so nice to come. It is so good to have you."

"It's been good to come."

She smiled. I said, "There will be others there—you will not be alone. And the Master will be there." I started to pray, "Eternal Father, we lift our eyes to Thee."

She interrupted. "Will you pray that I can go tonight?"

"Would you like me to?"

"Yes. I'm so tired. There is so much pain. And I would like to go. It seems so nice."

Eternal Father, hear this humble prayer of gratitude:
Wouldst Thou, in Thy great mercy and affection
Take this one unto Thyself,
Relieve her from the pain and the weariness.
For her great courage and endurance we are truly thankful;
In the quiet of the night may she go unto Thee,
And in her going may she not regret leaving her loved ones;
May she know they will come soon,
For we are all soon to follow.
If it be not Thy will that she come unto Thee tonight,
Give her strength to complete so nobly the race thus far run.

The grace of the Lord Jesus be with thee,
The communion of the Holy Spirit uphold thee,
The love of God the Father possess thee
And give thee peace. Amen.

"You will not go away?"

"No, I will not if you want me to stay."

"If it's convenient. Thank you." Presently she said, "You will come and see my sister tomorrow?"

"Yes. I will see her."

She smiled. "Come tomorrow to see her. I hate to think of her going home alone. And mother and father are so broken up."

She seemed to stop breathing, then breathed again. Several times during the next minutes I thought she was gone. I would have called the nurse if I could have, but she seemed to want me to be there. Again she said, "You will see my sister tomorrow?"

Each time she smiled, gratefully. I suddenly felt nervous—then I was quiet again as I thought of the tremendous fact of her peace. She became sleepy.

"I want to sleep. If I can just sleep an hour it will be so good." She loosened my hand. "I am going to try to sleep now. Good-night."

I went to the nurse inquiring if she thought I should stay. She said, "I've no idea. It might be all right to go. She is so peaceful. It makes her easy to take care of, her wanting to go as she does." We decided that the nurse would ask her if she wanted me to stay. She came out saying she would call me when the patient asked for me.

I stopped to see Miss L.'s sister. She said, "Isn't it nice to see J. so peaceful? Two weeks ago she was so apprehensive. She wanted to see a minister and yet she hated to call in a stranger."

It was interesting that the patient, her nurse, and her sister spoke of the patient's peacefulness in almost the same words. Since yesterday the same feeling had been growing on me, but I was grateful to have it corroborated.

April 3, 10:30 A.M. Miss L. was somewhat weaker. I said, "It was not last night."

She said, "No, it wasn't."

I prayed:

> Eternal Father, for Thy wondrous ways we are thankful;
> Thou hast brought us through many paths in our lifetime;
> Wouldst Thou bear us up at this time in our need,
> Wouldst Thou comfort us and claim us for Thyself;
> We lift up our eyes unto Thee and are certain of Thy presence.

Patient started, saying, "Where am I?" Then realized I had been praying. She said, "Oh, I'm so sorry!" I continued:

> May the Lord be with you and keep you;
> May the Lord make His face to shine upon you;
> May the Lord lift up the light of His countenance upon you
> And give you peace. Amen.

(This prayer had not gone well from the beginning. I could not relax my own tension—it had been too long. From the beginning the patient had been confused. The instant after she had interrupted me and had realized what had happened she was lucid for a moment.)

April 3, 8 P.M. I had come by in the afternoon. Miss L. was asleep so I had not gone in. When I saw her tonight she seemed much stronger than this morning, although her face had less color. She said, "I have not seen you much today." At first I did not understand as she spoke with difficulty; she repeated the remark.

"No, I came by but you were asleep."

"Yes, I knew you came. Do you have any way of feeling if it will be tonight?"

"No, do you?"

"No. I thought it would be last night. Let's ask that it will be tonight. I would so like to go."

I said, "Yes, let's do." She smiled.

> Eternal Father, for Thy peace and strength we are grateful,
> For Thy grace, mercy and comfort we give Thee thanks.
> Take us now unto Thyself and Thy eternal peace.
> If it be Thy will take this one unto Thyself tonight;
> She is tired, wouldst Thou give her rest
> And strength unto the end.
> In her patience and her faith we do truly rejoice;
> In the peace of the Lord Jesus, the communion of the Holy Spirit
>   and the fellowship of God the Father Almighty. Amen.

(I did not feel it would be that night.)

April 4, 10:30 A.M. Patient looked very tired. But she smiled, as she said "Good morning." After a time she said, "I'm ready to go. I'm very tired. I wish it might be now." I prayed:

> For so great a peace we are eternally thankful,
> Our Father. Thou hast been good to us.
> Wouldst Thou ease our weariness and give us rest eternal,
> Thou who hast brought this one unto so noble an end,
> May she now begin anew that which is without end,
> The new life in the new day.
> We commend her unto Thee;
> In the name of Him who doth bear us up in the hour of our
>   great need,
> Jesus Christ, our Lord. Amen.

April 4, 5:00 P.M. Patient wanted to talk. I knew that her mother and her sister had been to see her in the afternoon. "My mother and sister were here. And a man whom I admire very much."

"It was good to see them, wasn't it?"

"Yes, it was nice. We have been so close as a family. Five of us. This is the first break. I think that is hardest."

"Yes, that is hard."

"But I am all ready to go. I hope it will be soon. There are two or three things I would like to do, but my mind isn't clear enough."

"Everything is all right."

After a time she said, "The doctors don't say anything is going to happen," she smiled, "but I'm just waiting."

I prayed:

> May the Lord bless thee and keep thee,
> May the Lord make His face to shine upon thee,
> May the Lord lift up the light of His countenance upon thee,
> And give thee peace. Amen.

She said, "That is beautiful, beautiful. . . ." After a time she said, "Will you do me a favor?"

"Yes."

"Will you stop at the desk and leave your telephone number so they can call you. I want you here with my sister."

"Yes, they have it and will call me. Miss B. is with your sister now and will come too."

She was pleased. "That is nice. Miss B. is so nice."

April 4, 8:30 P.M. Miss L.'s sister was with her. She sent her nurse to call me when she heard I was there. "I thought it would be nice if you came with us both here together."

I put my hand on her head:

> The Lord is my shepherd, I shall not want.
> He leadeth me in green pastures,
> He maketh me to lie down beside the still waters.
> Yea though I walk through the valley of the shadow of death
> I will fear no evil,
> For thy rod and thy staff they comfort me
> And I shall dwell in the house of the Lord forever.

> For Thy peace and Thy comfort we thank Thee,
> For the spirit of this one and for her confidence;
> Take her unto Thyself, Our Father, and give her peace,
> And wouldst Thou be with her loved ones,
> May her spirit strengthen them and her peace comfort them.
> The grace of the Lord Jesus be with you,
> The communion of the Holy Spirit comfort you,
> The fellowship of God the Father give you peace. Amen.

The patient smiled, said, "How are you?"

At first I did not understand, this being unexpected. She repeated it. I said, "I'm fine."

She smiled. "You appreciate being fine, don't you?"

Her sister left, I stayed a little longer. She said, "You will come when they call, won't you?"

"Yes, I'll come. Good night."

"Good night. Thank you."

April 5. Shortly before six a.m. I was called. At six-fifteen I was at the hospital. Her sister was sitting by the bed. The nurse said, "She has gone." I put my hand on her head.

> May the Lord bless thee and keep thee,
> May the Lord make his face to shine upon thee,
> May the Lord lift up the light of His countenance upon thee
> And give thee peace, now and forever more. Amen.

She had gone quietly, just before I was called. I had arrived shortly after her sister. She said, "This is something you don't get used to."

It was a tremendous experience for all concerned. To the patient's sister it was the terrific experience of parting with someone she had loved dearly; to Miss B., the social worker, it was the experience of standing by the sister and waiting; to the doctors it was the humbling experience of bowing before the mystery of disease, helpless except for opiates; to the nurses it was the difficult task of a losing fight, for one who needed constant care and showed a noble courage. To the patient and myself it was a stepping into the Presence of the Divine. To us no tragedy was involved: it was terrific, peaceful, quiet, possessing.

One hesitates to speculate upon what happens in such an experience—yet I saw, felt, knew that in the end all was not as it had been before. The sister, the special nurses, and the doctor felt the same change in her.[3] Never have I been so conscious of the significance of the ministry and of the tools at its command. Experiences like this do not happen often, yet I am convinced they might happen more often if we gave them a chance.

To the sister of the patient, the day following her death:

April 5, 1934,
Mass. General Hospital,
Boston, Mass.

Dear Miss L.,

You and J. have been very much on my mind all day. Although I knew you both only a few days, during that time we touched heights which are seldom experienced. I have ministered to several people during the past months facing the same experience J. faced, but never have I witnessed so complete an attainment of peace and confidence, nor

---

[3] Some weeks later the attending surgeon stopped me in the hall to express appreciation for my having seen Miss L. and for the difference it had made.

have I felt the Divine Presence so keenly. It was a tremendous experience for me as it was for you both.

You now feel the loss of her but I am convinced you have lost her only for a little while. These days are the hardest—I wish I might relieve them somewhat for you, and for your sister, mother and the others of your family. Express to them my complete understanding.

Be assured of my long remembrance and appreciation.

Yours cordially,

From the sister:

April 11, 1934.

My dear Mr. D.,

You were so thoughtful in writing me such a lovely letter. It was such a comfort to my folks to know you were with J. so much. I tried to tell them everything, but hearing from you meant so much more to them.

My mother is really "carrying on" beautifully and you will never know how much of this we owe to you.

There is no adequate way of thanking you but I just want you to have the book as a remembrance of all you have done for both J. and me.

With kindest thoughts,

Sincerely,

Massachusetts General Hospital,
17th April, 1934.

My dear Miss L.,

Thank you very much for the nice book you sent, and for your letter. I am glad to have such a note of appreciation from you, not for anything that I did but rather for your confirmation of my belief that J. was helped by that which I was able to suggest. After that Easter Sunday noon when I saw her and she had come to realize what she was facing, she seemed immediately to set her face towards something else. One could not help but be lifted up after seeing her, it was all so natural and so real. You perhaps know, that both the special nurses spoke of this fact also.

J. felt badly about breaking the family circle. She said, "I think the first is the hardest." But she knew also that although you would miss her very much, you would carry on. I was glad to have the word of your mother's feeling better. I don't think I mentioned being pleased at the way you stood up that Thursday morning yourself. Miss B. and I were proud of you.

With very best wishes,

Sincerely,

P. S. I am enjoying the book very much, your selection was to my taste.

4. IN THE AFTERNOON

One afternoon I received a call from the front office of the hospital saying that Mr. S., a patient in Ward E, was dying, that his wife wanted to see a minister. I was admitted to the room by a special nurse. I explained to the wife who I was. She was a woman of forty but looked older; she was plain, humble, patient, quiet. She had taken the vow to "love, honor and obey," and one knew that through the years of her married life she had been true to that vow. She looked at me out of patient eyes saying, "I don't know what I will do without him. I don't know what I will do." I asked, "How long has he been sick?" "Since last Thursday. I brought him to the hospital on Sunday." It was then Tuesday. "If I had brought him sooner the doctor here might have been able to do something for him. I asked the doctor but he said 'maybe not.' The doctor at home wasn't doing anything." She turned to the patient who was breathing with difficulty. She rose and took his hand. "Are you all right, dear?" He opened his eyes, seemed to try to smile, then closed them again. I stepped up beside him and put my hand on his. She said, "Say a prayer for him." I put my other hand on her arm:

> I will lift up mine eyes unto the hills,
> From whence cometh my help?
> My help cometh from the Lord,
> Maker of Heaven and earth.
> Thou art our rock and our fortress, Eternal God,
> For underneath are the everlasting arms;
>
> Unto Thee we turn in this hour of our need,
> And unto Thee we commend our spirits in this hour of turmoil
>   and sorrow;
> Take this one unto Thyself and give him peace and quiet;
> Wouldst Thou grant this wife comfort to bear the grief of
>   this hour;
> May she know that Thou dost come unto us in this hour with
>   Thy strength and Thy salvation.
> The Lord be with you and keep you,
> May the Lord make His face to shine upon you,
> May the Lord lift up the light of His countenance upon you
> And give you peace, now and forever more. Amen.

I stayed a while longer and then excused myself. When I returned two hours later he had just died. I went to the front office to see Mrs.

S. The House Officer was talking to her in the admitting office. He came out and called a man who was standing nearby. Soon another man came to the front desk near which I was standing and asked for Mr. S. The girl at the desk asked him if he was Mr. S.'s brother. He replied that he was. She said, "Mr. S. just died a few minutes ago. Mrs. S. is in the office talking to the doctor. That lady there," nodding to a little woman sitting nearby, "is a friend." He turned and spoke to her. I walked over to where they were standing, explained who I was, and said that I had seen Mr. S. shortly before he died. The brother said, "I was afraid of this when I brought him in Sunday. But this is something that comes to us all." He turned away. Presently he came back asking, "Was he conscious when you saw him?" "He was semiconscious." He said, "A year ago I brought my wife here. She did not leave either." Some one beckoned to him from the office.

I turned to the woman standing by. She explained that she was the wife of Mr. K., Mrs. S.'s brother, who was with her in the office. She said, "This is something that comes to all of us. We had a son who died in this hospital. My husband was here and nearly died but he is stronger now. Her husband was a good, hard-working man, I don't know what she will do without him. She has four children. The oldest is eighteen. He will graduate from trade-school in June." She said, "He didn't hold with life insurance. I don't myself, but it would help her now if he had had some. Did she send for you?" "Yes." "I'm glad she did. I'm glad she had the Word of God said for him. I did for my father. She was raised a strict Episcopalian. But he didn't hold with religion and never allowed her to send the children to Church School. He was very stiff-minded. She has been very patient with him, but he was a difficult man. A hard worker and good to her but strong-willed.

"They are talking about an autopsy but I don't expect she will give it to them because he didn't hold with touching the body. I told her to do it if it would help heal somebody else, because they do everything they can for you at this hospital. The rich and the poor are treated alike."

After a time the other three came out of the office. Mr. S. came up to me saying, "I want to thank you for what you have done. There doesn't remain anything else but to get him to his final resting-place." I turned to Mrs. S. "You may be certain he's resting now and in peace." She said, "Yes, he is resting now. I did everything I could.

I stayed with him to the very last. He asked me this morning how long I was going to stay and I said, 'As long as you want me to,' and I stayed as long as he was here. I could do no more. Thank you for coming to see him." Mr. K. said, "Yes, he's at peace now." I said to Mrs. S., "You will find strength to go on." She said, "Yes, I will find strength." They left.

ON THE MEANING OF THE WORD "GROWTH"

Growth, as we use the word in this book, is to be sharply distinguished from simple *enlargement* as it occurs, for example, when a city grows in population and is perhaps distinctly the worse off for it. The enlargement of the human body may be due to fat or to dropsy. In this case the enlargement spells not growth but degeneration.

Growth is not to be certified by watching any increase in size. When children grow up we are satisfied that their increase of stature and strength goes along with the development of other powers, and is, therefore, one phase of true growth. But the giants of the dime museums and circuses usually exemplify a degeneration due to tumor of the pituitary gland. The individual is slowly going to pieces though he is getting taller all the time. This proves that we cannot identify growth merely by the evidence of enlargement.

Growth should also be distinguished from simple change. We say, for example, "It is growing dark," or, "The world is growing worse," and we mean nothing more than alteration. As we watch ocean waves break on a seashore there is constant change, the forming and reforming of waves which are swiftly broken up again. In these changes there is no suggestion of growth. Many of the rhythmic processes, such as the heart beat or the flow of the seasons and of the fashions, exemplify changes that have nothing to do with growth.

Growth always involves an element of loss, though not a net loss. The mature man does not keep all the virtues and beauties of childhood, though we are usually convinced that on the whole he has grown and not degenerated. Growth, then, does not exclude attrition and loss; but in growth these destructive processes never predominate. There must be a gain in spite of them.

This gain is shown in the realization of a single purpose. The main purpose of a person's life may develop even though he loses in physical strength, in the graceful lightness of childhood, and in many other respects. His main purpose nevertheless is attained, and this purpose supplies the element of *continuity with the past* throughout all the changes that occur.

Growth may be defined, then, as *the production of novelty within the range of a purpose without dominant self-destruction*. Learning, experimenting, admiring, and sharing, exemplify growth. When self-destruction predominates we have degeneration. This definition enables us to exclude such processes as the "growth" of bad temper or of deceitfulness through the years of a man's life. These are degenerations as above defined.

Growth takes place in character, not toward character; in wisdom, not toward it. There is no goal which we approach.

Growth comes by the appropriation of the energies of the universe taken in both through our food and the air we breathe and through all that we learn from the world and from other people. Any one who does not turn away from reality and refuse to learn from it cannot help growing. The opposite of growth, therefore, degeneration, results from refusing to learn the lessons which cumulative experience teaches to all who do not refuse them.

Men refuse to grow because they are defending themselves in some little citadel of habit and comfort, which they fear would be broken up if they absorbed the teaching which God gives us through reality. A mixture of laziness and self-deceit, then, is the essence of evil in the moral sense. Growth as we here use it connotes all that is morally good and all that is morally good must appear as growth.

These points are discussed at much greater length in Chapters V and VI, of *The Meaning of Right and Wrong*, by Richard C. Cabot (Macmillan, 1933).

BIBLIOGRAPHY

The Pastoral Ministry, H. Adams (Nashville, Tenn., Cokesbury Press, 1932). Specially good on ministry to the bereaved.

Ministerial Practices, C. B. McAfee (New York, Harpers, 1928). Chapters 14, 19, and 20.

Feed My Sheep, Francis Underhill, ed. (London, Mowbray, 1927).

The Soul of the Hospital, E. F. Garesché, S.J. (Philadelphia, Saunders, 1928).

The Cure of Souls, William Cunningham (Cambridge University Press, 1928).

Modern Methods in Church Work, G. W. Mead (New York, Dodd, Mead & Co., 1897).

Manual of Parochial Work, J. Ellerton, ed. (London, Society for Promoting Christian Knowledge, 1892).

Spiritual Ministration to the Sick, C. Arey (Salem Press, 1891).

Parish Problems, Washington Gladden, ed. (New York, Century Co., 1887).

Church Thought and Church Work, C. Anderson (London, W. S. King, 1874). Good chapter on visiting the sick.

Directorium Pastorale, J. H. Blunt (London, Murray, 1888). (First edition 1856).

INDEX